A Midwestern Mosaic

A
Midwestern Mosaic

Immigration and Political Socialization in Rural America

J. CELESTE LAY

TEMPLE UNIVERSITY PRESS
Philadelphia

TEMPLE UNIVERSITY PRESS
Philadelphia, Pennsylvania 19122
www.temple.edu/tempress

Library of Congress Cataloging-in-Publication Data

Lay, J. Celeste.
  A midwestern mosaic : immigration and political socialization in rural America /
J. Celeste Lay.
     p.   cm. — (The social logic of politics)
  Includes bibliographical references and index.
  ISBN 978-1-4399-0792-4 (cloth : alk. paper)
  ISBN 978-1-4399-0793-1 (pbk. : alk. paper)
  ISBN 978-1-4399-0794-8 (e-book)
  1. Cultural pluralism—Iowa.   2. Ethnicity—Iowa.   3. Immigrants—Iowa.
4. Political socialization—Iowa.   I. Title.

  HM1271.L39 2012
  305.8009777—dc23   2011048802

♾ The paper used in this publication meets the requirements of the American National
Standard for Information Sciences—Permanence of Paper for Printed Library Materials,
ANSI Z39.48-1992

Printed in the United States of America

2 4 6 8 9 7 5 3 1

Dedicated to Buck and Helen Lay

Contents

Preface and Acknowledgments

There is so little work in political science on rural America. Sociology has a small subfield in rural sociology, including a journal and an annual meeting. Anthropologists have long studied rural areas around the world. Political scientists, especially those studying American politics, have focused on national and international issues; those who examine local politics nearly all study urban areas. This is especially true in the study of racial and ethnic politics. Political science theories about interracial and interethnic relations are steeped in the experiences of cities. This made some sense when small towns—especially those in the Midwest—were 99 percent White. Today, however, rural America is no longer full of White farmers and ranchers, where the only people of color are migrant workers who are not full members of the communities in which they work. This study examines five small Iowa towns that are substantively different in only one respect: the presence or absence of ethnic diversity. Perry and Storm Lake have undergone "rapid ethnic diversification" in the past 20 years, while Boone, Carroll, and Harlan are what most would picture in a small Iowa community—nearly all White, aging, and trying to survive. This book analyzes natives' responses to the changes in their communities, focusing on adolescents and on the effects of diversity on political socialization.

As usual, many people made this project possible. The initial research was funded in part by grants to James Gimpel from the William T. Grant Foundation and the Ahmanson Community Trust Foundation. Portions of the book were originally developed as part of my dissertation, funded in part by a grant from the Center for Information and Research on Civic Learning and Engagement (CIRCLE). A grant from the Dean of the School of Liberal Arts at Tulane University was also instrumental in funding the more recent trips to these communities. Members of the office staff in the Political Science Department, Jo Ellen Miller and Jennifer O'Brien, were helpful in their administration of this grant. I had two outstanding undergraduate research assistants: Joanna Bak and Samuel Worth. I am grateful to Brian Brox, Tom Langston, Aaron Schneider, Mark Vail, and Dana Zartner, my colleagues in the Political Science Department at Tulane who read drafts of chapters. I also received invaluable feedback on portions of the manuscript from Richard Niemi and Carl Bankston. Finally, Alex Holzman and Scott McClurg were supportive of the project and extremely helpful in getting it through the publication process.

The support of the high school administrators was absolutely critical to conducting the surveys and filling in the context about their students. The principals at each school gave permission to survey their students: Steven Haluska (Carroll High School), Michael Hanna (Storm Lake High School), David Kapfer (Boone High School), Klint Klinkefus (Harlan High School), and Dan Marburger (Perry High School). The teachers also allowed us into their classrooms to speak with their students and interrupt the school day. Of course, had the students in these schools not taken the surveys seriously and been willing to talk, this all would have been for naught. In subsequent trips to Iowa, I spoke with many residents of these communities, especially in Perry and Storm Lake. I thank them for their time and willingness to talk with me, especially about issues that are sometimes difficult to open up about with someone who is an outsider. I am also grateful to Ganeen Tibben at the *Perry Chief*, who helped me dig through the newspaper's archives for many hours.

When this research started, I was a graduate student under the direction of James Gimpel at the University of Maryland. He allowed me to advise on the survey instrument, travel with him to Iowa, and administer the surveys and talk with students. He later released the data to me entirely, making this book possible. Although this project is very different from my dissertation, the advice I received from the other members of my committee—William Galston, Karen M. Kaufmann, Judith Torney-Purta, and Clarence N. Stone—was instrumental to my thinking about these issues.

Finally, writing this book has been a rollercoaster. The past ten years have included several happy events: graduation and completion of my doctorate, my wedding, and the birth of my child. They also included, however, the flooding of our house and, sadly, the illnesses and deaths of my parents. The book would not have been possible without the support and encouragement of my friends, especially Karen Kaufmann, and, of course, my family. My husband, Chris Fettweis, convinced me that I could do this. In addition to providing emotional support and home-cooked meals, he took great care of our young daughter, Lucy, so I could complete the research and write the manuscript. He also makes me laugh every day.

Finally, my parents, Buck and Helen Lay, were always my biggest advocates. In writing about growing up in small towns, I came to appreciate them in new ways. Armed with little more than a dream for their family, they left their tiny hometowns in northern Louisiana to embark on lives that must have seemed unimaginable at the outset. Although they left their hometowns, they passed along the values they learned there—faith in God, respect for and kindness to others, generosity, and an appreciation for underdogs. For their courage and commitment to our family, I dedicate this book to them.

A Midwestern Mosaic

INTRODUCTION

Places and Political Learning

I think it's gotten a lot better. 'Cause I remember when I was little—
it's not that I was scared of Hispanics, but like, everyone else hated
them, or they hated us or whatever. I think it's gotten a lot better,
'cause the kids—we're so used to it. It's not a big deal if you have,
like, eight Hispanics in your classroom.

—Student, Perry High School, 2002

When I was ten, my family moved from New Orleans to Paducah, Kentucky. The move has caused me to wonder how growing up in a relatively small town has influenced who I am and how I might be a different person if my family had stayed in New Orleans. Unfortunately, the literature on political socialization has not given a great deal of insight into the effects of local context. Political science has been especially quiet with regard to small towns and rural communities. This book hopes to shed some light on the political socialization effects of growing up in small towns. It is an analysis of adolescents being raised in small communities in Iowa and examines one important aspect of the community: the influence of ethnic diversity.

The most common reaction when people hear about my book is surprise: "You're studying ethnic diversity in Iowa? That must be a short book." Most analyses of diversity take place in major urban centers or in suburbs. However, in small communities across the Midwest and South, towns are rapidly diversifying through immigration. Most of the towns have not experienced foreign immigration since the nineteenth century, and as recently as 1990 their racial compositions, especially in the Midwest, were almost completely White and non-Hispanic.

This book focuses on the political attitudes and inclinations of native adolescents who are growing up during a time when their communities are undergoing dramatic change. It compares them with young people in nearby communities of similar size whose populations have remained static. Group conflict theory predicts that White majorities may be initially threatened by ethnic minorities and respond with intolerance or hostility. Research on social capital formation also suggests that the initial reaction of many people is to withdraw from politics in the wake of rapid demographic change.

This book asks the following questions: How does rapid and significant demographic change affect the political socialization of native White youth? Does this contact with people from different ethnic groups and cultural backgrounds lead to increased tolerance for diversity, or does it lead these native young people to become more intolerant? Does it make them more (or less) knowledgeable about politics; does it affect their political efficacy or the sense that their voice matters and they are heard by those in power; are they more likely or less likely to say they will vote and to participate actively in their schools?

It looks at the next generation and whether young people choose to reject the transformation occurring within their communities, or whether they accept and welcome these changes. Based on the assumption that adults' political behavior is shaped primarily by experiences during adolescence, this book gives a glimpse into how demographic change is likely to influence politics in the future. The main argument of this study is that over time, native adolescents in ethnically diverse rural communities begin to accept and welcome newcomers. The book also shows that native adults in these communities also become more tolerant of newcomers over the 20 year period. The arrival of immigrants in small towns was initially accompanied by reduced levels of political knowledge, efficacy, participation, and tolerance among native students compared with native youth in similarly situated, predominantly White towns. Over time, however, the gaps between these groups shrank. Like the young man in Perry whose statement opens this chapter, young people adapt rather quickly to their environments. In his words, "It's not a big deal."

This book is the result of a ten-year research project that uses a natural experimental design of five small towns in Iowa. Three of these towns are "traditional" Iowa communities, in which residents are nearly all White and most are longtime residents (Boone, Carroll, and Harlan). These towns have almost no ethnic or racial diversity. The other two towns have experienced dramatic population changes since 1990, due in both cases to the arrival of Latino immigrants attracted to jobs at local meatpacking plants (Perry and Storm Lake). In Storm Lake, a small influx of Asian refugees in the 1970s and 1980s gave the community a head start in coping with demographic change. These towns now have substantial portions of the population who are non-White, including many who are foreign born or are the children of those who are foreign born. In the fall of 2001, a team of researchers traveled to each community and surveyed students at the public high schools within each town. We returned in 2002 and surveyed many of the same students again. The following year, we conducted focus groups with students, and for the past several years I have spoken with school and town officials about changes taking place, both good and bad. Although certainly not a true laboratory experiment, this design allows me to compare five very similar towns with one major difference: the presence of immigrants.

The study has three major aims. First, I want to expand the literature on the effects of social context on political socialization. Most scholarship on socialization examines the process outside of time and space, and very little of the literature on social context considers adolescents. Second, I hope to push others to realize that there are very interesting phenomena outside urban and suburban areas. Millions of Americans live in small communities, but political scientists are especially guilty of failing to systematically analyze the politics of small places. Finally, this study sheds light on the increasing cultural and ethnic diversity of the United States and how some communities are coping with these changes. The remainder of this introduction examines the rationale for looking at the influence of social context on political socialization and outlines the book to come.

Political Socialization and the Influence of Local Communities

Political socialization is the process by which young people develop their political attitudes and inclinations to participate in politics. Thanks to the vast scholarship on this process, we know a great deal about the agents and outcomes of political socialization. Not surprisingly, parents have considerable influence on their children, especially when it comes to party identification.[1] Peers and schools are important agents of socialization.[2] Recent research has focused on the apathy, mistrust, and general disdain that young people, especially Generation X, have toward government and how the millennial generation seems to have a different perspective on politics from that of its predecessors.[3] One of the major problems with most literature on political socialization, however, is that it treats the process as if it occurs in a vacuum, outside of time and space.[4]

Intellectual Foundations of Examining Political Socialization in Context

With some notable exceptions, in most political science literature on political socialization, communities are ignored altogether or, in some cases, accepted as important but not examined.[5] Until recently, most of our knowledge about how places influence attitudes and behavior comes from outside political science. The school of symbolic interactionism posits that human behavior is best understood in relation to the environment. According to Herbert Blumer, who coined the term, humans behave based on the meanings they ascribe to objects and events, and these meanings are derived from interaction with others.[6] To Blumer's predecessors and mentors, Charles Cooley and George Herbert Mead, individuals' beliefs about themselves (and other objects) are based on one's interpretations of the imagined impressions of others.[7] Like other pragmatists, these scholars believed that reality is created as activity in the world; it is a dynamic process based on the interaction between the individual and society.

As people interact with the world around them, their interpretations of the meanings of objects form the basis of their knowledge and beliefs. One's "mind" emerges only through one's interaction with others within the social environment. Sociologists from Karl Marx, Max Weber, and Emile Durkheim to Edward Shils and David Reisman all wrote, at one level or another, about the inextricability of the individual from society.[8]

Social and developmental psychologists also have more fully developed theories about how individuals are embedded within physical places that influence their experiences and opinions about the world. Kurt Lewin argued that to understand individual behavior, one must look at the person's "life space," which includes his or her immediate social circle. The well-known psychologist Urie Bronfenbrenner constructed the ecological theory of child development. This theory contends that humans develop not in isolation but, rather, in relation to their families, schools, communities, and society.[9]

In the study of political behavior, however, most political scientists fail to adequately consider the influence of social context. One of the basic tenets of *The American Voter* is that adults' attitudes are shaped by the process of adolescent political socialization, especially the adoption of party identification.[10] The authors depict vote choice as a product of a "funnel of causality" in which the effects of group membership, religion, and, presumably, the local community are found at the far end of the funnel, indirectly influencing vote choice through candidate evaluations and partisanship. Angus Campbell and his colleagues recognized not only that political choices are internal, but also that private decisions are greatly influenced by the people by whom one is surrounded. Even so, scholars have spent most of the past 50 years closely examining political behavior outside the contexts in which it takes place. Due in part to the influence of rational choice theory and the reliance on survey data that have failed to account for the social environment, most research in political behavior assumes, either implicitly or explicitly, an individual making political choices in isolation from those around him.[11]

Disciplinary boundaries have kept many of the ideas from sociological and social psychological theory outside of mainstream political science. Even before Campbell and his colleagues wrote their classic study, behavioral social scientists across disciplines worked closely on theories of voting. These early studies showed that informal social pressures from one's family, neighbors, and friends can have a powerful impact on vote choice, and scholars theorized that vote choice, like other preferences, is a social activity.[12] In *The People's Choice,* Paul Lazarsfeld and his colleagues state, "There is a familiar adage in American folklore to the effect that a person is only what he thinks he is, an adage which reflects the typically American notion of unlimited opportunity, the tendency toward self-betterment, etc. Now we find that the reverse of the adage is true: a person thinks, politically, as he is, socially."[13]

In recent years, there has been a return to the early ideas of Bernard Berelson and Lazarsfeld, to the notion that we cannot understand political behavior by plucking people out of the time and space in which they live. Political scientists have begun to attempt to account for the influence of "social context" on political behavior, but few have examined political socialization. These scholars focus on how communities structure the types and frequencies of social interaction and how this interaction imparts information that people use in making political choices.

Adults' Political Behavior and Social Context

Borrowing from schools of symbolic interactionism and ecological theory, some political scientists again understand that through the process of social interaction, one's social context exerts powerful influences on political behavior. For example, regardless of where they live, people receive much political information from the mass media, but local perceptions of media bias in news stories are more influential on political behavior than actual news content, indicating that voters filter national news through their local climate of opinion.[14] Further, the mass media are not the only sources of information. In 2008, when my neighbors put signs for Barack Obama in their yards, I did not need the national press to tell me that New Orleans was Obama territory. People rely on their friends and neighbors for information, and they place great value on the opinions of their spouses, co-workers, and community leaders.[15] Informal social interactions expose people to knowledge that can expand their understanding of politics by offering different information than one possesses individually.[16]

There are many forms of social interaction that transmit information about politics. Face-to-face encounters with close friends and family members, as well as relative strangers, impart information about the community's expectations and preferences. Models based on "social cohesion" contend that intimate relationships are responsible for considerable personal influence on political attitudes.[17] For example, having friends who are active in politics makes people more likely to get involved themselves.[18] Relationships that may be considered "weak ties" also have profound implications for one's choices and attitudes. Discussions with co-workers and neighbors provide information and, often, social pressure to think or behave in a particular way, even politically.[19] Citizens who are more socially connected to larger communities—for example, to groups outside their immediate families—are generally more politically active.[20] Diana Mutz finds that political differences of opinion are better tolerated within relationships characterized by weak ties than by strong or intimate connections.[21] And, of course, a great deal of information is translated through nonverbal communications, such as my neighbor's yard signs.[22]

Through normal, everyday interactions in a variety of settings, we are constantly bombarded with information. Scott McClurg, however, points out that social networks tend to influence political participation only "when they carry political substance."[23] Although there are many forms of social interaction, it is the *substance* of the communications that matters in predicting political outcomes. Talking about the latest George Clooney movie or episode of *Project Runway* may tell you something about another person, but it is unlikely to impart much politically relevant information and is unlikely to significantly influence political attitudes or participation. Many studies show that the heterogeneity of one's social networks is an important mediating factor. Those whose social networks or neighborhoods are more politically or ethnically heterogeneous are less likely to discuss or participate in politics, largely because, it is thought, exposure to dissonant information creates ambivalence.[24] This is especially true for people who find themselves a political minority within their neighborhood or community.[25] These findings form part of the basis for expecting young people in ethnically diverse communities to be less politically engaged than those in homogeneous places.

In addition to the content of the information, the local setting also helps to determine the salience of particular issues and make certain information more cognitively accessible. In Los Angeles, debates about farm subsidies are unlikely to be profoundly interesting to most people or take place very often, just as information about gang violence may be of only peripheral concern to people in rural Montana. In this way, the environment "may alter which content is most likely to be used" in making political decisions.[26] Individuals develop a heightened sensibility to particular information based on the biases in their environments. Because individuals consume massive amounts of information, that which is most accessible is likely to be used in making judgments about new information.[27]

Political Socialization and Social Context

Most of the research on social context and politics has focused on adults' political behaviors and attitudes—voting and other types of political engagement, political discussion, and partisanship. These theories and findings are also relevant to the process of adolescents' political socialization. Just as people do not make political choices in a vacuum, they do not turn eighteen and suddenly become political animals. Although one certainly could go back (and some have gone back) to young childhood to study socialization, this study looks at the period of middle adolescence (age 14–18). This is when individuals begin to develop their self-identities, including their civic identities.[28] During adolescence, individuals begin to settle on the opinions and values that many will maintain throughout their lives.[29] It is also when most young people live at home with a parent or parents and have not ventured much beyond their local communities.

Thus, we should expect the local context to exert a significant influence on adolescents' socialization—even, perhaps, a more substantive one than for adults' political behavior. In one of the few comprehensive contextual studies of political socialization, David Campbell argues that "the civic norms within one's adolescent social environment have an effect on civic participation well beyond adolescence: *what you do now depends on where you were then.*"[30] He shows that homogeneous communities instill in young people a strong sense of civic duty that compels them to vote later in life, while heterogeneous communities provide an incentive to participate primarily to protect their interests. Both motivations, however, are instilled within the community in which one grows up.

Context operates through the same mechanism as for adults: social interaction. But there are important differences between adolescents' socialization and adults' political attitudes, both in how interaction operates and in the influence of the local context. In many ways, social interaction operates for young people in much the same way as it does for adults. Face-to-face discussions with family and friends, interactions with relative strangers, and nonverbal communication all serve to teach young people about their community's culture and expectations. The main difference is that for young people, many of these interactions, especially about politics, are not among equals.

Of course, adolescents talk about politics with their friends, but in their childhood and early adolescence, most of the knowledge they obtain about whether politics is a worthwhile enterprise, or which party best suits their preferences, or what these preferences ought to be, is learned from adults who have some measure of authority in the eyes of young people. These include teachers, parents, coaches, church leaders, grandparents and other extended-family members, and other adults in the community. When adults discuss political parties, candidates, or hot-button issues, such as the arrival of immigrants in their town, children are listening and absorbing this as information, even at perhaps unconscious levels, about what is appropriate and good. How often have we parents been shocked by our child repeating something we have said when we thought he or she was not listening? Or saying something at odds with our values and beliefs and wondering, "Where did that come from?" In all likelihood, depending on the child's age, he or she heard it from a trusted adult. While it is certainly true that not all adult interactions are between equals (bosses and employees or pastors and parishioners, for example), it is often the case that adults have chosen to enter into these situations.

This is one of the main ways in which the context is likely to affect children and adults differently. Young people do not choose their context; adults do. Children have almost no control over where they live. This solves one of the greatest hurdles for those who study the effects of social context. For adults, it is difficult to know whether contextual effects are not, at least in part, products of self-selection. Have people chosen their residence because of its inhabitants' views, or do the interactions with other residents exert significant effects on their behavior and attitudes? This suggests a much clearer causal chain between the community and political behavior for young people than for adults. For young people, the culture and norms of the surroundings almost certainly precede their attitudes and inclinations. With the exception of friendship groups, children cannot self-select into any particular community or school. Adults, especially parents, have a significant influence on the "nature of their child's social networks by seeking out schools or activities characterized by differing degrees of class-based, ethnic, gender and/or religious diversity/homogeneity."[31] Though young people do pick their friends, youth networks tend to be shaped primarily by the school and leisure activities that have been chosen by their parents.[32]

Another important difference between adults and youth with regard to the influence of social context is that adolescents are more confined to their local environment than are adults. Even though the Internet and cable television may have expanded the opportunities for young people to experience some of what the larger world has to offer, most teenagers' lives revolve around family and friends in their immediate local area. Adults, however, may have to commute to work outside their residential area and may have friends in places all over the country. Their information environment is larger than it is for the typical adolescent.

The small nature of the local environment is especially true in rural areas where the population is relatively homogeneous and stable. In fact, one of the advantages often mentioned about rural areas is that everyone knows one another, that people share the same values and goals, and that there is a great deal of predictability about life. According to Sonya Salamon, "Daily life [in rural areas] thus takes place among a cast of familiars whose social networks are overlapping rather than segmented."[33] Youth may encounter the same adults in several different settings, serving to homogenize the information available to young people. For those who may leave the community only to attend an event in a neighboring community (that probably looks much like their own town), it may be rare to encounter anyone with dramatically divergent views or life experiences. According to William Freudenberg, "In a stable small community with a high density of acquaintanceship, socialization can often be as much a community effort as a familial one, and hence it can also be vulnerable to disruption in the face of community change."[34]

There are, of course, many aspects of the community that get translated through social interaction. Studies of adults have shown that one of the most important aspects of the social context is its ethnic composition. This research is reviewed extensively in the coming chapters. In particular, this book looks at diversity in the context of rural America. Ethnically diverse communities and neighborhoods in the heart of rural America are a relatively new phenomenon. How do young people in diverse communities feel about their new neighbors? Do they reject the changes occurring around them, or have they welcomed the increasing diversity in their communities?

Outline of the Book

The first chapter describes population change in rural America in the past 30 years. It discusses the extent of foreign immigration into new destinations, focusing especially on Iowa. It reviews the literature on the economic, social, and political effects of immigration. The chapter also reviews, in some detail, the extensive demographic changes in two immigrant-receiving communities: Perry and Storm Lake. It is important to note that these communities underwent a greater volume of in-migration than cities in traditional destinations in California and Arizona. Demographic changes were substantial, and given the original homogeneity of these populations, most would have expected to see significant friction.

The second chapter discusses the natural experimental survey research design. Because there is no appropriate pre-test, one of the best ways to measure the effects of ethnic diversity is to use the natural setting in Iowa. Several communities have undergone rapid ethnic diversification in the past 20 years, while most have had populations that have remained fairly static. This chapter discusses the selection of Iowa and the communities within the study. It demonstrates that the five cases were similar across nearly every social, political, and economic indicator prior to the arrival of immigrants in the 1990s.

Chapter 3 looks at the effects of ethnic diversity on support for immigrants. Based on the results from the 2001 surveys, the findings indicate that on some indicators, ethnic diversity dampens sympathy for immigrants. On closer inspection, however, this occurs only in Perry, the community with the least experience with diversity. In Storm Lake, where the diversification process began with a small group of Southeast Asian refugees in the 1970s and 1980s, young people are just as tolerant as the students in the homogeneous communities. The chapter shows that tolerance in Perry is a function of both positive affect toward Hispanics and an older, stubborn form of prejudice based on negative attitudes related to African Americans, a group that has very little presence or history in either community.

The fourth chapter examines the effects of rapid ethnic diversification on civic outcomes: political knowledge, efficacy, generalized trust, intention to vote, participation in school activities, and political discussion. On the whole, the findings do not support the idea that diversity lessens civic engagement. Native-born youth in Storm Lake and Perry have lower levels of political knowledge than their counterparts in the homogeneous communities. In Perry, youth have lower levels of external efficacy and are less trusting of others. There are no significant differences on any of the other measures of social capital or engagement. Furthermore, in Storm Lake, young people are significantly more engaged in school activities than youth in any of the other towns. These results suggest that as communities become more accustomed to diversity, differences in civic engagement decline.

Chapter 5 examines change over time. Chapters 3 and 4 rely on survey data from only one point in time: the fall of 2001. The differences between Storm Lake and Perry are primarily due to the fact that Storm Lake had slightly more experience with diversity than did Perry, owing to the Asian refugees who began to arrive in Storm Lake in the 1970s. Community leaders in Storm Lake began officially to come to terms with the demographic changes before those in other diversifying communities. By the early 2000s, White high school students in Storm Lake had more experience with diverse cultures than did those in Perry. This chapter demonstrates that in a relatively short time, native-born youth in Perry became more supportive of immigration and more civically engaged. This chapter also chronicles the towns' responses to the demographic changes throughout the 1990s and 2000s.

Chapter 6 asks, "What happened to my town?" Native-born residents of small towns are often worried about the negative effects if immigrants move to their communities in large numbers. This chapter examines several of the most serious concerns and the extent to which they were realized over a 20-year period in Perry and Storm Lake. It looks at natives' concerns about becoming a minority group, about losing power to Latinos, about public costs, about the quality of the schools, and about immigrants' desires to assimilate into mainstream American culture. Chapter 6 also brings the demographic profiles of these communities up to date. Most of the fears about the potential negative effects of immigrants have not been borne out in either Perry or Storm Lake.

The final chapter discusses the implications of the findings, including the implications for immigration policy and rural communities. People adapted fairly quickly to their new environments. Given the dearth of rural research in political science, this may be surprising to those who assume that rural America is a bastion of intolerance, full of hostile and dangerous rednecks. My results challenge scholars to conduct more systematic research on small towns.

1

Transformation of Small-Town America

Change there will be . . . For he who rejects change is the architect of decay. The only human institution which rejects progress is the cemetery.

—British Prime Minister Harold Wilson

D riving into Perry, Iowa, one finds a quintessential American small town. There are the nicely mowed lawns, picket fences, and turn-of-the-century homes, many of which have been recently restored. There is the high school at the edge of town, with its Friday night football games where one can get the local delicacy: pork chop on a stick.[1] Heading into downtown Perry, the Carnegie library sits across the street from City Hall and a restored boutique hotel. Turning off the main drag on Willis Avenue and onto Second Street, one notices more small-town must-haves: a variety store, a locally owned bank, an old-fashioned ice cream shop, and a three-screen movie theater.

At first glance, travelers would think they had been dropped into any typical small, Midwestern town—until, that is, they look a little closer. Across the street from the Benjamin Franklin variety store sits Restaurante El Buen Gusto, an authentic El Salvadoran *pupuseria*. A few blocks down, one can wander into the Panaderia Mexican bakery for pastries or a bottle of Jarritos strawberry soda, or stop in for lunch at Casa de Oro, a Mexican restaurant on the same block. Drive past St. Patrick's church and it is hard to miss the sign listing three weekly services in English and two in Spanish. For those who grew up in small towns in the Midwest and South, this picture is incongruent with our childhood memories.

Since the early 1990s Perry, a town with fewer than 10,000 people, has become home to many immigrants from Latin America. Along with dozens of other communities in the Midwest, this town has undergone a significant transformation in the last twenty years. Rural communities in the Midwest are no longer seas of white faces with German and Scandinavian surnames. First- and second-generation immigrants from Latin America and Southeast Asia have migrated to small towns, drawn by low-skill jobs and in search of new permanent homes for their families. Communities where "everyone knows your name" have had to adapt to newcomers who look and speak differently from those who have lived there for generations. These communities can be seen as microcosms of ethnic changes taking place in the United States as a whole. More important to the residents of the communities themselves, however, is that they are some of the few small towns in rural areas escaping the risk of becoming ghost towns.

This study examines the effect of immigration into small towns in the Midwest—in particular, its effects on political socialization. How have rapidly changing demographics in formerly homogeneous communities affected the political attitudes and inclinations of young people? Are young people "architects of decay," angry about the changes in their communities and prejudiced toward their new neighbors? Or are they generally accepting, even welcoming, of this transformation? This chapter examines the demographic changes in rural America and the initial changes in Perry and Storm Lake, Iowa.

Immigration in Rural America

For most of the twentieth century, immigrant gateways were in urban areas. In fact, from 1971 to 1993, nearly half of all immigrants went to five U.S. cities: New York, Los Angeles, Chicago, Houston, and Miami.[2] Starting in the late 1980s, but picking up dramatically in the 1990s, immigrants began to head toward entirely new destinations, including the rural Midwest. Scholars argue that both "push" and "pull" factors are responsible for this migration.[3] On the push side of things, several factors converged to precipitate movement to new gateways, including a profound economic crisis in Mexico, pushing out many of those who were not too poor to afford to leave.[4] Similar economic and political crises in other parts of the world have served to push immigrants and refugees to seek a better life in the United States.

Within the United States, other forces shaped where these immigrants would end up. Sociologists refer to the "context of reception" as determining migration flows and immigrant incorporation in the host country. The context of reception includes the interaction of the following elements: (1) the condition of the host labor market; (2) government policies (both national and local); (3) the resources of the existing co-ethnic community; and (4) the response of the native population to newcomers.[5] With regard to national policy, the passage of the Immigration Reform and Control Act (IRCA) of 1986 granted legal status to some 3 million people and gave them greater freedom and mobility, enabling them to move to new destinations. Further, the Border Patrol was strengthened along the California and Texas borders and served to channel immigrants to less visible locations in Arizona and the lower Rio Grande Valley. An important state-level policy also helped push immigrants out of one traditional destination: Proposition 187 in California prohibited undocumented migrants from using publicly provided services and sent an explicit message to immigrants that they were not welcome.[6]

The labor market also has a significant role to play in determining the numbers of immigrants seeking to come to the United States and where they will go when they arrive. In the late 1980s, economic growth began to slow in New York and California. Due in part to increasing labor supply in traditional gateways because of IRCA, but also to economic downturns in the early 1990s, the job market hardened in traditional gateways.[7] Between 1990 and 2000, the percentage of Mexican immigrants in California dropped 10 points and reached an all-time low in Texas in 2000.

Job growth was more significant in rural areas in the Midwest and South. One of the growth industries in rural areas during this time was the food-processing industry. Throughout the 1980s, old-line meatpacking companies began to fail or sell to larger corporations. These new companies, dominated by the "big three"—Iowa Beef Packers (IBP; now Tyson Fresh Meats), Excel (now Cargill), and ConAgra (now Swift)—changed their business plans dramatically. The industry began to prioritize proximity to animal supplies over labor supplies. They moved their operations to small, rural communities in Kansas, Iowa, Nebraska, and Minnesota to cut down on transportation costs and because they were right-to-work states.[8] The new breed of packers gutted the unions that had existed for many years in the old-line plants, slashed wages and benefits, and increased productivity. Between 1967 and 1982, the meatpacking industry's output per hour increased at an average yearly rate of 2.8 percent; after 1976, the rate increased 3.2 percent.[9] The reduction in wages was partly a product of the redesign of plants, such that skilled butchers were no longer necessary. Their jobs were broken down into smaller tasks that could be performed by unskilled workers.

With line speeds increasing each year and workers having fewer skills and less experience, the job became increasingly dangerous. When inevitable labor shortages erupted in the small towns, the "new-breed packers . . . relied increasingly on recruitment of Hispanic workers into these rural counties to make up for local labor shortages."[10] Corporations even began formal recruitment procedures in U.S. urban areas and in Mexico.[11] The meatpacking companies argued that they had to hire immigrants because Americans did not want to work in these jobs under these new conditions. Meatpacking jobs today carry a stigma that discourages Anglos from applying.[12]

Simultaneously, the rest of the rural economy, especially in agriculture, was suffering its worst economic crisis in decades, a crisis that contributed greatly to the ethnic diversification that was to come.[13] Over the twentieth century, rural America has consistently declined as a proportion of the U.S. population, as demonstrated in Figure 1.1. The late 1970s and early 1980s were disastrous, especially for farmers. In the 1970s, agricultural prices skyrocketed, and farmers planted more than ever, leading many to take on a lot of debt. High prices on commodities led to higher supplies and an ultimate drop in prices by the late

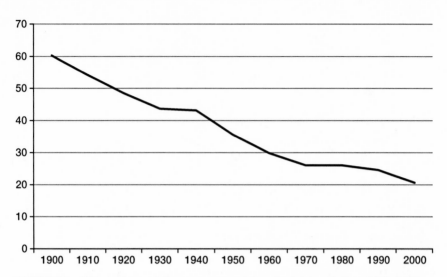

FIGURE 1.1   U.S. rural population as a percentage of total population, 1900–2000

1970s. Further, the national economic crisis of the late 1970s exacerbated the problems for farmers. High interest rates made it difficult for farmers to borrow money at the beginning of each planting season and many farmers lost their land. By 1990, the farm population had declined so much that a record low of only 1.8 percent of Americans still lived on farms, compared with nearly 25 percent in 1940. David Danbom states, "Even in the countryside farmers were becoming anomalous."[14] In addition to the rural exodus, birthrates in many Midwestern states began to drop. The populations of many rural communities were rapidly aging. Mining and oil industries declined in rural areas, and the few existing railroads closed shop. The economic crisis hit Midwestern farming-dependent communities particularly hard.[15]

All of these factors led states and small towns to roll out the welcome mat for meatpacking companies seeking to move their operations to their ever shrinking communities. IBP received $7 million from the State of Iowa to expand its business within the state, even though IBP was already making a hefty profit.[16] Many towns gave the companies tax incentives and promised to take a hands-off approach to their daily operations, essentially giving them free rein to hire non-union, low-wage workers. The idea, of course, was that the companies would provide jobs to displaced local workers, but in reality employers who took advantage of the towns' offers ended up recruiting immigrants from other U.S. states and outside the country.[17] Storm Lake offered IBP industrial revenue bonds, tax abatements, and favorable water rates. For IBP's $3.9 million investment in the Storm Lake plant in 1982, the city received only $253,640 in taxes, a pattern that continued well into the 1990s.[18]

For immigrants, other aspects of the labor market also made moving to small towns more attractive. The jobs were year-round, allowing families to settle in one place; they also paid more than migrant labor and allowed for some upward mobility. According to Helen Marrow's research in small towns in the rural South, meatpacking plants offered "newcomers a strategic hole of opportunity within which to establish themselves and make a go at moving up and achieving the American dream over time, precisely when similar opportunity has begun to stagnate, become saturated, or even decline in the traditional immigrant gateways."[19] Although the plants had extraordinarily high rates of turnover in the first several years of reliance on immigrant labor, this declined over time. The jobs allow for some within-company mobility, as well as, for some, outward mobility to less dangerous jobs within the community.

The last elements of the context of reception are the resources of co-ethnics within the host communities and the reception immigrants receive from natives. Traditional gateways came with many drawbacks: crime-ridden neighborhoods, bad schools, and high costs of living. Many immigrants perceive rural areas as safer, more affordable, and offering better opportunities for their children.[20] In Perry, a woman who moved from Mexico described the town as "*tranquilo* (quiet, peaceful)." These attributes helped the first wave of immigrants overcome the lack of existing social networks within new destinations.[21] After the initial waves, new immigrants used social networks based on the first settlers. In many communities, for example, a significant proportion of the immigrants originated in the same town in Mexico. Men would come first, usually without their wives and children, to scout the scene and determine whether it would be a good move for their families. After several months or years, families would follow, in some cases, while other immigrants would choose to leave the community altogether. The remainder of this book examines the final aspect of the context of reception: the response of the natives within two small Midwestern towns.

Rapid Ethnic Diversification of Small Communities in the Midwest

Between 1980 and 2005, two out of every five individuals added to the Midwest were Latino.[22] This region's growth has been tied to increasing ethnic diversity, especially to the growth of the Latino population. Further, much of the growth has been outside major metropolitan areas. Since 1980, the Hispanic population in U.S. rural areas and small towns has doubled, from 1.5 million to 3.2 million.[23] Hispanic population growth in non-metropolitan areas exceeded that of metropolitan counties from 1990 to 2000 and accounted for more than 25 percent of all non-metropolitan growth during the 1990s.[24] In the Midwest during this period, the Hispanic non-metropolitan growth rate was 113 percent, second only to its growth in the South and far exceeding the rates in the traditional

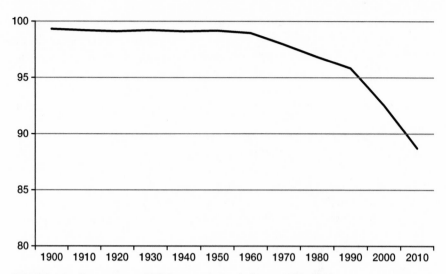

FIGURE 1.2   Percentage of White population in Iowa, 1900–2010

gateways in the Southwest and Northeast. In the Midwest, the growth of the foreign-born population (an astounding 206 percent increase) explains 61 percent of the increase in the Hispanic population, indicating that the majority of Hispanic newcomers to the Midwest in the 1990s were born outside the United States.[25]

Taking a closer look at Iowa, its population remained relatively static from 1960 to 1980 (growing at about 3 percent with each census) but was devastated with the farm crisis in the 1980s, losing 4.7 percent of its population from 1980 to 1990. In the next decade, the population grew by 5.4 percent, a rate not seen since the period between 1910 and 1920. Much of this growth was the result of immigration. By the 1990s, state leaders had recognized the looming population shortage. The substantial growth from immigration led Governor Tom Vilsack to propose in 2000 that Iowa become an "immigrant enterprise zone" and recruit more than 500,000 immigrants to fill jobs that would be lost as the native population aged. Vilsack's plans hit several roadblocks, including a widespread lack of support from the predominantly White communities throughout the state. Within a year, he had dropped his initiative.[26]

Throughout the twentieth century, Iowa's non-Hispanic White population hovered near 100 percent but dropped below 95 percent in 2000 and then below 90 percent in 2010 (Figure 1.2). The growth in the Latino population jumped significantly between 1990 and 2000, from 1.2 percent (32,647) of Iowa's population in 1990 to 2.8 percent (83,473) in 2000. By 2010, more than 150,000 residents of Iowa were Hispanic, composing about 5 percent of the population. These figures are comparable to other Midwestern and Southern states. At 170 percent, Iowa had the eleventh-fastest-growing Hispanic population in the

United States from 1990 to 2000 and the third-fastest growth rate in the Midwest.[27] The Asian and Pacific Islander population also grew over the 30 year period, from 0.4 percent of the population in 1980 to 1.8 percent in 2010.

Economic, Social, and Political Effects of Immigration

Many scholars across the social sciences have examined the effects of immigration, especially on the economy and society. Some studies claim that immigrants are primarily a drain on the U.S. economy. According to these arguments, immigrants displace American workers (especially African Americans and low-skilled Whites); they enjoy more government benefits than they pay into the system; and they cost communities a great deal for social services.[28] Other studies show just the opposite: immigrants pay more into the system than they cost it; they do not take Americans' jobs but, rather, keep corporations from leaving the country; and they are not more likely than similarly situated natives to participate in the social welfare system.[29] In downtrodden areas, such as small, mostly rural communities and Rust Belt towns, immigrants occupy housing that otherwise would be vacant; their children boost the enrollments of the public schools, helping to keep teachers and staff employed; and some open businesses along commercial streets that have been boarded up for years.[30] Most economists today believe that immigrants are primarily a net gain for the country, especially over the long term.

There is a similar debate about the social effects of immigration. One side defends the position that immigrants, particularly in this wave, are unlikely to assimilate or attempt to integrate themselves into their communities.[31] According to this view, immigrants pose a significant danger to social cohesion and national identity.[32] Language has become one of the most important factors in this debate. Natives tend to want immigrants to learn English immediately upon arrival, if not before they come. These concerns are not new or exclusive to this wave.[33] To many, "English language proficiency [is] perceived not as a skill but as the reflection of core American values."[34] Natives see immigrants' inability to speak English as unwillingness to assimilate to American values and culture. Just as with past waves, linguistic challenges "constitute an important component of [immigrants'] symbolic threat [for natives], both as a determinant of prejudice and as a justification for preexisting xenophobic attitudes."[35]

In addition to the pluralistic and multicultural critiques about the inherent ethnocentrism of assimilation, other social scientists argue that immigration has a primarily positive effect on society. Immigrants typically have a lot of ambition and drive; they bring energy to their communities and workplaces. They revitalize their communities by bringing new ideas and diversity.[36] Instead of giving up their native cultures and giving in to a static, dominant American culture, immigrants change mainstream society and culture, primarily for the better.[37] Many also point out that it is not uncommon for first-generation immigrants to struggle with the language, to rely on co-ethnic groups, and to avoid getting involved in the larger community. The second and third generations, however, typically learn the language much more quickly and are often indistinguishable from native-born Americans in their cultural, social, and political preferences.[38] Still others point out that most immigrants, particularly those who take low-skill jobs and do not speak English, find anything but a promised land here in the United States. They often must live in oppressive settings, suffer with poverty and lack of basic services, and are the victims of exploitation and discrimination.[39]

Political scientists studying the impact of immigration on politics have focused on the potential changes to elite coalitions, parties and partisanship, turnout, and voting behavior. As the number of immigrants from Latin America and Asia began to increase, many scholars believed the prospects for minority representation would be enhanced, especially in cities where most immigrants arrived. Among some, this raises fears about a coming White minority and its loss of political power. The reality, however, has shown that in urban areas "immigration-induced diversity may actually threaten the prospects for future Black empowerment" and that minority coalitions have not emerged in most cities.[40] A growing body of evidence suggests that relations between African Americans and immigrants are increasingly hostile.[41] In addition, there are substantial differences between Latino subgroups, who are motivated to participate by somewhat different factors.[42]

The "Latinization" of the United States could also have repercussions for national politics, political-party strength, and voting behavior. Many scholars believed that once mobilized, Latinos would automatically eschew the Republican Party in favor of the Democratic Party. Although the Democrats have recently won more support from Latinos, especially in 2008, Republicans made inroads in the Hispanic community in 2000 and 2004.[43] Further, Latinos and other immigrants have not dramatically changed the makeup of partisan coalitions or the political agenda. Latinos tend to have lower overall participation rates than the general population and lower rates of civic organizational activity. Because so many Latinos are foreign-born and ineligible to vote, they are generally uninterested in politics.[44] The 2006 Latino National Survey, for example, shows that even though a plurality of Latinos (46.7 percent) are "somewhat interested" in politics, nearly one-third of the Latinos group still is not interested in politics.[45] Current levels of interest and participation, however, are likely to increase. Turnout and partisanship among immigrant groups tends to increase with years of residence in the United States and English proficiency.[46] Further, political parties have not begun to effectively mobilize Latinos or other immigrant groups.[47] For Latinos, mobilization makes a substantial difference in turnout and other types of participation.[48]

As for the political effects of immigration in rural areas, there is very little analysis, but there is some indication that immigrants are likely to play a limited role in local politics, at least in the first generation. Latinos who remain isolated from other Americans are less likely to obtain information about mainstream

American politics and institutions than those who are more socially integrated.[49] Immigrants in rural America, in many ways, are more isolated than their urban or suburban counterparts. And although native-born residents of small towns tend to be very active in civic organizations, there are relatively few strong social or political organizations serving the interests of immigrants in rural communities. Community organizations are very important in providing services and support to newcomers and in helping them adapt to their new communities. Immigrant political mobilization is difficult without a strong civil society.[50] A strong immigrant-focused civil society, however, is limited in areas of new migration.[51] The absence of strong networks and organizational activity in small towns and rural areas may inhibit political activity among new immigrants.

Even so, Jonathan Benjamin-Alvarado and his colleagues show that in 2006, immigrant groups in nontraditional gateways organized and actively protested H.R. 4437, a bill that would have criminalized illegal status.[52] On a national day of protest in which the media focused on protests in U.S. major cities, about 15,000 marchers in Omaha, Nebraska, took to the streets; protests also spread to other parts of that state, including South Sioux City, where 5,000 people marched; Lincoln, where 4,000 protestors marched; and Schuyler and Grand Island, where thousands more marched. Melissa Michelson also finds that old-fashioned door-to-door canvassing by members of co-ethnic groups can have a significant effect on Latino participation in rural areas of California.[53] These studies are unique, however, because political scientists have largely ignored rural immigrants.

Immigration in Perry and Storm Lake, Iowa

One of the problems with much of this research is that most studies examine immigration's effects on the nation or in the traditional gateway states or cities. Rural areas and small towns that have little or no experience with recent immigrants have some special challenges and opportunities. Given the negative response to Governor Vilsack's proposal to increase the number of immigrants to Iowa, many would assume that Iowans would be unwelcoming to immigrants. The state fueled these assumptions when it passed a bill in 2002 to make English the official language of the state. Using Perry and Storm Lake as models of other Midwestern small towns that have undergone rapid ethnic diversification, the remainder of this chapter examines the specific demographic changes in these communities and the initial responses to the changes in these communities.

Immigrants are not evenly distributed across Iowa's population. Certain communities have experienced the brunt of the population shifts, while others are nearly as homogeneous as they have always been. The towns examined in this study illustrate this phenomenon. From 1980 to 1990, each of the five communities in this study lost population, mirroring the substantial population loss in rural areas nationwide during that period (see Table 1.1). Storm Lake's losses were smaller than the others', in part because of the growth of the Asian

TABLE 1.1 Population Change and Asian and Hispanic Growth in Five Iowa Towns in Study, 1980–2000

	Boone	Carroll	Harlan	Perry	Storm Lake
Population (1980)	12,602	9,705	5,357	7,053	8,814
Population (1990)	12,392	9,579	5,148	6,652	8,769
Population (2000)	12,803	10,106	5,282	7,633	10,076
Percent change (1980–1990)	−1.7	−1.3	−3.9	−5.7	−0.5
Percent change (1990–2000)	+3.3	+5.5	+2.6	+14.7	+14.9
Asian population (1980)[a]	64	38	32	38	76
Percent Asian (1980)[a]	0.5	0.3	0.6	0.5	0.8
Asian population (1990)	49	38	14	17	304
Percent Asian (1990)	0.4	0.4	0.3	0.3	3.5
Asian population (2000)[b]	27	52	25	71	790
Percent Asian (2000)[b]	0.2	0.5	0.5	0.9	7.8
Percent change in Asian population (1980–1990)	−23.4	0	−56.3	−55.3	+300
Percent change in Asian population (1990–2000)	−44.9	+36.8	+78.6	+317.6	+159.9
Hispanic population (1980)[c]	65	58	29	77	39
Percent Hispanic (1980)[c]	0.5	0.6	0.5	1.1	0.4
Hispanic population (1990)	48	35	11	47	102
Percent Hispanic (1990)	0.4	0.4	0.2	0.7	1.1
Hispanic population (2000)	112	58	33	1,873	2,121
Percent Hispanic (2000)	0.9	0.6	0.6	24.5	21.1
Percent change in Hispanic population (1980–1990)	−2.2	−39.7	−62.1	−39.0	+161.5
Percent change in Hispanic population (1990–2000)	+133.3	+65.7	+200	+3,885	+1,979

Source: The population figures for 1990 and 2000 are from American Factfinder, available online at http://factfinder.census.gov. The 1980 figures are from the State Data Center of Iowa, available online at http://data.iowadatacenter.org/DemographicProfiles/ISU%20Profiles/1980/City/BooneCity1980.pdf.

[a] The Census 1980 figures for Asian population include those who identified themselves as Japanese, Chinese, Filipino, Korean, Asian Indian, Vietnamese, Hawaiian, Guamanian, Samoan, and Other Asian.

[b] The Census 2000 figures for Asian population include those who identified themselves as Asian, Native Hawaiian, or Other Pacific Islander.

[c] The Census 1980 figures for Hispanic population include those who identified themselves as Persons of Spanish Origin.

population during the 1980s. Between 1975 and 1979, twenty-four Tai Dam (a subgroup of Laotian) families settled in the community after the Vietnam War. This population grew in the 1980s by 300 percent as relatives and friends of the original refugees followed.

During the 1990s, the population recovered in all of the towns. From 1990 to 2000, the populations of each community increased, but at very different rates. In Perry and Storm Lake, the dramatic increase in population is due to

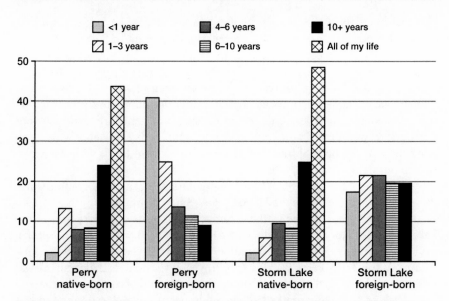

FIGURE 1.3 Immigrants' and natives' length of residence in Perry and Storm Lake as reported in 2001 survey

substantial increases in the Asian and Hispanic populations. Although all of the communities increased their numbers of racial minorities in the 1990s (with the exception of the Asian population in Boone), the gains are staggering in Perry and Storm Lake. In Perry, the Asian population increased by 318 percent, and in Storm Lake, it increased by 160 percent; the Hispanic population increased in Perry by 3,885 percent and in Storm Lake by 1,979 percent. It is important to note that these rates of change greatly exceed the national rates. During this same period, the nationwide Latino population increased by 58 percent, and the Asian population increased by 48 percent.[54] Even in traditional gateway areas, such as the five-county area around Los Angeles, the rates of change came nowhere near what Perry or Storm Lake experienced.[55]

Another way to look at the increases in the minority populations in these communities is to consider their proportions in the overall populations of the towns. The Hispanic population went from 1 percent of Storm Lake's population in 1990 to 21 percent in 2000; in Perry, it went from less than 1 percent in 1990 to 24.5 percent in 2000. Although the Asian population in Perry was still minuscule in 2000 (only .9 percent), it increased from 3.5 percent of Storm Lake's population in 1990 to 7.8 percent in 2000.

Figure 1.3 demonstrates an important difference between Perry and Storm Lake. Looking at results from the representative sample of high school students in these communities in 2001, a greater proportion of Storm Lake's immigrant youth have lived in the town for many years than those in Perry. In 2001, only 9 percent of the immigrant youth in Perry had lived there for longer than ten years, while nearly 20 percent of immigrant young people had called Storm Lake home for more than half their lives. Similarly, 18 percent of Storm Lake's foreign-born youth said they had lived there for less than one year, compared with 41 percent in Perry. The majority of the foreign-born youth who had lived in Storm Lake for ten or more years were the children of Asian refugees. These refugees gave longtime Storm Lake residents an opportunity to learn about living with people who had different cultural backgrounds, histories, and religious practices. As we will see in the coming chapters, this early experience with diversity helped native-born Storm Lake residents to come to terms with the explosion of immigrants in the 1990s.

As in other small towns that have undergone significant demographic shifts, these dramatic increases in the Hispanic and Asian communities can be attributed to substantial changes in the meatpacking industry in Perry and Storm Lake. Perry's history with meatpacking began in 1920 with the Hausserman Packing Company, which closed in 1925 and was reopened as Perry Packing Company and, later, Perry Packing and Provision Company. The company was sold to Arnold Brothers Packing Company in 1933 and became a subsidiary of Swift Packing Company until 1956 when this aged facility closed for good.[56] A new plant was built on the west side of town, and in 1962 the Iowa Pork Company employed 200 workers on the kill floor and planned to increase retail sales and provide an outlet for local farmers to sell their hogs.[57] Its quick merger with IBP brought in more capital to enlarge the Perry plant and include a cut floor in addition to the kill floor. An upstart, IBP had little interest in adhering to the rules that had been negotiated between the packing unions and management, leading to a strike in 1965. Oscar Mayer bought the plant soon thereafter, quickly enlarging and upgrading it to employ more than 600 workers. According to Jim Olesen, the president of the local branch of the United Food and Commercial Workers, the Oscar Mayer plant was a "close knit" group, where one "had to know someone" to get hired.[58] One Oscar Mayer employee stated that there was "one colored guy" and a woman but no other minorities at the plant.[59]

After several years of attempting to compete against nonunion IBP plants, including a variety of worker concessions, Oscar Mayer sold the plant back to IBP in 1988. The company cut wages and began aggressively recruiting Latinos from East Los Angeles.[60] IBP merged with Tyson in 2001, which runs the company today.[61] Today, Tyson is Perry's largest employer (1,200 employees). Its plant packages pork specifically for Nippon Meat Packers, Japan's largest meat company. Twenty percent of the men in Perry are employed in the food industry, the vast majority at the Tyson plant.[62] And 10 percent of the women are employed in the food industry, second only to health care.

Storm Lake has been home to significant meatpacking operations since 1935 and became a major slaughtering center for Kingan (later, Hygrade).[63] Hygrade was an "old-line" pork plant that shipped meat in whole sides to groceries, where butchers cut it for retail sale. The plant paid generous wages to its unionized employees. As they did the jobs at the Oscar Mayer plant in Perry, many people in town coveted positions at the Hygrade plant, which were considered some of the most secure jobs for the local middle class, especially those who did not go to college. By the late 1970s, workers earned an average of $30,000 per year (or $102,000 in 2011 dollars).[64] In 1981, the plant closed and was purchased six months later by IBP. The new plant hired very few former Hygrade workers and dramatically expanded the facility. It brought new methods, such as faster line speeds, that required a larger workforce. Starting wages were significantly lower, at about $6 per hour, and benefits were slashed.[65] IBP hired several Southeast Asian refugees who had settled in Storm Lake. Over the next few years, the company began to offer incentives to those who could recruit other refugees, offering $150 to any Laotian who recruited relatives or friends to settle in Storm Lake and work at the plant.[66] By 1992, more than 300 Lao worked at the Storm Lake IBP plant, making up more than a quarter of the company's work-force.[67] Around this time, IBP recruited about 70 Mexican Mennonites, signaling a change from the use only of refugees to more aggressive recruiting of Latinos.

Today, the largest employers in town are two meat processing facilities. Tyson Fresh Meats (the former IBP plant) operates a large hog slaughterhouse, and Sara Lee Foods has a turkey processing plant. Tyson employs about 2,000 workers and slaughters nearly 15,000 hogs per day. Sara Lee has 700 employees slaughtering 30,000 turkeys per day.[68] Thirty-two percent of men and 17 percent of women in Storm Lake are employed in the food industry. Only the local schools employ more women.[69] The plant is central to Storm Lake's economy; in addition to employing labor, it purchases millions of hogs from local farms.[70]

The Importance of Time in Understanding Responses to Immigration

The early years of demographic change in both diverse communities were described by most residents as turbulent. Several people expressed how the number of immigrants "sneaked" up on the community. According to many residents, what started out as a few men coming to work in the meatpacking plant "exploded" into several hundred new community members within a very short period of time. The coming chapters examine the responses in detail over nearly two decades. It is critical to examine the responses to and effect of immigrants over time. Dennis Chong refers to an "adjustment process" that must take place when there is significant change in a community's composition. He states, "Tolerance . . . depends also on the ability of people to assuage fears and anxieties and to reconcile themselves to new ideas and groups."[71] This reconciliation takes time, but many studies fail to adequately capture this process.

Chong describes tolerance as a dynamic process of adaptation. Likewise, this study argues that the native-born residents of these diverse communities adapt and adjust to the demographic changes occurring within their borders. White residents of Perry and Storm Lake started out by ignoring newly arriving immigrants—denying their existence and the changes being wrought by their presence. At some point, a critical mass had arrived, and longtime residents could ignore the newcomers no longer. Many became suspicious and anxious about the new groups. With the exception of a small minority, this anxiety generally did not manifest itself as hostility; rather, it was a more subtle discomfort some native Iowans had about their new neighbors. Over time, however, they have developed a "fair-minded assessment of [immigrants'] characteristics and the consequences of not censoring or repressing [them]."[72] In other words, White residents became less fearful, less anxious, and less suspicious of ethnic minorities and in doing so became more accepting of changes in their communities. This did not happen overnight; nor did it occur without some bumps in the road.

I do not mean to suggest that *all* residents became happy about the changes that have taken place. Instead, the important first steps of prejudice reduction—a renunciation of prejudice—have occurred among the majority of those now living in these diverse communities. According to Chong, people are often in a process of prejudice reduction, and "fully overcoming the 'prejudice habit' presents a more formidable task and is likely to entail a great deal of internal conflict over a protracted period of time."[73] Change is driven partly by declines in bigotry among longtime residents and partly by young people who have been raised in diverse communities and never accumulate the level of prejudice once held by their adult counterparts. When researchers ignore the element of time, they can be too quick to argue that dominant groups are intolerant of minority groups.

It is particularly interesting to examine this process in rural areas. Katherine Fennelly points out that there is one unique issue with regard to immigration in rural areas: nostalgia. Rural people often think of their small communities as idyllic: as safe places to raise children; as sheltered from the urban problems of crime, drugs, and bad schools; as less stress-inducing by giving life a sense of predictability; and as places where so-called traditional values are shared by community residents.[74] Attitudes change *very* slowly in small communities, especially among adults. Rural nostalgia leads many residents of small towns to believe that demographic changes, particularly immigrants, are primarily the cause of rural problems. Immigrants become scapegoats for rural America's economic and social problems. Further, part of the nostalgia is wrapped up in ethnic solidarity and a selective remembering of how long it took their immigrant forefathers to learn English and integrate fully into the community.[75]

Looking at a variety of formerly ethnically homogeneous communities as immigrants begin to arrive, Mark Grey and his colleagues argue that most small towns follow a "20–60–20 rule" with regard to attitudes about newly arriving foreign immigrants. Twenty percent of longtime residents openly welcome immigrants and view them as an opportunity for the community; 20 percent hate them and actively attempt to get them to leave and prevent others from coming; and 60 percent are indifferent.[76] When asked about the initial reactions to immigrants in Perry, former Mayor Viivi Shirley supported Grey's contention: "I think it probably went on the continuum from 'Gosh am I glad to see you' to 'What in the hell are they doing here?' And that's polite. Like most continuums, most people were in the middle. [In the beginning] the 'go away' side was probably bigger than the welcoming side, and obviously more vocal."[77] This study will show that this rule changes over time as residents adapt to their new surroundings and as the immigrants settle down and plant roots.

The Dunghill Ideas of Cow Country

This chapter has outlined the demographic changes in rural America, in Iowa, and in the communities examined in this study. As we will see throughout the book, some residents welcomed the changes for cultural and economic reasons, and others resented the immigrants whom they saw as a threat to the way of life in their small towns. One important assumption forming the basis of this study is that communities shape the information environment for young people and that although adults certainly adapt and alter their views as a result of demographic changes in the community, these changes strongly influence young people as they develop their political and social attitudes. We should expect, then, that young people in Perry and Storm Lake will have different attitudes toward immigration, as well as different inclinations with regard to civic engagement, from those of young people in nearby homogeneous communities. The findings indicate that rural, native-born young people are adapting quite well to the changes in their communities. After some initial reluctance, adolescents in these towns become just as tolerant and engaged as those in similarly situated, predominantly White Anglo communities. Given the dearth of empirical work on rural communities, the results may surprise many people.

Urban America has long been preferred over rural places, as a destination and an avenue for research. Frank Bryan, the author of the only comprehensive study of rural politics in the United States, states that it is as if "the rural has been wiped from the consciousness of American political scientists."[78] We believe we know a great deal about rural Americans, but a search through political science journals indicates only a handful of systematic studies exclusively about rural places and people.[79] The journalist H. L. Mencken wrote about the "dunghill ideas" of "cow country," a view probably shared by most political scientists (but without Mencken's overt disdain or artful form).[80] To many coastal elites, rural Americans are backward hillbillies—inbred, uneducated, and unsophisticated. It was relatively easy for many scholars to buy Thomas Frank's argument about something being "the matter" with Kansas.[81] Of course, many believe, rural folk would allow themselves to be politically manipulated.

There are also those who look on rural America with great longing. Robert Dahl, a father of urban politics who grew up in a small town, once quipped, "Occasionally one still runs across a nostalgia for the village—a nostalgia strongest, I suspect, among people who have never lived in small towns . . . I suspect that the village probably never was all that it is cracked up to be."[82] Reminiscent of Eddie Albert's character in the television sitcom *Green Acres,* many people consider small towns safe, unchanging, idyllic places from which to escape the hectic life in the big city. In either case, rural people are simple and unsophisticated. Bryan writes about the characterization of rural people:

> They are honest, God-fearing, hardworking, and courageous or shrewd, hypocritical, lazy, and cowardly. . . . Rural people are either saluting the flag, saying their prayers, or eating a hearty breakfast, or they are lurking behind billboards in unmarked sheriffs' cars. They are either offering cool drinks to weary travelers or ambushing weekend canoeists on whom they intend to bring down insidious perversions. . . . The common denominator that links both aspects of the stereotype is parochialism or naiveté.[83]

My hope is that this study contributes to dispelling both myths. The people of these communities are neither perfect nor hideous. Although some young people certainly learn prejudice from the adults in their lives, many others learn tolerance and acceptance. In many ways, rural residents understand the complexities of immigration better than those in urban or suburban environments. When given time to adapt, the vast majority do so quite well.

2

A Natural Experiment in Iowa Towns

It is not the strongest of the species that survive, nor the most intelligent, but the one most adaptable to change.

—Clarence Darrow

As Clarence Darrow points out, adaptability is critical for every living species. It also has been crucial for U.S. small towns. Over the past half-century, many small towns in rural areas literally have died off. In spite of the fact that for most Americans rural imagery is synonymous with farm imagery, the mass rural-to-urban migration and declining family size meant that in one generation, farmers became a marginal group in the United States. Between 1946 and 1970, more than 21 million people moved from farms into urban and suburban areas.[1] Migration made it nearly impossible for communities to maintain themselves. The major bedrocks of rural communities—churches, civic organizations, and schools—could not continue with so few people and ceased to operate. As rural schools consolidated throughout the Midwest, some communities became ghost towns. The middle class left small towns, leaving behind those too poor or too rooted to pick up and start over and leading to increases in rural poverty. Despite a growth spurt in the late 1970s and early 1980s, the farm crisis that followed decimated what was left of many of the smallest communities.

Scholars and pundits have cited many reasons for these phenomena: labor-saving technological change, increasing ease of transportation, the growth of agribusiness, improvements in public health that allow people to have fewer children and to live longer, economic change and globalization, the arrival of big-box stores in small towns, the necessity of a college degree to obtain a well-paying job, a materialist culture, changes in family structure, government policies on social welfare and agriculture. The list goes on and on. Regardless of the source of change, the landscape of small-town America looks very different today from how it did 60 years ago. To survive, communities have had to adapt.

Although immigration from Latin America and Asia is not the only survival strategy for small communities, the survival and growth of many towns have depended on it.[2] In communities where residents were nearly all of European descent, and most were third-, fourth-, or even fifth-generation Americans, these newcomers meant substantial change to the composition of their communities.

Examining the effect of immigration on the attitudes of native residents in small towns poses several problems. Most significant, to study change of any kind, the best designs involve a pre-test—measures of the outcomes of interest prior to the change. In this case, it would be great to have measures of how young residents felt about immigration, diversity, and civic engagement before immigrants arrived in their communities. Without a crystal ball, however, most of us miss the appropriate window of opportunity to gauge attitudes before change occurs.

In the absence of a pre-test, this study utilizes a natural experimental design. It compares attitudes in two immigrant-receiving communities—Perry and Storm Lake, Iowa—with those in three non-immigrant-receiving towns of Boone, Carroll, and Harlan, Iowa. This chapter demonstrates the appropriate nature of this design by establishing that, prior to the arrival of immigrants in Perry and Storm Lake, the five towns were similar across many of the most important social, political, and economic indicators. In doing so, it provides the background necessary for the subsequent chapters to interpret the book's findings and discuss their implications.

Natural Experiments in the Social Sciences

A natural experiment is a naturally occurring instance of an observable phenomenon that approximates the properties of a controlled experiment. The control and treatment groups self-select into these groups in ways that are not associated with the outcomes of interest. The approach consists of comparing systems that are very similar, but "differ with respect to the factors whose influence one wishes to study."[3] One advantage of natural experiments is that those being observed do not know they are part of an experiment and therefore behave naturally, a problem with some controlled experiments in the social sciences.[4]

One of the major problems with natural experiments, as with most social science research, is the possibility that some other explanation is the "true" cause of the outcomes under investigation. Researchers refer to this as a problem of an omitted explanatory variable. Because the phenomenon under study is naturally occurring, and the researcher does not control assignment to the comparison groups (as in a controlled experiment), it is possible that researchers miss an important potential explanation for the phenomenon being studied. The best solution to the potential omitted variable bias is to select cases that are as similar as possible. If indeed the cases are exactly the same except for one factor, then it is reasonable to suggest that the outcomes were caused by this factor.

However, within political science, as in all social sciences, most of the phenomena we wish to study are products of the interactions between multiple actors in the political and social world, such that it is difficult to isolate one particular cause from any of the others. In other words, the explanatory variable is likely to be part of a "linked package of changes."[5] In the case of this study, many factors contribute to political socialization. There are individual factors, such as parents' income or education, discussion of politics in the home, and the educational aspirations of the young person; there are school-level factors, such as civic education classes, the quality of the schools and teachers, and the availability of extracurricular opportunities; and, there are community-level factors, such as the partisan composition of the town or its level of social capital. Each of these factors contributes, often in overlapping ways, to the development of political attitudes in young people. Thus, the ethnic diversity of the community is one of potentially dozens of possible explanations for variations in socialization outcomes.

Even with such complex interrelationships between the potential factors responsible for the outcomes of interest, it is possible to eliminate some concern about an omitted variable in two ways. First, one must identify alternative explanations and demonstrate there is no significant variation on these factors across the cases. Second, it is possible to control for individual factors using statistical analysis. Multiple regression analysis explicitly tests the effects of other possible factors. The main goal of this chapter is to demonstrate the similarities and differences across the five towns in the study to eliminate explanations other than the treatment: the arrival of immigrants.

Case Selection

Another important concern with natural experiments is the technique for selecting cases. Cases must be selected independently of the outcomes we wish to study, and subjects must not self-select into treatment and control groups because of the outcomes of interest. In this case, the five communities in this study should have been selected not because of their socialization outcomes but, rather, solely on the basis of the treatment (ethnic diversity) under investigation. This is fairly easy to demonstrate, considering that we (and anyone else in the communities) did not know the results of the socialization outcomes until after we selected the towns and surveyed the respondents.

It must also be true that residents of these communities do not choose to live in these communities because of the outcomes in this study: tolerance, political knowledge, efficacy, and participation. Many native-born residents have lived in these communities for generations, with no consideration of the political socialization of their children. Immigrants say they come to these towns primarily because of the availability of jobs. They stay in rural communities because they are quiet and peaceful, especially compared with urban areas. They feel safe and believe these communities are good places to raise children.

The lower cost of living than in many traditional gateway destinations makes it possible for some immigrants to save money to buy a home or to leave the meatpacking plant to work at a less dangerous job or open a small business.[6]

It is a stretch, then, to believe that anyone would choose to live in a community because of the political socialization to which his or her children may be exposed. It is possible that the quality of the schools is related to political socialization and can be a legitimate rationale for residential selection. However, when people consider the quality of the schools, they generally think of state test scores, the quality of the teachers, or the availability of school activities. Most never consider political socialization outcomes. Typically, this information is impossible to obtain, even if one is interested.

In terms of case selection, the research team sought to eliminate as many of the potential differences between communities as possible. For this reason, all of the towns are located in one state. State policies on education, immigration, and many other arenas vary considerably. For this reason, it was important to hold constant any potential differences across states. Further, although immigration has increased in nearly all states, there are a few in the Midwest that have seen dramatic increases in their foreign-born and non-Anglo populations. Between 1990 and 2000, Minnesota, Indiana, Iowa, Nebraska, and Missouri had the highest rates of change, respectively, among Midwestern states in their nonmetropolitan Hispanic populations.[7] Iowa had one of the fastest-growing rates of population change in the Midwest. Geographically, it is truly the "heartland" of America. It is at midpoint of all states in terms of size (thousands of square miles) and location (latitude and longitude).[8] Iowa is also a politically relevant state because of its first-in-the-nation presidential caucuses and its position as a swing state in general elections. On most economic indicators, Iowa is fairly representative of the United States as a whole.[9] The state also has the characteristics of interest to this study: small towns with immigrants neighboring communities that are nearly all White.

Within Iowa, the immigrant-receiving towns were selected first. Because the object of this study is to examine small towns, communities with populations greater than 5,000 but less than 15,000 were selected. In this way, communities would be large enough to include all of the major institutions that make a community a town, such as schools, retail outlets, and places of worship. However, they would not be so large that they would border on being medium-size towns or bedroom communities. Significant regional differences exist between the western and eastern parts of Iowa, so all towns are located in the central or western portion—the most rural parts of the state. Under these parameters, there are only three potential immigrant-receiving communities—Denison, Perry, and Storm Lake. Because Denison and Storm Lake are located in the west, and Perry is in central Iowa, one from each region was selected: Perry and Storm Lake. Under these parameters of case selection, there were 27 towns that were well over 90 percent White. Because there is potentially more variation across

TABLE 2.1   Pre-treatment (1990) Comparisons of Iowa Communities across Population, Ethnicity, and Socioeconomic Status

	Iowa	Boone	Carroll	Harlan	Perry	Storm Lake
Population	2.8 mil[a]	12,392	9,579	5,148	6,652	8,769
Ethnic composition						
Percent non-Hispanic White	96.1	99.1	99.3	98.7	99.2	94.8
Percent Latino	1.1	0.1	0.3	0.4	0.7	0.9
Percent foreign born	1.6	1.1	1.1	0.5	1.2	3.9
Socioeconomic status						
Percentage with bachelor's degree or higher	16.9	14.9	14.1	18.9	13.4	17.0
Percentage of individuals below the poverty line	11.5	10.7	9.7	6.5	11.5	10.0
Median household income	$26,229	$24,296	$32,732	$21,406	$21,999	$23,755
Per capita income	$12,422	$12,171	$12,236	$11,884	$12,653	$11,229

Source: U.S. Census 1990 Summary File (SF 1).
[a] mil, million.

twenty-seven communities than across three towns, three predominantly White communities were chosen: Boone, Carroll, and Harlan.

Table 2.1 shows the pre-treatment (1990) demographic profiles of each of the five communities and the State of Iowa. The towns' populations in 1990 ranged from 5,148 in Harlan to 12,392 in Boone. Otherwise, there were few substantial differences across these communities. In 1990, all of the communities were composed of more than 94 percent non-Hispanic Whites. They all had similar proportions of impoverished residents and college graduates. Carroll had a slightly higher median household income than the other towns, but the per capita incomes were comparable. The aim of this chapter is to demonstrate that the five towns in this study were similar across other indicators prior to the arrival of immigrants. It discusses any other possible linkages that may confound the outcomes under investigation here. I examine the main aspects of each community that may affect political socialization: geography and history, social and civic indicators, politics, educational system, and local economy.[10]

Comparing the Five Study Communities

Geography

Most of Iowa, including each of these towns, is characterized by rolling plains. Iowa's location between the Mississippi River in the east and the Missouri River in the west gives it some of the most fertile topsoil in the world, making it ideal for farming. Iowa leads the nation in its production of corn, soybeans, hogs, and

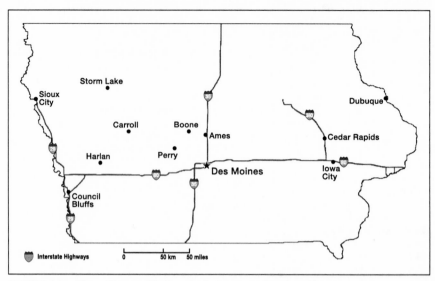

FIGURE 2.1   Map of Iowa with five study towns and major cities

eggs and is third in total livestock sales. Figure 2.1 shows a map of Iowa with each of the five communities in the study.

All five communities are in central or western Iowa. Boone is in central Iowa, only 17 miles from a midsize city, Ames (pop. 50,731). Carroll sits farther west, about 85 miles from Ames and about 95 miles from the state's capital, Des Moines. Harlan is in southwestern Iowa and sits along the West Nishnabotna River. The nearest midsize city is Council Bluffs, Iowa (pop. 58,268), and Omaha, Nebraska (pop. 390,000), is 55 miles away. Perry is in central Iowa about 25 minutes from Des Moines. Storm Lake is in northwestern Iowa, about 83 miles from Sioux City, Iowa, the nearest midsize city.

History

This region was settled during the mid-nineteenth century, after Iowa officially became a state in 1846. After the Civil War, the state's population grew dramatically. Initial settlers came from other parts of the United States, but after the war, foreign-born settlers found their way to Iowa. In 1869, the state published the booklet *Iowa: The Home of Immigrants* and instructed that it be published in English, German, Dutch, Swedish, and Danish to represent the ethnic groups that were settling the state.[11]

Each of these communities traces its founding and early history to the expansion of railroads across the Midwest. Boone was laid out in 1865 by John I. Blair, an executive in the Northwestern Railroad. He named the town Montana, but the name was later changed to Boone. The Chicago and Northwestern Railroad was closely involved in the town's early success. The railroad invested large sums of money in Boone: in equipment, in employees, and in bringing tourists by running a hotel and restaurant at the station.[12] In 1888, Boone was made the seat of Boone County. Also a railroad town for many years, Carroll was laid out by the Chicago and Northwestern Railroad in 1869. According to a newspaper account from 1874, "One fact cannot be ignored. If there had not been a railroad, there might not have been a Carroll."[13] Carroll is the seat of Carroll County.

Harlan was named for one of Iowa's early U.S. senators, James Harlan, and the first plat or lot was executed in 1858.[14] Harlan became the seat of Shelby County in 1859 and was incorporated in 1879. In the 1860s, Harlan was the terminus of a branch of the Chicago, Rock Island, and Pacific Railway (CRI&P).[15] In 1878, the Avoca, Harlan, and Northern Railroad Company was incorporated to construct and operate a rail line from a point in the line of the CRI&P at Avoca, Iowa, by way of Harlan. The company eventually was sold to the CRI&P in 1899.[16]

Perry was founded in 1869 by Harvey Willis when he convinced railroad surveyors to put tracks on his land.[17] He named the town in honor of Colonel C. H. Perry, a railroad official on the Des Moines and Fort Dodge Railroad. Located in Dallas County within Spring Valley Township, Perry is not the county seat. For nearly a century, Perry was a Midwestern hub for the Milwaukee Railroad.

Storm Lake also began with links to the railroad. The arrival of the Dubuque and Sioux City Railway in 1870 led to the town's development around the depot, just west of the 3,200 acre natural lake. The town was incorporated in 1873, and in 1878, after a fire destroyed the original county courthouse, the Buena Vista County seat was moved from Sioux Rapids to Storm Lake. "The City Beautiful," Storm Lake's nickname, expanded in the early twentieth century when the Chicago, Milwaukee, and St. Paul Railway was built into the town from the southeast and the Minneapolis and St. Louis Railway was built in the town from the north.[18]

Measures of Social Capital

Small towns in rural areas are renowned for their high levels of social capital and civic engagement. One of the defining features of rural America is that people know one another well, trust one another, rely on one another, and participate in civic activities. Theoretically, children brought up in these kinds of communities, compared with their counterparts in places where people do not participate or trust one another, have a different—arguably, better—political socialization experience. If these five communities vary considerably in social indicators, this may explain a great deal of the variation in socialization outcomes across the towns.

According to Robert Putnam, there are several components of a comprehensive social capital index, including measures of community organizational life, engagement in public affairs, informal sociability, and social trust.[19]

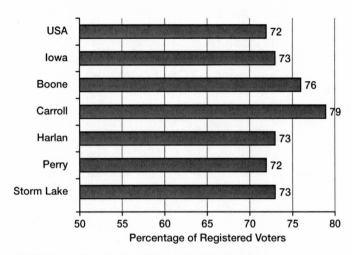

FIGURE 2.2   Turnout in 1988 presidential election

Unfortunately, many of these components can be measured only by surveys conducted at the community level, an expensive and rare endeavor. Several U.S. communities were included in Putnam's Social Capital Benchmark Survey, but none were in Iowa. It is possible to get a sense of a community's engagement in public affairs through its turnout in elections, arguably one of the easiest components to measure. Iowa typically has one of the highest rates of turnout in the nation. In the last national election in the pre-treatment period, the 1988 presidential election, 73 percent of registered voters in Iowa voted. The rates were slightly higher in some of the communities, but turnout generally was similar across these communities (see Figure 2.2).

We can also get a sense of the civic life of each of these towns by looking at tax-exempt organizations. According to an archive of data on these organizations in Iowa, there were few differences in the organizational activity within these towns.[20] By counting the number of tax-exempt organizations that existed in these communities in 1990 and dividing by the population, we see that there was roughly one organization per 775 people in Boone, per 550 people in Carroll, per 1,000 people in Harlan; per 830 people in Perry, and per 975 people in Storm Lake. It is not surprising to see more organizations in the larger towns of Boone and Carroll. Although this is certainly a rough estimate, it does not seem to be the case that there were substantial differences in the civic life of these towns before the arrival of immigrants.

Religiosity and Religious Affiliations

One of the most important aspects of social capital and social structure is religious involvement. Attendance and participation in church embeds people in their communities and increases the likelihood of staying in a community.[21] Religious structures are also strong sources of volunteerism in both church-oriented and secular activities in the community.[22] With regard to church attendance and affiliation, there are no substantial differences between the towns in this study. Based on church attendance rates, Iowa would be considered a fairly religious state. According to one estimate, 26.7 percent of Iowans attended a Christian church on a given Sunday in 1990, higher than the average rate of attendance in the United States.[23] These figures are not available at the county or town level for 1990, but figures on religious adherence are available. As a percentage of the county's population, Carroll County had by far the highest proportion of residents who were affiliated with or members of a religious congregation: 93.2 percent. The other five counties trail by at least 10 percent. In Shelby County (Harlan), 82.2 percent of people were adherents to a religion; in Buena Vista County (Storm Lake), 77.6 percent; in Boone County, 57.9 percent; and in Dallas County (Perry), 54.1 percent.[24] Thus, there was some variation with regard to religiosity across these counties, but it was not the case that Dallas and Buena Vista counties were systematically different from the others.

Statistics on religious affiliation do not demonstrate much difference across the communities (Table 2.2). Mirroring the state's founding primarily by Germans and Scandinavians, the largest denominations in Iowa today, in order of

TABLE 2.2 Religious Affiliation in Iowa Counties, 1990

	Boone (Boone Co.)	Carroll (Carroll Co.)	Harlan (Shelby Co.)	Perry (Dallas Co.)	Storm Lake (Buena Vista Co.)
Roman Catholic	18.9	67.0	46.0	25.9	18.0
Lutheran[a]	28.9	15.9	23.3	16.3	42.9
Methodist[b]	21.2	10.3	15.9	30.0	19.5
Church of Christ[c]	3.6	0.5	7.4	1.2	5.3
Baptist[d]	6.6	—	5.1	2.4	2.5
Presbyterian (USA)	3.0	4.2	1.2	3.6	8.1
Other[e]	17.8	2.2	1.1	20.7	3.8

Source: Martin B. Bradley Norman M. Green Jr., Dale E. Jones, Mac Lynn, and Lou McNeil, *Churches and Church Membership in the United States, 1990* (Atlanta: Glenmary Research Center, 1992).

Note: Values are percentages within each denomination as a proportion of total religious adherents. Columns may not total 100 percent due to rounding.

[a] Includes Lutheran Church (Missouri Synod) and Evangelical Lutheran Church of America.

[b] Includes Free Methodist Church of America; United Methodist; and Primitive Methodist, USA.

[c] Includes Churches of Christ and United Church of Christ.

[d] Includes General Association of American Baptist Churches in the USA and Southern Baptist Convention.

[e] Includes Assemblies of God, Brethren in Christ Church, Christian and Missionary Alliance, Christian Church (Disciples of Christ), Church of Christ Scientists, Church of God, Church of God of Prophecy, Church of Jesus Christ of Latter-day Saints, Church of the Brethren, Church of the Nazarene, Episcopal, Evangelical Free Church of America, Friends (Quakers), Old Order River Brethren, Salvation Army, and Seventh-Day Adventists. The only county with a Jewish population is Dallas County.

size, are Catholicism, Lutheranism, and Methodism. In each county, small numbers of people attend churches of smaller denominations. Very few people in Carroll and Shelby counties, however, adhere to the smaller denominations. Carroll continues to have a very high proportion of Catholic residents—the highest by far of the five towns in the study. The Lutheran church dominates Buena Vista County, and because of Buena Vista University, a Presbyterian college, this denomination is larger there than in the other counties.

Information Environment

The information environment within a community is also an important part of the social fabric. Where do people receive their information about local, national, and international events? Do local people own, and thereby control, the main sources of information? In terms of television news, the majority of Americans watch local news.[25] Further, older people, who make up significant proportions of small-town populations, are significantly more likely to read a newspaper. Local television and print news may be especially important in small towns. None of these communities is large enough for its own local television station. Local television news comes from Des Moines (in Perry, Carroll, and Boone), Sioux City (in Storm Lake), and Omaha (in Harlan). All of the towns have at least one FM radio station; Boone and Carroll each have two.

Each of the towns has a local newspaper, but none of the papers is issued daily. The *Carroll Daily Times Herald* is published five days per week and is locally owned. The *Boone News Republican* is published four times a week but is not locally owned. Harlan Newspapers owns and publishes two weekly papers, the *Harlan News-Advertiser* and the *Harlan Tribune*. The *Perry Chief*, in business since 1874, comes out once a week and is locally owned and published. Storm Lake has two newspapers. The oldest is the *Storm Lake Pilot-Tribune*, established in 1870, is published three times per week but is not locally owned, and the *Storm Lake Times*, which opened in 1990 and is locally owned, is published twice a week. The information environment in the pre-treatment period was similar across the towns. Most residents relied on a non-daily local newspaper, television news from the largest nearby town, and, of course, national news.

Politics

For at least the past 60 years, Iowa, unlike many predominantly rural states, has been a highly competitive political arena. The U.S. congressional delegations have been split between Democrats and Republicans. Since 1985, Iowa's two U.S. senators have been the Democrat Tom Harkin and the Republican Charles Grassley. Since the 1960s, Iowa's U.S. delegation in the House of Representatives has been fairly evenly split between the two major parties. In 1993, after Iowa lost its sixth congressional seat and when immigration was increasing rapidly in some Iowa communities, three of the remaining five seats were held by

TABLE 2.3   Percentage of Democratic Vote Share in Presidential Elections in Case Study Towns, 1988–2008

	1988[a]	1992[a]	1996	2000	2004	2008
Boone	62	48	55	52	47	55
Carroll	59	40	50	48	43	52
Harlan	48	32	38	36	31	45
Perry	60	44	61	60	57	61
Storm Lake	52	36	[b]	45	45	56

Source: Secretary of State of Iowa, available online at http://www.sos.state.ia.us/elections/results.

[a] The 1988 and 1992 results are reported only at the county level. Results from 1996–2008 are reported at the precinct level.

[b] No results available.

Republicans. For a short period, from 1995 to 1997, all of the state's House districts were held by Republicans. Since 2007, three of the five districts have been represented by Democrats.

Since 1955, the governorship in Iowa has switched parties six times. Terry Branstad, a Republican, served four terms as governor from 1983 to 1999 and was reelected in 2010. In the years between his terms, the office was held by Democrats Tom Vilsack (1999–2007) and Chet Culver (2007–2011). In 1990, both houses of the state's General Assembly were controlled by Democrats. Today, the General Assembly is split: the Senate is controlled by Democrats, while the House is controlled by Republicans. The period from 2006 to 2011 was the first time in four decades that both houses of the legislature and the governor were of the same party.[26]

In presidential elections, Iowa is generally considered a swing state. Since 1960, voters have supported Republicans in seven of thirteen presidential elections. Since 1988, the state's electoral votes have gone mostly to Democrats, but in 2000 and 2004, razor-thin margins separated the winning candidate (Al Gore in 2000 and George Bush in 2004) from his opponent.[27] Barack Obama not only won the Iowa Democratic caucuses, but he had a substantial victory over John McCain in the general election in 2008 (9 percent). Iowa is probably most famous for its first-in-the-nation caucuses in presidential elections.

Within the five communities in this study, only one town could be called a Republican stronghold: Harlan has overwhelmingly supported the Republican presidential candidate in every election since at least 1988 (see Table 2.3). Currently, Harlan's representatives in the state's House and the Senate are Republicans. They are longtime incumbents who have little trouble getting reelected. Harlan's representative in the state's House was elected in 1992; its state senator was elected in 1994 and is the assistant Republican leader. Harlan, along with the rest of western Iowa, has been represented by Republicans in the U.S. House of Representatives since the mid-1980s.

After redistricting in 2002, Steve King, also a Republican, was elected to represent the Fifth Congressional District. He is known for being a social conservative and outspoken critic of gay rights and illegal immigration.[28] King is a rising star in the Republican Party and in 2010 was praised for introducing H.R. 4972, a measure that would completely repeal the health-care bill signed by President Obama. King is well known for making controversial statements about illegal immigration. For example, in 2007 he stated that any senator who voted in favor of comprehensive immigration reform should "wear a scarlet letter 'A' for amnesty."[29] In 2010, 63 percent of Harlan's voters supported King. In 2011, Iowa lost a congressional district. Shelby County will become part of the new Fourth District, along with the counties housing the towns of Carroll, Boone, and Storm Lake.

None of these communities is a Democratic stronghold, although Perry usually supports Democratic presidential candidates by substantial margins (see Table 2.3). Perry is located in a county, however, that often elects Republicans to state offices.[30] In the U.S. House, Perry and Boone are currently represented by Republican Tom Latham. In 2010, Latham even garnered wide support in Perry (54 percent). Politically, in the pre-treatment period, the five communities in the study were all fairly moderate, with the exception of Harlan.

Educational Systems

Another factor that could make a difference with regard to political socialization is the quality of schools. Each of the towns in this study has one public high school, each of which would be considered a small to medium-size school. In addition to the public schools, Carroll has a Catholic high school, Kuemper High School, with enrollments reaching about two-thirds of the number of students who attend the public high school. In Storm Lake, about 20 students graduate from a K–12 Catholic school each year. Each of the other towns has a Catholic elementary and middle school but no high school. Storm Lake also has a K–6 Lutheran school.

As Table 2.4 shows, there were few significant differences across the five public schools in the pre-treatment period. All of the schools had similar enrollments, although Boone High School was slightly larger, and Carroll High School—likely due to the Catholic school in town—was slightly smaller. In each school, 10–15 percent of the school population was eligible for the free or reduced school lunch program. And, with the exception of Storm Lake's Asian population, there was very little racial or ethnic diversity. In Storm Lake, 6.6 percent of students were Asian, reflecting the wave of Tai Dam/Laotian immigration into the community during the 1980s.

A long line of research on political socialization examines the impact of civics curricula on political knowledge, efficacy, and other outcomes.[31] Because all of the schools in this study are in one state, there are unlikely to be many differences in the civics requirements across the schools. High school students in Iowa are required to have five units of social studies, including citizenship education, history, and the social sciences.[32] There were likely to be differences in pedagogical techniques used in individual classrooms, but the data suggest

TABLE 2.4   Pre-treatment Comparison of Public High Schools in Iowa Study Towns

	Boone High School	Carroll High School	Harlan High School	Perry High School	Storm Lake High School
School size/enrollment[a]	624	356	592	437	473
Percentage on free/ reduced lunch[a]	13	14	13	12	11
Percent White[a]	99	99	98	99	92
Percent Latino[a]	—	0.6	0.1	0.2	0.6
Percent Black[a]	0.2	—	—	0.2	0.8
Percent Asian[a]	1.1	0.6	0.8	0.7	6.6
Average teacher salary[b]	$24,161	$23,842	$26,238	$22,856	$22,809
Average teacher years of experience[b]	16.3	15.7	19.9	14.4	14.4
Percentage of teachers with master's degree[b]	48	37	49	42	35

[a] *Source:* National Center for Education Statistics in the Common Core of Data for 1990–1991 academic year.

[b] *Source:* Iowa Department of Education based on the academic year 1985–1986.

that the five schools were also quite similar in quality during the pre-treatment period. School quality is often measured by the performance of students on standardized tests and several indicators of teacher quality. There are no available scores on students' performance at the school level prior to 2003 when the reauthorization of the Elementary and Secondary Education Act (commonly known as No Child Left Behind) was passed. As shown in Table 2.4, there are few pre-treatment differences with regard to teachers' salaries, years of teaching experience, or average level of education.

It is worth noting that Storm Lake had (and continues to have) one distinct difference from the other communities: its access to higher education. Buena Vista University, affiliated with the Presbyterian Church, was founded in 1891. Its enrollments increased in record numbers in the late 1980s, leading it to expand with new majors and several new buildings in the 1990s. Today, the college has about 1,400 students on its main campus in Storm Lake and employs 84 faculty members and nearly 200 more in staff and support.[33]

Local Economy

In the pre-treatment period, the local economies of these small communities were very similar. In 1990, unemployment in each of the counties was lower than the state average of 4.5 percent. Buena Vista County, home of Storm Lake, had the lowest unemployment level at 3.0 percent. The highest was 3.8 percent in Shelby County, home of Harlan.[34] Tables 2.5 and 2.6 show other economic data for these towns and counties. In the four towns that reported data in 1992, the economic profiles were relatively similar. (No data were reported for Shelby County or Harlan.) Partly because of its smaller size, Perry's economy was

TABLE 2.5   1992 Economic Profiles of Iowa Communities

	Manufacturing[a] (receipts)	Retail (sales)	Wholesale (sales)	Services (receipts)
Boone	28	101	15	81
	($82)	($122)	—	($20)
Carroll	36	129	44	98
	($310)	($134)	($166)	($29)
Perry	37	59	20	53
	($319)	($49)	($96)	($13)
Storm Lake	24	117	31	100
	—	($124)	—	($29)

Source: 1992 Economic Census, U.S. Bureau of the Census.

Note: Values are numbers of establishments. Numbers in parentheses are receipts or sales in millions of dollars. No figures were reported for Shelby County or for Harlan. Dashes indicate that information was withheld to avoid disclosing company data.

[a] Manufacturing figures are available only at the county level. Other figures are at the town/place level.

generally less vibrant than the others', with less revenue from retail sales, wholesale sales, and services. Dallas County's most significant economic sector was manufacturing; we cannot tell how many of these establishments were located in Perry, but it is no stretch to presume that manufacturing made up a substantial part of the town's economy. The other three towns look much alike, with few differences between Storm Lake (the other community that became ethnically diverse) and Boone and Carroll. The data in Table 2.6 demonstrate few differences in the classes of workers in these towns. There are a slightly higher proportion of government workers in Boone County than in the other towns. Shelby County has the highest percentage of self-employed workers due to its continued reliance on agriculture as an important part of its economy. Although there are, of course, slight economic differences across the towns, there are no dramatic variations. In the pre-treatment period, all of these communities relied heavily on manufacturing and retail sales.

TABLE 2.6   Class of Workers for Iowa and Case Study Counties, 1990

	Private wage and salary workers	Government workers	Self-employed workers	Unpaid family workers
Iowa	73.9	14.3	10.9	0.8
Boone County	68.2	21.9	9.2	0.7
Carroll County	72.2	9.6	17.1	1.2
Shelby County (Harlan)	63.2	12.3	22.5	2.0
Dallas County (Perry)	73.5	15.2	10.5	0.8
Buena Vista County (Storm Lake)	72.7	10.3	15.9	1.1

Note: Values are percentages. Rows may not total 100 percent due to rounding.

Source: 1990 Census: STF 3, American FactFinder, Table P079.

Interviewing Young People in
Iowa Communities

Once the five towns were selected, researchers traveled to the communities and distributed surveys to students at each of the five public high schools in the fall of 2001 and the spring of 2002. The sample of student respondents could not be randomly drawn from school enrollment lists because cooperating school administrators considered such data-collection procedures too disruptive to the school day. Thus, entire classrooms of varying achievement levels were surveyed, along with very large proportions of the student population at each school (sampling more than a third of all students in all communities, except Boone). The resulting sample is a good representation of the underlying population. Table A.1 includes information demonstrating the representativeness of the sample. Table A.2 includes the wording of the questions and descriptive statistics for each item used in these analyses.

Limitations of Research Design

Although this chapter demonstrates that the case studies were similar across all major indicators in the pre-treatment period, there are some limitations to this design. As with all survey research, there were some questions that were not asked that would have been useful in this analysis. For example, the survey did not include questions asking specifically about whether the young people felt threatened—physically or economically—by the arrival of immigrants. Nonetheless, I believe that with few exceptions, the data allow for a good examination of questions related to the effects of ethnic diversity on adolescents' acceptance or tolerance of immigrants and civic engagement.

The book does not rely only on the surveys conducted in the high schools, and also relies on qualitative methods. Many students participated in focus groups in two of the communities (Perry and Harlan) during the 2002–2003 school year. Once again, students could not be selected totally at random. School officials selected students at varying achievement levels across the four grades, and within Perry included a mix of immigrants and natives. The results of these discussions are included throughout the book to help make sense of the quantitative results and to provide support for the conclusions. I took students' responses at face value and was not particularly concerned with social desirability. The setting was very comfortable for these youth. The groups were composed of small groups of peers—kids who have known one another for most of their lives. Because of their familiarity with one another, it would have been obvious to them if someone was lying or distorting his or her views. No school personnel were in the room, and their responses were not divulged to anyone else. In the manuscript, I changed the students' names to protect their anonymity. For those who still may be skeptical about the students' honesty, it is also important to note that in almost every case, the survey results back up the responses in the focus groups.

In addition to surveys and discussions with young people, the study relies on dozens of interviews with adult residents of each community. These interviews focused primarily on Perry and Storm Lake. I interviewed the principals at both high schools, along with some teachers and administrators. I also talked with elected and appointed town officials. I talked with editors and former editors of the local newspapers and spoke at length with longtime community residents. They gave me tours of the towns and discussed the towns' histories—and, of course, their opinions about the changes that had taken place. I also spoke to several first-generation immigrants in each town.

One obvious limitation of the study design is that there could be an issue with external validity. There was a tradeoff between internal and external validity. To examine the effect of diversity at the local level, it is necessary to do in-depth research in a small number of communities instead of using a more generalizable nationwide study that may only include one or two people per locality. Given the large sample sizes within each school and the number of people included in the interviews, it is not, however, unreasonable to assume that communities with similar compositions would return comparable results. Even so, I am appropriately cautious in the conclusions and encourage others to conduct additional studies in similar settings. This is the only way to reveal whether these findings are generalizable across unexamined locations.

Summary

This chapter describes this study as a natural experiment and has presented data on the pre-treatment (i.e., pre-immigration) period within the five communities. It shows that there are few substantial differences between these communities in terms of their geography, history, social capital, political participation, local media, political composition, educational systems, and local economies. Although there is some variability across each of these indexes, there is no systematic pattern to the differences. It is reasonable, then, to presume that any differences we see in the coming chapters related to political socialization outcomes are due primarily to the demographic changes that took place in Perry and Storm Lake.

Over the period 1990–2000, Perry and Storm Lake experienced significant change. The demographics of the communities had shifted significantly by 2000. The composition of the schools became very diverse. Longtime White residents had to confront their own prejudices, and young people experienced communities that were very different from the ones just a generation earlier. The next two chapters examine how young people felt about immigration and civic or political engagement about ten years after immigrants had begun to arrive in their communities and compare these responses with those of young people in the towns that did not experience an influx of newcomers.

3

Seeing Race

Attitudes toward Immigrants and Symbolic Racism

Now, I don't see race. People tell me I'm White and I believe them because I have a lot of Jimmy Buffett albums.

—Stephen Colbert

S tephen Colbert's claim is funny not only because he contends he knows his race because of his poor taste in music but also because in the United States, it is ridiculous to believe that anyone does not notice race. Colbert probably would not even need the second statement to get a laugh. Race and ethnicity, many argue, are not only important aspects of individual identity but also an inextricable part of American politics. Many of the most contentious issues in U.S. history have been racial and ethnic issues.

As immigrants from Latin America and Asia have settled in formerly homogeneous communities in the Midwest, residents of small towns have had to confront their own racial and ethnic biases. Residents of these communities could, for most their existence, easily believe that they were tolerant without any empirical test. Iowa is known for its graciousness and hospitality, but as stated succinctly by David Evans, "Iowans have considerable goodwill toward people in general, and are a pretty welcoming bunch, but lack of experience with diversity leads to mistakes out of ignorance and stereotyping."[1] Given the political climate around the immigration debate since the 1990s, and these small towns' lack of experience with diversity, it would be surprising if townspeople did *not* react with some reservations about the changes in their communities.

Although prejudice certainly exists in communities with very little diversity, there is substantial evidence that a community's ethnic composition is significantly related to its residents' attitudes and behavior.[2] One popular theory suggests that the size of the minority population is directly related to the level of hostility and prejudice expressed by Whites.[3] Its major counterweight is the idea behind racial integration in the United States: the belief that Whites' greater proximity to racial and ethnic minorities leads to less prejudice. A third important idea relates to "symbolic politics," which suggests that ethnic composition is not as important in explaining racial attitudes as are predispositions developed through childhood socialization.

This chapter reviews these theories and provides expectations for how young residents of small towns might react to large influxes of immigrants with cultural and ethnic backgrounds different from theirs. Are young people in diverse small towns more tolerant toward immigrants than their peers in homogeneous places? Does proximity to immigrants heighten threat perceptions or is it associated with empathic responses? And are there substantial differences between Perry, a community where the influx of immigration began recently, and Storm Lake, where residents have had more time to manage the changes in their town?

Using the surveys of high school students in these communities conducted in 2001, the evidence suggests that the relationship between ethnic diversity and tolerance for immigrants is complicated. The results first demonstrate that ethnic diversity has a negative influence on sympathy for immigrants, but later we see that this association exists only in Perry, where ethnic diversification and official responses to it began later than in Storm Lake. Positive feelings toward Hispanics and negative racial attitudes about African Americans are the primary explanations for sympathy of immigrants, especially in Perry.

The chapter discusses the three main theories about the relationship between ethnic diversity and tolerance. It then examines the evidence from the surveys by comparing the ethnically heterogeneous towns with the homogeneous ones, as well as the differences and similarities between the two diverse communities of Perry and Storm Lake. The final section of results examines the attitudes of immigrants about tolerance of other ethnic groups.

Proximity to Diversity and Political Socialization

One of the central assumptions of this study is that political socialization does not occur in a vacuum. The agents of socialization—parents, peers, schools, churches, and the media—are located within time and space. Adolescents are raised within a specific structural context, a local socialization environment that influences what they learn and the identities they adopt. Social interactions structure the information flow on the basis of which individuals develop their attitudes toward ethnic groups, including their own group, as well as related beliefs about equality and morality.[4] In particular, "When features of settings make race [or ethnicity] highly salient, as when settings are ethnically integrated or highly discriminatory, parents are more likely to communicate messages about ethnicity and race to their children."[5] If nearly everyone has the same cultural background, parents and teachers often believe there is not much reason to discuss racial or ethnic differences.[6] However, in heterogeneous places, adults find it necessary to guide young people about how to think about and act toward members of other ethnic or racial groups. Thus, there are likely to be differences in the socialization experiences in diverse and homogeneous communities. On the idea that the racial and ethnic composition of one's community influences racial and ethnic attitudes, three theories have formed the basis for much of the research for the past 60 years.

Power Threat

Power threat theory is the idea that as the proportion of racial and ethnic minorities in the community increases, the majority group, Anglos/Whites, begins to feel threatened. On Black–White relations, evidence has shown that Whites are more hostile to racial integration, vote at higher rates, engage in more racial violence, and are more ideologically conservative in response to the threat posed by African Americans to their social, economic, and political power.[7] Whites in places with high proportions of African Americans also erect barriers to political participation to keep Blacks from gaining too much power.[8] At least one study indicates, however, that this theory does not hold when it comes to Anglos' attitudes about immigrants.[9]

Power threat theory leads to several expectations about how young people in small, ethnically homogeneous towns might react to sudden increases in immigration. One young girl in ethnically homogeneous Harlan predicted that if immigrants moved into her community, the main effect would be power struggles and tension, merely because of the presence of diversity:

> Liz: I have nothing wrong with different races, except that I think more along the lines of, like, when Americans first came here, we were all—we were all like a group. . . . When you have lots of different racial groups, they tend to fight and want to be more powerful—one more powerful than the other. And that seems to cause a lot of problems. So I think a little bit of racial difference is good, because then you get different points of view. But when you get lots of different racials in one group, they tend to fight, and you don't get anything done because you're all wanting something else. And I think it's harder to get things done. So—and sometimes when you're all the same you can—it's like you get a bond, a special bond between the people, and then you, I don't know, you feel more comfortable.

Although Liz's expectations about there being a lot of conflict and disagreement were not expressed by other students, several did say that there are strong bonds among members of ethnically homogeneous communities. Some believe these bonds may be threatened whenever there is significant demographic change. Because these attachments are one of the defining features of small-town life, many longtime residents are protective of them. They may not embrace changes to the community even if those changes are unlikely to affect them directly. Rural areas are thought to be particularly resistant to change, and "cultural inertia," or the desire to avoid cultural change, is significantly related to attitudes about immigration.[10] Some residents of small towns see changes in local culture due to immigration as threatening to the traditional culture of the community, or to the rural "way of life."[11] We might then expect perceptions of this type of threat to be especially high among those living in small communities that have undergone rapid ethnic diversification and even more so among those within these towns who are strongly rooted to their community.

One of the main differences between small towns and larger communities is residents' sense of rootedness in the community. Small towns are often composed of multiple generations of families. For young people, the presence of older generations as socializing agents, who are strongly rooted in the way of life in the local community, may sustain traditional forms of discriminatory thinking that date to a time when open expressions of intentional prejudice were more widely accepted. Exposure to these expressions introduce youth to older stereotypes that create and sustain intolerance. James G. Gimpel and I have found that hostility to immigrants in small towns is concentrated among youth from well-rooted families, including children whose parents are full-time farmers.[12] The youth whose families are longtime members of, and major stakeholders in, the community have the most to lose from shifting demographics. Among this group, anti-diversity attitudes are also the expression of a more general sense of anxiety based on collective memories of how things used to be.

In the Harlan focus group, students were asked what they think of when they are asked about a neighboring town, Denison, which has a slaughterhouse and many immigrants. One young man said that he thinks about

> *Eric:* Good Mexican food. [They've] got authentic cooks, but a lot of it is just with that being there, it's easy to be able to appreciate more, I guess, if you appreciate that sort of thing. The kind of life we have in Harlan where we don't have a lot of immigrants going through or things like that. It's just—for someone who's very conservative, who doesn't really want a lot of immigration, this would be—this is more of a town for them, where if someone who's a little less conservative wants more cultural diversity, they can live in somewhere like Denison. It's good that they have places like that, you know, in, like, this part of Iowa where for a long time it's just been, you know, German farmers or, you know, people of different ethnic—you know, different German tribes came here.
>
> *Interviewer:* What would you think if a plant opened up in Harlan [like the one in Denison]?
>
> *Eric:* I don't think it would fly very well in this community. It's just— this community is not one for that sort of—something like that

coming in. They're OK with the one up in Denison because it's not in Harlan. This is a very—I don't want to say racist, but it's a very non- . . .

Interviewer: Diverse? It's not diverse?

Eric: Yeah.

Although this young man did not explicitly say that he was one of those very conservative people, or that he did not want immigrants in Harlan, he did indicate that immigrants would not be entirely welcomed by longstanding members of the community. It is nice, he thinks, that *other* places have immigrants, but it is not right for Harlan, a town that he later describes as welcoming to everyone:

Interviewer: What is one of the things you like most about this town?

Eric: Everybody loves you. Everybody watches out for you and your property and your family. Like if your kid—I had this happen to me when I was little—riding my bike down the middle of the road not paying attention to the street signs or nothing. People would call my mother or my father and be like, "You know, you've got to keep your son—you've got to keep an eye on that kid. He ain't paying attention. You know, he might get hurt." That kind of stuff you will never see in Omaha. You walk down the street you might be shot and does anybody care? No . . .

Interviewer: Does it ever bother you that people know you so well, and, you know, can recognize you?

Eric: No, and I think, because you're brought up right. You're not brought up—you're not brought up on the street doing drugs, you know, and games.

Jane: Because people know about it.

Eric: Because the gain here is your friends and family. That's your gain. You—no matter where you go, you feel loved. And you feel like you belong—people will make you belong.

Eric does not see his statements as contradictory. On the one hand, he reports that immigrants would not be particularly welcome in Harlan, but on the other, "everyone" loves and takes care of their neighbors. Of course, he is speaking about his experiences of being cared for by the members of his community and projecting that onto "everyone" else. His comments represent many of those young people whose families have lived in these small towns for multiple generations, especially those in the towns that remain racially and ethnically homogeneous. Residents believe them to be havens from the cities, safe places where everyone knows and trusts everyone else. Even though they see their communities as nurturing and welcoming, they recognize that some people—"others"—would not fit in. These residents have no particular animosity toward immigrants, but they do not necessarily want to see them in *their* towns. In other words, things are just fine the way they are for these youth and their families. Based on these comments alone, it is difficult to predict whether young people like Eric or Liz would react with hostility if significant numbers of immigrants moved into Harlan. However, it is fairly clear that it would make them, and probably others in the town, uncomfortable and anxious about the changes that might be wrought.

A second expectation stemming from power threat theory is the effect of personal economic threat. Hubert Blalock contends that a sense of threat is likely to be highest among those who are in direct competition with the minority groups.[13] Since many of the jobs immigrants hold, especially in small towns, are low-status positions, there may be more hostility among lower-status Whites who may feel a direct personal threat from immigrants. In some research, lower-status individuals or those who are concerned about the economy are less supportive of immigration and more willing to deny immigrants citizenship and other societal benefits.[14] The disadvantaged may believe immigrants are stealing their jobs, reducing wages, and contributing to the loss of workers' rights. Other studies have shown, however, that income and other socioeconomic character-istics are largely unrelated to attitudes about immigrants.[15]

Keeping in mind that this study examines adolescents, it is unlikely that many high school students feel an immediate, personal economic threat from immigrants. Rather, lower-income teenage Anglos may feel a prospective sense of threat on their own behalf (i.e., they are less likely to obtain jobs when they need them in the future) or a threat to their family on behalf of parents and other family members who are in direct competition with immigrants for jobs and other advantages. In the focus groups in Perry and Harlan, for example, some Anglo young people commented that immigrants will "work for cheap" and that this puts jobs at risk for White people. However, it was very common for students to tell us that they do not believe immigrants take jobs from natives because if local people wanted the jobs, they could get them. There was a com-mon sentiment that the immigrants were mostly doing "dirty" jobs that Anglos did not want. It was not entirely clear from the interviews, then, whether native young people feel a sense of economic threat from immigrants.

Contact Theory

There is a great deal of evidence that proximity to diverse groups breeds not contempt but friendship. The "contact hypothesis" holds that an individual's prejudices can be alleviated by new, positive information derived from contact with people from different racial or ethnic groups.[16] A recent study shows that Whites embedded in "core networks" with non-Whites are much more likely to hold pro-immigrant attitudes than those whose networks are all White.[17] Under this paradigm, Whites' negative attitudes about racial minorities are primarily due to ignorance about these groups, not perceptions of threat. Ignorance leads to negative stereotyping, and contact introduces information about out-groups that contradicts negative stereotypes through the exchange of intimate information. In the process of breaking down stereotypes, contact heightens perceptions of intergroup similarity.[18]

Some have attempted to reconcile these two theories. Where power threat theory examines *exposure* to out-groups, contact theory tends to focus on face-to-face *interactions* with members of other groups.[19] Robert Stein and his colleagues demonstrate that Anglos who are exposed to Latinos because they reside in counties with a high proportion of Hispanics report more negative feelings about this group than do those with little proximity to this group. However, Anglos who live in proximity to Hispanics *and who have frequent contact with Hispanics* have more positive feelings toward this group.[20] Similarly, Eric Oliver shows that living in a metropolitan area among people of other races is associated with greater racial animosity, but living in integrated neighborhoods is related to less racial resentment.[21]

We should not expect all types of contact to elicit positive responses. For example, Gunnar Myrdal differentiates between intimate contact, such as intermarriage, and casual contact.[22] Gordon Allport argues that, for the best possible outcomes, interracial and interethnic contact should take place in settings that are institutionally sanctioned, groups should not be in competition with one another, and groups should work together to achieve common goals.[23] When groups are not equal, it is easier for the majority group to hold on to negative stereotypes. Thus, having a single African American neighbor does little to affect overall levels of prejudice toward Blacks, in part because status differences between Whites and Blacks remain.[24] Positive affect toward an individual may not transfer to the group as a whole.[25] When Allport's conditions are met, however, people are more likely to have friends outside their own racial groups than they would in segregated settings.[26]

Camaraderie is especially likely among young people, because the earlier in life interracial contact begins, the more likely the experiences will be productive of friendship and understanding.[27] The absence of firsthand information about other groups makes individuals less able to counter unfavorable stereotypes.[28] According to Drew Nesdale's "social identity development theory," children first learn about racial categories and show bias in favor of their ethnic group, and only later do they transition from ethnic preference to ethnic prejudice.[29] There is some disagreement among psychologists about the age at which this transition takes place, but most scholars agree that by middle to late childhood, and certainly by high school, young people not only identify with a racial or ethnic group but have opinions about these identities and their meaning.[30] Thus, interethnic contact can be particularly important among young people.

We should expect the effects of interethnic contact to be manifested somewhat differently among young people than adults. Compared with adults in urban and suburban areas, adults in small towns are likely to interact more closely with immigrants because of the sheer size of the community and its resources.[31] In these towns, everyone shops at the same local stores, goes to the same few churches, and sends their children to the same public schools. Even so, young people in small, diverse communities are likely to interact more closely with people in other ethnic groups than are adults. In small communities with small schools, young people are in classes and extracurricular activities with the same overlapping group of other youth. As we will see in the next chapter, foreign-born young people participate in school activities at the same rate as native-born children. Importantly, these interactions take place on more equal footing. Given the nature of public schools' public mission, the treatment of students is likely to be more equal than we would find in private enterprises or other heavily stratified public services. The opportunities for interethnic contact, then, are likely to be even closer than their adult counterparts to Allport's ideals, suggesting that interethnic contact may have a positive effect on native-born kids in small towns.

The focus groups in Perry and Harlan demonstrated, however, that interethnic contact—at least in 2001–2002—had not been all together productive of cultural understanding and friendship. These conversations also demonstrated that information travels easily between these communities and how the negative experiences and beliefs in the diverse towns influence the young people in largely White communities. For example, the Harlan youth discussed how the White people they knew in Denison (a nearby ethnically diverse town) make fun of the immigrants in their schools. One young lady said she had heard a friend in Denison say about the immigrants, "You can't drive a block to school without running over a little one." She said, "They [the White kids in Denison] don't like it, either, I don't think." Others agreed that they heard only negative things about immigrants from acquaintances in diverse communities. They perceived the diverse communities as very divided, as demonstrated when Matthew stated, "Their town [Denison] is, like, divided. They have Hispanic grocery stores now. I mean, Denison's one of the few towns of their size around here that I know that had a strip club, and now even the Hispanics have their own strip club in Denison." The common perception among the young people in Harlan seemed to be that immigration and diversity led to division and that interethnic contact was a net negative for those towns with immigrants.

In Perry, the comments from the White youth displayed a great deal of ambivalence about immigration. Students discussed how the plant brought jobs and revived the economy and about how they believed they were benefiting from cultural diversity. Just as many of the comments, however, were negative. Many of the young people in Perry commented about how difficult it is when newcomers arrive and do not speak English and how strange it is to see new kids come in for a few months and then leave, never to return. These youth had not seen much turnover among the White population in Perry because they were born at the end of the population losses of the 1980s. Some young people made comments about increases in crime in town and how they feared walking by groups of "Mexicans" outside of school. It is not at all clear, then, that interethnic contact was always positive, especially in the early 2000s in Perry.

Symbolic Politics Theory

The major theory that counters both the power threat theory and the contact theory is symbolic politics. It posits that childhood socialization leaves individuals with attitudinal predispositions that can later be evoked by symbols. As adults encounter new stimuli, they rely on these early predispositions to figure out how to process information. Because attitudes are based on longstanding inclinations cultivated through socialization, the diversity of one's adult surroundings may be unrelated to his or her attitudes about the groups that make up that diversity. Racial policy attitudes are more stable over time than most other policy attitudes, heightening the importance of early messages about racial and ethnic groups.[32] If this theory is correct, attitudes about immigrants and immigration, and feelings toward a variety of ethnic groups, are unlikely to be significantly different in communities that have undergone rapid diversification compared with nearby, ethnically homogeneous towns.

According to this theory, the "most salient symbols in a political controversy determine its 'symbolic meaning,' and therefore which predispositions are evoked."[33] Salient symbols include political issues that may be directly or indirectly associated with racial groups. For example, welfare and affirmative action trigger negative inclinations toward African Americans, predispositions that have endured since childhood socialization.[34] Immigration debates may play a similar role in generating attitudes about Latinos and Asians. One study shows that aversion to Latinos is strongly associated with support for more restrictive immigration policy.[35]

The research on each of these theories has largely focused on Black–White relations. These ideas were born out of the African American struggle for civil rights in the mid-twentieth century. V.O. Key's work on Southern politics and the behavior of "black belt" Whites is still the basis for many hypotheses related to interracial relations. However, it may not be appropriate to assume that the responses to ethnic minority groups, specifically Latinos and Asians, will be the same as the beliefs about and feelings toward African Americans.

David Sears and his colleagues argue that in the United States, attitudes about African Americans are unique. Many White Americans tend to hold negative stereotypes about Blacks—particularly that African Americans violate traditional American values, such as hard work and self-reliance—and many believe that racism is no longer a serious problem in the United States.[36] The "black exceptionalism" hypothesis suggests that Blacks are likely to have been the focus of prior stigmatizing socialization that does not compare to any other minority group's experiences of discrimination.[37] In contrast, relatively few Americans, White or Black, have had long socialization histories that would influence their attitudes about Latinos or Asians. Most Whites' attitudes about "minorities" have been disproportionately influenced by their beliefs about African Americans, so much so that these beliefs have a lopsided effect on attitudes toward any minority-related issue, even those involving non–African

Americans. Joe Feagin also suggests that the United States has a bipolar racial structure and that racism against Latinos and other people of color is an extension of an "anti-black orientation."[38]

Comments from focus groups in Harlan demonstrate how easy it is for native-born, White young people to conflate opinions on immigrants with their opinions about Blacks. The interviewer asked about their parents' reactions if immigrants moved into their community. The responses that followed quickly veered into discussions related to African Americans:

Interviewer: What would your parents say if immigrants moved into Harlan?

Monica: Well, you know, Mexicans—my dad works with a bunch of them up there [in Denison], and they can get paid for less, you know, and they don't get taxes taken out, and if they're going to be moving in the U.S., I think they should have to pay taxes.

Caitlyn: They should.

Monica: If they're going to be a U.S. citizen, then . . .

Jim: Exactly.

Monica: And that's just what I don't like about immigrants coming in here and they should only be able to come in here not legally . . . they should . . . like . . .

Interviewer: Right

Monica: . . . you know, I don't like that idea.

Interviewer: OK.

Monica: —of coming . . .

Jim: That's . . . because you hear a lot about people talking about how it's unfair. We pay a high amount of taxes when they're running away with cash. And if you're going to be working in this country, you're going to be doing what every other person does in this country: pay taxes.

Monica: But we're going to become the minority pretty soon, I'm thinking. And now they have . . . they still have those things for black scholarships, you know, and stuff like that. They have to get so many . . . or a number of jobs or . . . different races . . .

Interviewer: A quota?

Monica: Yeah. And pretty soon we're going to be the minority, and I guess we'll probably have to get that, too, then, but who knows if that will happen.

Jim: What I think is stupid in this country is how we say we're not racially based. But if you look at it, everything is sexually or racially based. There has to be so many women, there has to be so many colored this and that. That's stupid. And that's something that's just—it's unfair. Just like she said. Black don't—I mean, why should there be a Black scholarship? There should be a scholarship, period.

Monica: You should just send it in, you know, with a number; no name,
no sex, no race.

Jim: Yeah, it just should be . . .

Monica: . . . on merit.

Jim: Exactly. It's on who are and what you are.

Monica: I mean, we're starting a new, like, it's 2000 now and it should
be . . . like the Blacks. We kind of, we are starting repaying from. . . .
Well, I don't like what we did, like, you know.

Interviewer: In the past?

Monica: Yeah, if I would have been there, I—

Jim: Yeah, I couldn't imagine.

Caitlyn: Well, I think a lot people then would have, you know, if they'd
been brought up now. It's a lot of what you grow up with.

Jim: See, like my father. My father is racially inclined. He does not care
for Black people or Mexicans. Me, I'm open-minded.

Although the question was specifically about immigration, these youth
quickly segued into a discussion of affirmative action for African Americans.
They began by discussing the common misconception that immigrants do not
pay taxes. But in just a few minutes, they had jumped from the injustice they
believe exists around this issue to the injustice of affirmative action programs,
which they explicitly associated with Blacks. Their opinions on immigrants, in
this way, were associated with their attitudes about African Americans.

A growing body of research shows that attitudes about African Americans
are distinctive and are often good indicators of support for immigrants and
immigration.[39] Peter Burns and James G. Gimpel find that negative stereotypes about Blacks are highly related to negative attitudes toward immigration
policy.[40] Jeffrey Dixon shows that for Whites, "Large numbers of blacks may
arouse threat and give rise to prejudice, but large numbers of Hispanics and
Asians do not."[41] Further, superficial interethnic contact between Whites and
Latinos or Asians is associated with less intolerance toward those groups, but
similar contact with African Americans does not reduce prejudice against
Blacks. Only when Whites know *and feel close to* African Americans is prejudice
against them reduced. David O. Sears and his colleagues examine attitudes
about Latinos in Los Angeles, which show "an older and more intractable form
of group conflict: the pervasive influence of anti-black attitudes on whites' preferences about minority-related policy issues, even those, like multiculturalism
that scarcely involve blacks at all."[42] Negative affect related to Blacks is not
unique to White Americans. Studies of young Haitian and Dominican immigrants show that when given a choice, they choose not to identify themselves
with African Americans.[43]

This study offers an interesting test of this theory. In national samples, communities with high levels of ethnic diversity tend to be in urban areas. Sears and
his colleagues' study is on Los Angeles, a city with a long history of immigration

and a socially and politically significant African American community. The towns in this study are quite different. They have almost no history with ethnic diversity, except for differences between European ancestries. In addition, none of these communities has now or has ever had a substantial African American population. A few Blacks have lived in these towns over the years, but they have been a minuscule proportion of their populations and generally have not stayed long. How can young people in small towns with few African Americans have crystallized negative perceptions of this group? And should we expect these attitudes to influence opinions about ethnic groups with which they have contact?

It is also important to keep in mind that adolescents are still undergoing the socialization experience. Sears and his colleagues suggest that the environment "plays a key role both in nurturing the original socialization process and in determining which predispositions are evoked by political stimuli later in life."[44] Because these youth, age 14–18, are in the midst of their socialization process, they should be less likely to have ingrained, long-held beliefs about much of anything, including racial or ethnic stereotypes.

Results from Iowa Towns:
Attitudes toward Immigrants and Diversity

The survey contained seven questions designed to measure attitudes or opinions about immigrants and their effects on one's community. Three items attempt to measure stereotypes of immigrants, such as their work ethic ("Immigrants work harder than natives"), the importance of learning to speak English ("Immigrants should [not have to] learn to speak English ASAP"), and the idea that they take jobs ("Immigrants [do not] take jobs away from natives"). The other items attempt to get at respondents' ideas about the effect that immigrants have on their communities: "There would (not) be fewer problems here if there were (more) immigrants," "This town would be better with more immigrants," "Asian people will make life better here," and "Hispanic people will make life better here." The responses are coded so that higher values on each 0–4 scale indicate more sympathetic responses.

Attitudes about immigrants are not altogether negative or positive (see Figure 3.1). The analyses that follow examine only respondents who say they and their parents were born in the United States. In Figure 3.1, the middle category ("neither agree nor disagree") is not shown. A third of respondents believe that immigrants do not take jobs from natives, and another third contend that immigrants have taken jobs away from natives. A smaller proportion of young people believe that Hispanic people will improve their communities, compared with Asian people. This may be related to the stereotypes of Asians as a "model minority" in the United States.[45] A significant minority of young people believe their town would be better with more immigrants, while a majority disagree with this statement.

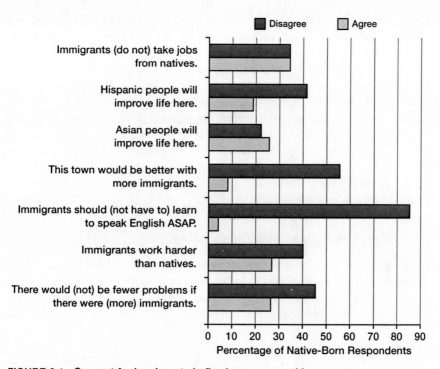

FIGURE 3.1   Support for immigrants in five Iowa communities

The question demonstrating the most consensus deals with the need for immigrants to learn to speak English. More than 85 percent of native young people in these communities believe that it is important for immigrants to learn to speak English as soon as possible. Less than 1 percent "strongly disagree" with this statement. The question undoubtedly measures both a belief about the importance of English skills to success and a commonly held stereotype that immigrants cannot and do not wish to speak English. A non-native language serves as a cue to others, and to the non-native English speaker, that he or she is a member of an out-group and is usually associated with many negative perceptions, such as less competence and intelligence.[46] Speaking English is seen as a prerequisite to being "American" and is one of the most contentious issues today in the national debate about immigration policy. As of 2010, thirty states (including Iowa) have passed laws declaring English the official state language, and in some rare cases students have been punished for speaking other languages at school.[47]

These attitudes are comparable in many ways to national studies of adults' attitudes about immigrants and immigration. A poll taken in May 2010 shows that 87 percent of adults favor making English the nation's official language.[48] Just as we see with the adolescents surveyed here, on other attitudes about immigration, American adults are split in their opinions. Francine Segovia and

Renatta Defever report that since 1993, polls have consistently shown that Americans are divided with regard to their beliefs about whether immigrants work harder than natives.[49] The young people in these Iowa communities are somewhat less likely than adults surveyed by other organizations to say that immigrants take jobs from native-born Americans, but both sets of opinion data indicate substantial ambivalence. A Fox News poll taken in May 2010 indicates that 41 percent of Americans say that "immigrants who come to the United States today help the country and make it a better place to live," as opposed to 31 percent who say that immigration "hurts the country and makes it a worse place to live."[50] As discussed in Chapter 1, there is disagreement among scholars about the empirical reality of immigrants' effects on labor markets. It is not surprising, then, to see public ambivalence.

Comparing Heterogeneous and Homogeneous Communities

Looking at Figure 3.2, we see that generally there are few attitudinal differences between native-born adolescents in the diverse communities compared with those in homogeneous communities. On four of the seven indicators, the differences are not statistically significant. On the other indicators, the results are

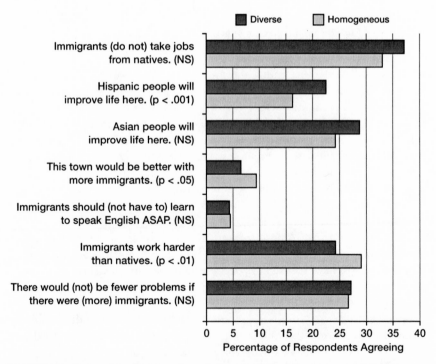

FIGURE 3.2 Support for immigrants and diversity in homogeneous and diverse communities

mixed. Young people in homogeneous communities are more likely to agree that immigrants work harder than natives and that their town would be better with more immigrants. One common anecdotal refrain in the homogeneous towns was that life was "boring" and that immigrants would add some interest to the otherwise staid existence of these towns. The youth in the diverse towns, however, are more likely to agree that Hispanic people will improve life in their communities.

These mixed results could be affected by several confounding individual factors. To conduct multiple regression analyses and control these factors, the next set of analyses uses a factor score consisting of each of these individual indicators of tolerance. This score is the dependent variable (see Table A.3). Within the regression models that follow, the indicator of the contact hypothesis is whether one lives in one of the diverse communities. The indicators measuring power threat theory are parental income and post–high school plans. The hypotheses suggest that lower-income young people and those who do not plan to attend college are the most likely to show low levels of tolerance because they are more directly threatened by the presence of immigrants.[51] With regard to both measures of interethnic contact and power threat, the measures are limited. It would be ideal to have measures about the frequency and type of personal interactions between respondents and individuals from another ethnic group. Even so, given the small sizes of these towns and schools, merely living in and going to school in these communities indicates respondents have interactions with immigrants. There are also more specific attitudinal measures of economic threat. Because these types of items were not asked on the survey, these results are suggestive, not definitive.

The models also include measures of rootedness to the community, because several studies have indicated that in rural areas people may feel a more diffuse sense of threat from immigrants to their way of life or rural culture. Three indicators measure the extent to which young people are rooted: the presence of grandparents nearby, parents employed as full-time farmers, and the length of residence in the community. In rural areas, grandparents are often active parts of young people's lives, and through the information they pass down to youth they serve as important resources.[52] Rural sociologists also have shown that young people from farming families are distinct in many ways from their non-farm counterparts.[53] Their families are more likely to have lived in the community for many years and to be well known by others. These young people and their families draw on social connections in the same way that highly educated parents draw on their professional experience in helping their children succeed.

The models also include feeling thermometers toward Whites, African Americans, and Latinos (1 = cold, 10 = warm). According to Donald Kinder and Cindy Kam, these scales allow respondents to "evaluate in-groups and out-groups in separate assessments, and they can express favoritism for their own groups without conspicuously violating norms of fairness."[54] They show that feelings about ethnic groups are associated with attitudes about immigrants. Jack Citrin and his colleagues also demonstrate that affect toward Hispanics and Asians is highly associated with attitudes about immigrants.[55]

In addition to several individual controls (grade level, sex, amount of civics coursework, parents' marital status, and generalized trust), the analyses test symbolic politics theory by considering two attitudinal questions that are related to beliefs about African Americans. One question asks whether respondents believe "it is better for people of different races to live in separate neighborhoods," and the other question asks whether "slavery has made it difficult for Blacks." These questions and many like them have been used by other scholars as measures of attitudes related to prejudice toward African Americans.[56] Although the latter question explicitly mentions "Blacks," the former question does not. However, in the United States, there is much evidence that residential segregation preferences are closely associated, in the minds of most White Americans, with the African American community.

Although Whites are more comfortable today than they used to be, there is a great deal of evidence that they are uncomfortable with the idea of living in neighborhoods with large proportions of African Americans.[57] Further, Black neighborhoods are less appealing to Whites than neighborhoods composed of other ethnic groups. Camille L. Zubrinsky and Lawrence Bobo find that, even though Whites find it less desirable to live in ethnically diverse neighborhoods than in all-White communities, they are least likely to want to live in communities with African Americans, followed by those with Hispanics and Asians, respectively.[58] Another study finds that Whites have no problem living in hypothetical neighborhoods with Latinos or Asians but are much less willing to consider living in neighborhoods with Blacks.[59] Bobo contends that residential racial segregation is the "structural linchpin" of American race relations.[60] Questions about segregation and slavery arguably are symbolic issues closely associated with attitudes about African Americans.

The results in Table 3.1 demonstrate that young people in the diverse communities are less sympathetic to immigrants than those in the homogeneous towns. Models 1 and 2 differ only in that the second model includes the measures of symbolic politics, allowing an examination of its effects over and above the other measures. Both models show that neither parental income nor educational aspirations is statistically significantly related to tolerance for immigrants, suggesting that young people's attitudes about immigrants may not be related to prospective economic threat. The rootedness measures are only minimally related to attitudes toward immigrants. The longer one has lived in the community, the more opposed one is to immigrants, lending some support to the idea that in small towns, those who are strongly rooted to the community are more concerned about potential changes to their way of life. Finally, young people who rate Hispanics positively are more supportive of immigrants. Similarly, those who evaluate Whites more positively are more opposed to immigrants. It is worth noting that attitudes toward Hispanics are more positive—that is, warmer—in the diverse communities ($p < .001$).

TABLE 3.1 Regression Results on the Influence of Ethnic Diversity on Attitudes toward Immigrants

	Model 1	Model 2
Lives in diverse town	−.05***	−.03*
	(.01)	(.01)
Power threat		
Family income	−.004	−.004
	(.01)	(.01)
Planning to attend a four-year college	−.01	−.002
	(.02)	(.01)
Rootedness to community		
Parents are farmers	−.01	−.0003
	(.01)	(.01)
Grandparents live in the state	−.03	−.01
	(.02)	(.02)
Length of residence in the community	−.01*	−.01*
	(.01)	(.004)
Symbolic politics		
Better for races to live apart		−.06***
		(.006)
Slavery has not made it difficult for Blacks		−.03***
		(.006)
Ethnic group evaluations		
Evaluations of African Americans	−.002	−.003
	(.003)	(.002)
Evaluations of Hispanics	.03***	.02***
	(.003)	(.003)
Evaluations of Whites	−.01*	−.01*
	(.01)	(.01)
Demographic/other factors		
Grade level	.01	.01
	(.01)	(.01)
Female	.06***	.05***
	(.01)	(.01)
Amount of civics coursework	−.002	−.004
	(.004)	(.003)
Parents are married	−.01	−.01
	(.02)	(.01)
Generalized trust	.05**	.04**
	(.01)	(.01)
Constant	.37***	.48
	(.10)	(.09)
	N = 538	N = 538
	R^2 = .32	R^2 = .46

Note: Values are ordinary least squares unstandardized regression coefficients. Standard errors are in parentheses. Foreign-born respondents and those with a foreign-born parent are excluded. Dependent variable is a factor score that includes each individual measure of tolerance and is rescaled to 0–1.

*p < .05; **p < .01; ***p < .001.

Although the results show that evaluations of African Americans are unrelated to attitudes about immigrants, Model 2 clearly demonstrates that both of the indicators of symbolic politics are highly significantly related to tolerance for immigrants. Thus, explicit feelings about African Americans as a group are not related to attitudes about immigrants, but symbolic attitudes related to Blacks are closely associated with these attitudes. Model 2 explains nearly half of the variance in measure of attitudes about immigrants ($R^2 = .46$). Native-born young people who believe that people of different races should live apart or that slavery has not made things more difficult for Blacks are significantly less accepting of immigrants. Once the model controls for negative symbolic attitudes related to African Americans, the diversity of the community makes less difference. The statistical significance between living in a diverse town and attitudes about immigrants falls from $p < .001$ to $p < .05$. Overall, these results indicate that ethnic diversity has a depressing effect on support for immigrants, and these attitudes are influenced most by positive attitudes about Hispanics and negative attitudes about African Americans.

Ethnic Change and Attitudes about Diversity

The level of diversity may not be the most important factor influencing perceived conflict. The timing of the change or experience residents have with diversity may matter more. Daniel Hopkins contends that residents of two communities with the same proportion of immigrants might have very different reactions to diversification depending on how recently the immigrants arrived.[61] Examining differences between Perry and Storm Lake allows us to examine this hypothesis. Storm Lake's diversification began before Perry's because of Asian refugees who settled there in the 1970s and 1980s, giving residents valuable experience with diversity before the rapid demographic changes in the 1990s. Table 3.2 compares differences between Perry and Storm Lake and Perry and the predominantly White towns on attitudes about immigrants. On five of the seven indicators, Storm Lake students were more sympathetic to immigrants than were Perry youth. There are no differences with regard to attitudes about immigrants' work ethic or whether Asian immigrants will improve life in the community.

Comparing Perry to the homogeneous White communities, we see that Perry youth are significantly less tolerant than are those in the less diverse places. Young people in Perry are less likely than those in the homogeneous towns to believe that there would be fewer problems with more immigrants, that immigrants work harder than natives, that their town would be better off with more immigrants, and that Hispanic immigrants will improve life in Perry. In contrast, there are no significant differences between Storm Lake youth and their counterparts in the predominantly White communities. These results lend credence to Hopkins's idea about the importance of ethnic change in predicting tolerance. In Storm Lake, where ethnic change occurred rapidly throughout the

TABLE 3.2 Difference of Means Tests on Support for Immigrants between Perry and Storm Lake

	Perry	Storm Lake	White towns
Immigrants (do not) take jobs away from natives.	1.73	2.01*	1.87
Hispanic people will make life better here.	1.39	1.76**	1.62**
Asian people will make life better here.	1.97	2.07	2.03
This town would be better with more immigrants.	0.98	1.26**	1.35***
Immigrants should (not have to) learn to speak English ASAP.	0.58	0.79*	0.69
Immigrants work harder than natives.	1.55	1.71	1.87**
There would (not) be fewer problems if there were (more) immigrants.	1.45	1.82**	1.73**

Note: Values are means within each category. Responses are coded 0–4, with higher values indicating more tolerance. Foreign-born respondents and those with a foreign-born parent are excluded. Significance levels correspond to comparisons between Perry and Storm Lake and Perry and the predominantly White towns. There are no significant differences between Storm Lake and the predominantly White towns.

*p < .05; **p < .01; ***p < .001.

1990s but had begun much earlier, young people were as sympathetic toward immigrants as those in similar all-White communities. In Perry, where ethnic change also occurred rapidly in the 1990s but there had been no previous experience with diversity, attitudes were more negative.

Multiple regression confirms these results. Native-born young people in Perry are significantly less sympathetic to immigrants than their counterparts in the homogeneous communities; the same is not true, however, in Storm Lake (Table 3.3). Positive evaluations of Hispanics are directly related to sympathy toward immigrants. Cross-tabs indicate that Storm Lake students have warmer evaluations of Hispanics than do Perry students (p < .01). Finally, once the model controls for symbolic attitudes related to Blacks, Perry students are as tolerant as young people in the other communities, suggesting that in Perry, but not in Storm Lake, negative attitudes related to African Americans were partly responsible for the students' negative beliefs about immigrants.

Immigrants' Attitudes toward Immigration and Other Ethnic Groups

While the focus of this study is primarily on the attitudes of the native-born youth in small towns, looking at tolerance among first- and second-generation immigrants offers an interesting window into life in these communities. The literature tends to suggest that there are two directions of immigrants' opinions on immigration.[62] The first, referred to as the cultural perspective, suggests that immigrants' natural affinity for co-ethnic members outweighs other cleavages,

TABLE 3.3 Regression Results of Attitudes about Immigrants in Storm Lake and Perry

	Model 1	Model 2
Perry High School	−.07***	−.03
	(.02)	(.02)
Storm Lake High School	−.03	−.02
	(.02)	(.02)
Power threat		
Family income	−.003	−.004
	(.01)	(.01)
Planning to attend a four-year college	.01	−.002
	(.02)	(.01)
Rootedness in community		
Parents are farmers	−.01	−.0004
	(.01)	(.01)
Grandparents live in the state	−.04	−.01
	(.02)	(.02)
Length of residence in the community	−.01*	−.01*
	(.01)	(.004)
Symbolic politics		
Better for races to live apart		−.06***
		(.01)
Slavery has not made it difficult for Blacks		−.03***
		(.01)
Ethnic group valuations		
Evaluations of African Americans	−.001	−.003
	(.003)	(.002)
Evaluations of Hispanics	.03***	.02***
	(.003)	(.003)
Evaluations of Whites	−.01*	−.01*
	(.01)	(.01)
Demographics/other		
Grade level	.004	.01
	(.01)	(.01)
Female	.07***	.05***
	(.01)	(.01)
Amount of civics coursework	−.001	−.003
	(.004)	(.003)
Parents are married	−.01	−.01
	(.02)	(.01)
Generalized trust	.05**	.04**
	(.01)	(.01)
Constant	.38***	.478***
	(.10)	(.09)
	N = 539	N = 539
	R^2 = .33	R^2 = .46

Note: Values are ordinary least squares unstandardized regression coefficients. Standard errors are in parentheses. Foreign-born respondents and those with a foreign-born parent are excluded. Dependent variable is a factor score that includes each individual measure of tolerance and is scaled to be 0–1.

*p < .05; **p < .01; ***p < .001.

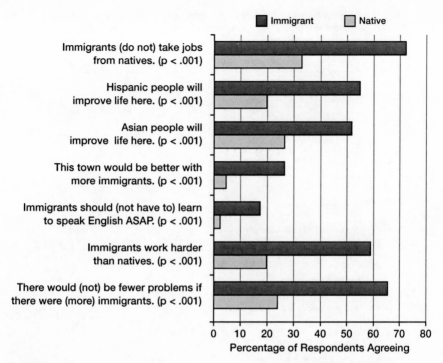

FIGURE 3.3 Support for immigrants among native and immigrant youth in Perry and Storm Lake

and therefore immigrants are opposed to restrictive immigration policies and feel closer to their brethren from nearby countries.[63] The other perspective is the structural, or SES, perspective, suggesting that because most immigrants are lower skilled and employed in low-wage jobs, they are more likely to support restrictionist policies because they fear economic competition from new arrivals.[64] Not only are higher-status immigrants thought to lack a personal economic threat from newly arriving immigrants, but those who have higher levels of education are thought to have benefited from the liberalizing influence of education.[65] Each theory is thought to be mediated by the immigrants' degree of acculturation: the more Americanized immigrants are, the more their attitudes resemble Anglos'.[66]

Bivariate relationships suggest that first- and second-generation immigrants are much more sympathetic toward immigrants than are natives (Figure 3.3). The immigrant group consists of young people in Storm Lake and Perry who were born outside the United States and those who have at least one parent who was foreign-born. In this study, 146 respondents in Perry and Storm Lake had a foreign-born parent (30 percent of the sample in these two schools), and this group captured all those who were themselves born outside the United States. The native group consisted of those in Perry and Storm Lake who were born in the United States and whose parents were born in this country.

TABLE 3.4 Regression Results of Attitudes about Immigrants Comparing Native-Born and Immigrant Respondents in Perry and Storm Lake

	Immigrant respondents	Native-born respondents
Power threat		
Family income	.004	−.01
	(.01)	(.01)
Planning to attend a four-year college	−.02	.01
	(.04)	(.02)
Rootedness in community		
Parents are farmers	−.04	.01
	(.02)	(.01)
Grandparents live in the state	.11*	−.01
	(.04)	(.03)
Length of residence in the community	−.03	−.004
	(.02)	(.01)
Symbolic politics		
Better for races to live apart	−.03	−.06***
	(.02)	(.01)
Slavery has not made it difficult for Blacks	−.01	−.03
	(.02)	(.01)
Ethnic group evaluations		
Evaluations of African Americans	−.002	.001
	(.01)	(.004)
Evaluations of Hispanics	.03***	.03***
	(.01)	(.004)
Evaluations of Whites	−.0007	−.01
	(.01)	(.01)
Demographics/other		
Grade level	.01	−.01
	(.02)	(.01)
Female	.05	.02
	(.03)	(.02)
Amount of civics coursework	−.0006	.04
	(.01)	(.01)
Parents are married	.01	−.01
	(.04)	(.02)
Generalized trust	−.04	.05*
	(.04)	(.02)
Constant	.35	.62***
	(.22)	(.14)
	N = 62	N = 209
	$R^2 = .63$	$R^2 = .59$

Note: Values are ordinary least squares unstandardized regression coefficients. Standard errors are in parentheses. All respondents in Perry and Storm Lake are included.

*p < .05; **p < .01; ***p < .001.

Although the vast majority of the immigrants in Perry and Storm Lake came from low-status backgrounds, on each item, immigrants were more likely to give the more sympathetic response, suggesting they do not feel a significant economic threat from other immigrants. It is also worth noting that the item with the lowest level of support concerned whether immigrants should learn English. We also saw that this is very important to Anglos. Although more immigrant children than native children disagreed with the statement that immigrants should have to learn English as soon as possible, this proportion was still a substantial minority of immigrant youth. Only 17 percent of immigrants believed it was not important to learn English. One of the common myths about immigrants is that they do not want to learn to speak English.[67] These results, and many others, dispel this myth.[68]

Regression analysis shows that differences between immigrants and natives remain significantly significant (p < .01; table not shown). I also ran separate models for immigrants and natives to examine whether there were differences in the predictors of sympathy toward immigrants (Table 3.4). The model with immigrant respondents should be read with some caution because of the small number of respondents. Nonetheless, these models demonstrate that there are few significant differences in the predictors of attitudes toward immigrants. The main difference is that symbolic attitudes related to African Americans are not significantly related to attitudes about immigrants among the immigrant group, while these attitudes are significantly related to attitudes among the native-born youth. Immigrant children and their parents have had less time to develop and internalize negative attitudes about African Americans than native children and their parents.

Summary

The findings do not suggest that young native-born residents are motivated by prospective economic threat. Although we cannot rule out the potential influence of power threat due to the limitations of the measures, the findings in this chapter demonstrate that two factors are primarily responsible for explaining attitudes about immigrants: feelings toward Hispanics and attitudes related to Blacks. First, positive feelings toward Hispanics were significantly associated with sympathy for immigrants in all of the analyses. Also, young people in the diverse communities—particularly Storm Lake—had warmer feelings toward Hispanics than those in the ethnically homogeneous ones. At a minimum, these results suggest that interethnic contact in Perry and Storm Lake has created some goodwill between natives and immigrants and that such contact has had positive effects on attitudes about Hispanics. Even though this interethnic contact improved their positive feelings about Hispanics, as of the fall of 2001, Anglo youth, especially those in Perry, showed a great deal of ambivalence about immigrants.

Second, negative symbolic attitudes related to African Americans contribute significantly to attitudes about immigrants. This is especially true in Perry. Once the models control for attitudes related to slavery and segregation, youth in Perry are just as supportive of immigrants as are those in the other communities. One potential explanation for such negative attitudes related to Blacks is the absence of exposure to and contact with African Americans. Although these communities have never been completely White, they have had very small African American populations. A few Black students per graduating class are not uncommon in these and other rural communities in the Midwest. In Perry, for example, Doug Bruce, a community and business leader, gave me a driving tour around town. He reported that one area of town was once an all-Black community, that Perry "used to have three or four Blacks that lived in town that worked on the rail line," and that a few African Americans live there now.[69] The Black section of town is where fewer than ten people had lived.

Even so, interracial contact may go only so far. Dixon discovered that interracial contact with African Americans only reduces prejudice against them if Whites feel close to them. Several other scholars have researched the existence of racist sentiments in communities with few very minorities.[70] In these contexts, racism is not the result of realistic group threat; nor is it based on negative experiences with these particular groups. Rather, there is a dominant, racialized discourse within the United States, fostered and maintained by residential segregation and structural inequalities and manifested in the form of racist beliefs and stereotypes about African Americans.[71] J. Eric Oliver and Tali Mendelberg, for example, argue that in places where people have low levels of education and employment, individuals are exposed to environments of social disorder that lead to anxiety, fear, and suspicion of "others," especially African Americans, who are "a salient target in a racially divided society."[72] Within these places, it is not just lower-status individuals who feel this way; a culture permeates the community. Rural Americans can be suspicious of outsiders, and these communities have little personal experience with minority groups that can counter negative beliefs and stereotypes that saturate the larger culture.

Symbolic politics theory posits that longstanding beliefs about Blacks explain attitudes related to issues associated not only with African Americans but with "minority" groups in general. Like P. J. Henry and David O. Sears, who show that "symbolic racism already is well crystallized when Americans reach voting age and the higher education system," these findings also show that "longstanding" is, indeed, *very* long-standing.[73] Teens as young as 14 or 15 in these communities have already internalized negative stereotypes and beliefs about Blacks. Some children undoubtedly grow up in families where overt racism still exists in the form of derogatory remarks and racist statements, but for many White American children today, these messages are more subtle, more covert, and, in this way, more difficult to eradicate. Young people, unlike Stephen Colbert, do indeed see race. In fact, the ways in which they see race have substantial, negative effects on their attitudes about immigrants.

The findings related to symbolic politics may seem to undermine one of the critical assumptions of this book: the importance of local context in shaping the socialization process. After all, if young people who have very little experience with African Americans already have internalized negative beliefs about them, and these beliefs are strongly related to attitudes about non–African American immigrants, then how can I argue that the local ethnic and racial context makes a difference? Theories about the influence of local context do not argue that context, by itself, determine outcomes. Urie Bronfenbrenner argued that there were multiple layers of context that affect a child's development. The local community is one of the most important contexts for socialization, but it lies within national and global contexts that also influence development. Even some of the most remote parts of the United States have cable television and access to the Internet, enabling young people to be exposed to the larger culture and its representations of African Americans. I contend that the local context has the most immediate influences on political socialization (with the exception of the family), but I certainly do not argue that the larger culture has no influence on these attitudes. These findings merely underscore a need in the scholarly community for nuanced theories and innovative tests that allow us to sort out how and when the local context shapes the development of political attitudes and beliefs.

Furthermore, it is important to note the differences between Perry and Storm Lake. Young people in each community are exposed to the same national culture and its messages about African Americans. At that time, neither community had a substantial African American population. To the extent that the larger, racialized culture alone—and not the local context—explains adolescents' attitudes about immigrants, we should see similar outcomes in the two communities. However, in Storm Lake, the Anglo youth are just as sympathetic toward immigrants as are those in the homogeneous communities. Further, negative attitudes related to African Americans have no effect on the attitudes of Storm Lake students about immigrants. These negative attitudes about Blacks influence the attitudes of only those young people in Perry. These differences can only be explained by differences in the local context.

Finally, the differences between Perry and Storm Lake suggest that time may have an important role to play in explaining attitudes about immigrants in small, diverse settings. Chapter 5 shows that because Storm Lake began to diversify several years before immigrants began to arrive in Perry, the community started coming to terms with demographic change before other towns undergoing the same changes. Further, the earlier wave of refugees in Storm Lake meant that native kids had some experience with diversity before Latinos started to arrive en masse. For them, the existence of ethnic minority groups had been common since they were young children. But first, the next chapter examines the extent to which ethnic diversity influences other civic outcomes.

4

No Retreat

Civic Withdrawal and Immigration

Residents of all races tend to "hunker down." Trust (even of one's own race) is lower, altruism and community cooperation rarer, friends fewer.

—Robert Putnam

Although not the first to conceptualize the concept, Robert Putnam's work on social capital helped set in motion a course of study in political science and other disciplines about the decline of political participation and civic engagement in the United States and around the world. This has included political socialization scholarship hastened largely by worries about recent generations' apathy, misinformation about politics, and lack of trust in public officials. Putnam argues that due to changes in technology and communication, citizens are less trusting of one another, less likely to vote, less sociable and neighborly, and less participatory in their communities.[1] He and others believe we should care about declines in social capital because it influences individual and societal well-being in a variety of forms.[2]

Rural America has some of the highest levels of social capital in the country. People living in small communities are more engaged in local and national affairs; they belong to and participate in civic organizations; and they are more trusting of their neighbors than are those in larger, more urban areas. They have dense social networks and routinely rely on one another for many purposes. Individuals who are not themselves active and engaged but live in communities characterized by high levels of social capital benefit from living in these places. Much evidence suggests that "where levels of social capital are higher, children grow up healthier, safer and better educated, people live longer, happier lives, and democracy and the economy work better."[3]

Putnam initially contended that social capital and equality, including racial equality, were highly congruent.[4] In recent years, several scholars, including Putnam himself, have come to different conclusions regarding the compatibility of ethnic diversity and social capital. It is hardly a coincidence, some have argued, that the places where social capital is highest are also very racially and ethnically homogeneous. In fact, Rodney Hero argues that the production of social capital may depend heavily on racial and ethnic homogeneity.[5] Putnam contends that the reason diversity is associated with lower levels of generalized trust and participation is not simply that heterogeneity leads to racial or ethnic conflict but, rather, that it is associated with less interracial *and* intraracial trust. In other words, "Diversity seems to trigger *not* in-group/out-group division, but anomie or social isolation."[6] Putnam uses the analogy of a turtle to illustrate: people react to diversity by pulling into their shells and disengaging from the world around them.

This chapter examines the effects of ethnic diversity on several measures of social capital and civic engagement in the Iowa communities in this study. Do native-born, Anglo young people living in heterogeneous communities "hunker down" and pull into their shell? Are they less likely than their native-born, Anglo counterparts in homogeneous communities to say they will vote? To participate in school activities? To feel they understand politics? To believe that public officials listen to them? To trust others? To discuss politics with others? Each of these measures is an important outcome related to political socialization, and because they are related to future adult measures of civic engagement, they tell us something about the potential future of social capital and civic engagement in these communities. Given the ever increasing diversity of the United States, they also shed some light into the future of civic engagement in the nation.

The results in Iowa suggest that ethnic diversity universally only depresses *one* indicator of social capital: political knowledge. In both Perry and Storm Lake, native-born young people have lower levels of knowledge than their counterparts in the homogeneous communities. In Perry, where immigration began later than in Storm Lake, levels of generalized trust and external efficacy are lower than in the Anglo towns, but in Storm Lake, this is not the case. In fact, in this community, young people are actually significantly *more* active in school activities than in the Anglo towns.

Ethnic Diversity and Civic Engagement

Conflict and contact theories, reviewed in the previous chapter, do not tell us much about why or how we might expect ethnic diversity to influence outcomes unrelated to tolerance. For example, why should heterogeneity affect generalized trust in others? Or civic engagement and political knowledge? Putnam argues that when thinking about these outcomes, the contact–conflict paradigm does not adequately explain people's reactions to diversity. He contends that in-group and out-group attitudes are not necessarily reciprocally related but, instead, can vary independently. This opens the "possibility that diversity might actually reduce *both* in-group *and* out-group solidarity."[7] In other words, even if ethnic diversity leads to negative attitudes about minority groups, this may not go hand in hand with enhanced feelings about one's own group or more active engagement in politics. In response to diversification, Putnam and others contend that people are less trusting more generally, contributing to lower levels of participation, efficacy, political discussion, and other aspects of civic engagement.

A growing body of literature across the social sciences demonstrates the deleterious effects of diversity on non-tolerance-related outcomes. Economists show that heterogeneous environments are accompanied by less support for public-good expenditures, less participation in social activities, and lower levels of trust.[8] Dora Costa and Matthew Kahn find that people are less likely to volunteer, to join organizations, and to trust others when they live in heterogeneous communities.[9] Robert Sampson's research shows that as racial diversity increases at the neighborhood level, people (especially Whites) perceive more social disorder in their communities.[10] Putnam discovers that ethnic diversity is associated with lower confidence in government, lower political efficacy, lower frequency of registering to vote, less expectation that others will cooperate to solve dilemmas of collective action, less likelihood of working on a community project, lower likelihood of giving to charity or volunteering, fewer close friends and confidants, less happiness and lower perceived quality of life, and more time spent watching television. A study in Iowa demonstrates that towns with greater *White* ethnic heterogeneity tend to have lower levels of community attachment, trust, and involvement in community activities.[11]

There are, however, many civic benefits from living in heterogeneous societies. In diverse locations, some argue, people have a greater incentive to participate because they find it necessary to protect their interests, whereas in homogeneous places, people may find that their interests are likely to be represented by those around them and do not have to get involved.[12] In theory, diversity should enhance the prospects for "bridging" social capital—informal contacts with people with varied backgrounds—that are beneficial for the production of generalized trust, political discussion, and civic participation.[13] In a cross-country analysis, Christopher J. Anderson and Aida Paskeviciute show that heterogeneity dampens interpersonal trust, but ethnic diversity has little effect on political discussion, membership in organizations, or political interest.[14] Similarly, although the bulk of his findings show negative effects of ethnic diversity, Putnam's research also demonstrates that in diverse places, people have more interest in and knowledge about politics and are more likely to participate in protest marches and social reform groups.[15]

This chapter uses the initial surveys conducted in five Iowa towns in 2001 to examine the effects of ethnic diversity on several outcomes often collectively called "social capital" or "civic engagement." The chapter first discusses each of the outcomes to be examined and why each is an important aspect of political socialization. Then the results focus on comparisons between native-born American young people in the immigrant-receiving towns versus those in the ethnically homogeneous communities. The next section disaggregates the two towns with immigrants to examine similarities and differences between these two contexts. Finally, the last section of findings compares foreign-born youth to their native-born counterparts in Perry and Storm Lake. The conclusions discuss the importance of considering differences between adults and adolescents in the development of theories about ethnic diversity.

Political Socialization and Civic Outcomes

The outcomes examined in this chapter are political knowledge, political efficacy, generalized trust, and three measures of participation: intention to vote, participation in school activities, and frequency of political discussion. Together they represent the fundamental measures of civic engagement among scholars of political socialization. Political knowledge is one of the most extensively examined outcomes in studies of the development of political attitudes but has been left out of much of the research on the effects of ethnic diversity. It is arguably the best predictor of political participation among adults.[16] High school students with more knowledge are also more likely to participate in school activities and to say they will vote in the future.[17] Political knowledge is an essential building block to all the other values studied here. When I use the term "political knowledge," my concern is with fundamental knowledge about political structures, historically significant events, and the identities and roles of officeholders in the political system.[18]

The fact that Americans have extraordinarily low levels of political knowledge is, by now, generally accepted within both the scholarly community and the public.[19] Americans are woefully unaware of many basic facts about how the U.S. government works and lack the ability to recall current events and personalities. Young people are no better than adults. A report from the National Assessment of Educational Progress (NAEP) in 2006 shows that only 22 percent of eighth-graders and 27 percent of high school seniors were considered at or above the proficient level on the civics assessment.[20] Only 5 percent of students were able to complete an open-ended question about three ways in which the power of the president can be checked by the legislative or the judicial branch.

For most democratic theorists, a knowledgeable citizenry is considered a prerequisite to democracy. As to an acceptable level of knowledge, William Galston's general definition of competent citizens captures a consensus on the issue: "Competent democratic citizens need not be policy experts, but there is a level of basic knowledge below which the ability to make a full range of reasoned civic judgments is impaired."[21] Without it, citizens are not able to effectively exercise their roles in the democratic process. In a representative democracy, elected officials are supposed to represent the "will of the people," and citizens hold them accountable for their decisions. However, when citizens are generally ignorant about the political process or about current affairs, it is harder for them to have a reasoned sense of what should be done, to communicate this effectively to their representatives, and, ultimately, to hold the representatives accountable for their decisions. Individuals with lower levels of political knowledge are less likely to vote; more likely to believe they are politically powerless; and generally less socially tolerant, trusting, and engaged in community affairs.[22]

Citizens with higher levels of political knowledge are more sophisticated in their understanding of the political world. Ilya Somin argues that political "ignorance potentially opens the door for both elite manipulation of the public and gross policy errors caused by politicians' need to appeal to an ignorant electorate in order to win office."[23] In other words, ignorant citizens are a problem not solely because they distort democratic representation and accountability, but because they compel elected officials to make bad decisions. To individuals who lack knowledge about politics, debate among elites "resembles a food fight," and thus they can be more easily manipulated by elites on all sides of political issues.[24]

Finally, in addition to its benefits to the political system, political knowledge is beneficial to citizens themselves. Knowledgeable citizens are, in normative terms, better citizens. A law-abiding, taxpaying citizen who remains ignorant about political affairs is not the citizen idolized by many democratic theorists. For Benjamin Barber and others, "Politics is something done by, not to, citizens. Activity is its chief virtue," and "If action is to be political, it must ensue from forethought and deliberation, from free and conscious choice."[25] According to Michael X. Delli Carpini and Scott Keeter, "No other single characteristic of an individual affords so reliable a predictor of good citizenship, broadly conceived, as their level of knowledge."[26]

Political knowledge is typically measured by asking respondents questions about current political officials and about fundamental aspects of the American political system. This study includes seven questions to test students' political knowledge (see Table A.2 for the wording of questions). As shown in Figure 4.1, students did relatively well on this test. A large majority of students answered four or more questions correctly. Half of the students earned a "passing" grade of 60 percent or more (answering five of seven questions correctly).

Based on the focus groups, it is unlikely that much of this information is coming from the media. Rather, it is learned in school and from parents. As the focus groups were conducted in 2002, a heated election campaign took place in Iowa. The interviewer asked the students about how closely they were following the campaigns:

> *Interviewer:* One of the things I've noticed is that there are a lot of ads on television. When I got over to the hotel and flicked on the TV, [there were] lots of ads about the political races going on in Iowa for governor and U.S. senator. What do you think about all those ads when you see them?
>
> *Tammy:* Yeah, I usually switch stations 'cause there's lame-ies at both ends. It's pointless.
>
> *Kevin:* Yeah, I think the same thing. I'd just as soon change the channel.

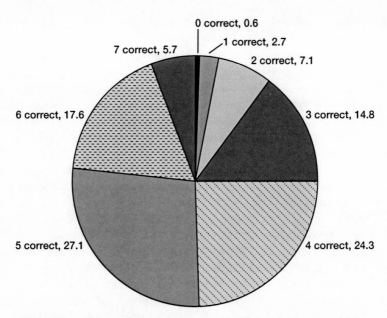

FIGURE 4.1 Percentage of students answering knowledge questions correctly

Tammy and Kevin were not alone. Most students told us they had paid no attention to the ongoing campaigns. Even so, many discussed that they were interested in their social studies classes and the debates that take place in class. Several students commented that they enjoy learning about American and world history. Not surprisingly, their interest in social studies—like most classes—depends on their evaluations of the teachers. A few students said they enjoyed the course material even though they had teachers they did not really like, but for the most part a student's assessment of his or her social studies classes was contingent on his or her assessment of the teacher. We heard many comments about "boring" teachers or "great" teachers with "interesting" assignments.

Political Efficacy and Generalized Trust

This chapter also looks at two main sets of attitudes that shape the nature of one's outlook on politics and his or her role in it: political efficacy and generalized trust. To be fully engaged in a democratic society, individuals should believe they have the capacity to understand politics and that if they participate, their voice is meaningfully heard at some level of government. Among the mechanisms of personal agency, "None is more central or pervasive than people's beliefs about their capabilities to exercise control over their own level of functioning and over events that affect their lives."[27] Political efficacy, like self-efficacy, is thought to be central to political participation, a necessary prerequisite for the exercise of duties as simple as voting and as complex as contacting government officials or volunteering for a campaign.[28]

Many scholars and practitioners are concerned with the very low levels of efficacy found among young people today. A survey of U.S. young adults age 15–25 conducted in 2002 had some disturbing findings about young people's attitudes about government, especially their roles in it. After the terrorist attacks of September 11, 2001, young adults expressed greater trust in government and its institutions, but this did not translate into beliefs that they could bring about changes or work to help solve problems in their communities.[29] Similarly, a bare majority (53 percent) believed government and elections address their needs, and 48 percent believed that political leaders paid at least some attention to concerns of people like them.

"Self-efficacy" has been defined as "beliefs in one's capabilities to organize and execute the courses of action required to produce given attainments."[30] In social learning theory, perceptions of self-efficacy influence one's choice of activities, the perseverance and level of effort one has in pursuing an activity, and, ultimately, the degree of success achieved. Political efficacy is a combination of one's sense of competence in the political sphere and one's assessment of the responsiveness of the system.[31] This characterization of efficacy encompasses two dimensions: internal and external efficacy.[32] Although it is possible for one to have high levels of one dimension and low levels of the other, the two are generally closely related.[33] Individuals with high levels of internal efficacy "feel they understand how to take part in politics, and are not intimidated by the challenges, conflicts or disagreements that occur in that arena."[34] One could characterize internal political efficacy as one's sense of self-confidence about involvement in politics.[35] Feelings of internal efficacy are developed early in life and become an important predictor of future engagement.[36] Internal efficacy motivates the acquisition of political knowledge.[37] For these reasons, many see enhancing internal efficacy as a central goal of civic education.[38]

External efficacy refers to an individual's belief in the openness and responsiveness of the political system. People with high scores on this dimension "believe the system reacts when pressure is applied by citizens, regardless of whether or not they are willing or able to apply that pressure themselves."[39] External efficacy is not simply a reflection of what one thinks of incumbent officeholders at a given moment; it reflects a more enduring attitude toward the regime.[40] It is theoretically and empirically different from internal efficacy.

The measurement of political efficacy has been somewhat contentious within political science. Scholars use a variety of survey items and combinations. In this study, there is an index for each concept based largely on the work of Stephen C. Craig, Richard D. Niemi, and Glenn E. Silver.[41] The index for internal efficacy consists of the following questions: "I am as well-informed about politics as others"; "Other people are better at understanding complicated political issues than I am"; and "I have a pretty good understanding of political issues." The external efficacy index consists of two questions: "Public officials don't care what people like me think"; and "People like me don't have any say in what government does."[42]

Generalized trust is thought to be an orientation one has toward those around oneself, an outlook about the world. Whereas external efficacy deals with attitudes about public officials, generalized trust is a measure of one's trust in other people, not in public officials. It is partly a product of the civil society in which one lives.[43] Generalized trust is a "lubricant" to foster productive social exchanges. It is part of the social fabric of societies and is said to produce economic prosperity and good government.[44] Interpersonal trust sustains social networks and cooperation and facilitates the transmission of democratic values.[45] Trust in others is an essential part of most conceptions of social capital, thought to influence how one interacts with others and the strength of one's social networks. Although it is theoretically possible that someone could be very suspicious of others and still be an active and engaged citizen, it is generally the case that those who trust others most of the time are likely to have higher levels of political knowledge, efficacy, and participation.

Students were asked to agree or disagree with the statement, "You can generally trust people to do the right thing." This is similar to other survey items used to measure generalized trust.[46] There is some disagreement within the literature about whether we should expect trust to be associated with changes in the environment. Eric Uslaner argues that for most respondents, questions about generalized trust elicit responses about the extent to which one trusts members of one's "moral community."[47] To him, generalized trust is "a value that we learn early in life" and is "largely resistant to bad experiences— or good ones."[48] According to this definition, generalized or "moralistic" trust is stable and reflects deep orientations about one's worldview. Thus, for adults who formed their opinions about the trustworthiness of others a long time ago, we might not expect trust to be susceptible to immigration or other changes in the environment in which one lives. For young people, however, this argument is largely moot. The context in which one grows up is likely to substantially influence their developing senses of whether people are trustworthy.

Table 4.1 shows the average levels of political efficacy and trust (as well as the other outcomes examined in this chapter) among all the students surveyed in these five Iowa communities. Young people in these communities had slightly higher levels of internal efficacy than external efficacy. They were somewhat more confident in their understanding of politics than they were in their beliefs about whether public officials care about them. This is not necessarily problematic, as some research indicates that low external efficacy combined with high internal efficacy can motivate participation.[49] In the focus groups, some of the students stated that politicians do not really care about them because they are children:

TABLE 4.1 Average Levels of Civic Engagement in
Five Iowa Towns

	Mean
Political knowledge	.63
Internal efficacy	.51
External efficacy	.41
Generalized trust	.34
Intention to vote	.80
Participation in school activities	.23
Frequency of political discussion	.34

Note: Values are means within each category. All values have been
recoded to 0–1. Figures include all respondents.

Interviewer: Do you think politicians care about what you think?
Jenny: I think a little bit. As much as most older people do.
Becky: I would say not really. But they don't really care what we think
because we're kids.

To them, politicians are no different from other adults who do not care
much about what children think. Several students commented that when they
turn 18, they will pay more attention to politics, and they believe politicians will
begin to pay more attention to them. Some young people were quite cynical (or
realistic, depending on one's beliefs about politicians). A minority of students
stated that politicians "only want to get elected" and that the only reason a poli-
tician cares about anyone's interests is to further his or her own cause. The most
common sentiment, however, was that their voices did not matter much only
because they were not old enough to participate in politics.

Intention to Vote, School Participation, and Political Discussion

Finally, this chapter looks at civic and political participation. If we were studying
adults, voting would be a central indicator. This study examines students' inten-
tions to vote. It also focuses on students' activities in school, such as athletics,
band, student government, and academic clubs. Numerous scholars have found
that young people who engage in school activities are more likely to participate
in politics and civic activities as adults.[50] It is no surprise that such activities help
adolescents "incorporate civic involvement into their [civic] identity."[51] Finally,
political discussion is one of the few forms of political participation in which
both young people and adults can engage. Discussing politics with others helps
people learn more about civic affairs and strengthens incentives to participate.[52]

Participating in extracurricular activities in high school has been shown to
foster higher self-esteem, greater academic achievement, reduced likelihood of

dropping out of school, and higher postsecondary educational aspirations.[53] Niemi and Jane Junn also find that students who are active in their schools have higher levels of political knowledge and efficacy.[54] Even non-academic activities, such as sports, have been linked to higher grades and greater likelihood of college attendance.[55] School activities offer young people opportunities to learn how to work with others toward a common goal, and often to become involved in their communities. Some activities, such as student government and programs such as Kids Voting, give students practice in using the skills necessary for participation as adults, introducing them to basic political roles and processes.[56]

School activities are important in their own right but are also critical because participation at a young age lays the foundation for future adult participation in politics and the community. High school activities "are an important formative process for the acquisition or further development of beliefs, attitudes, values, and skills that contribute to adult community and political participation. . . . Similar skills—leadership, organizational, expressive—are acquired and/or practiced in the associational life of the school and are transferable to adult community and political activities."[57] Using a panel study in which high school seniors were re-interviewed six years later, Jennifer Glanville finds "strong evidence that extracurricular activities increase adult political participation," especially campaign activities and political meetings.[58] Other studies show that extracurricular participation strongly predicts adult participation in voluntary associations, voting, and trust in political processes.[59]

Political discussion gives citizens opportunities to express their preferences and debate with others. Some argue that it has the power to "transform individual preferences to achieve a consensual collective decision of superior quality."[60] Nina Eliasoph contends that political discussion helps people understand politics, reconcile political points of view, and make informed decisions.[61] Face-to-face discussions with others help young people to develop "democratic habits."[62] Political discussion enhances one's confidence in his or her ability to affect the political system.[63] Those who frequently discuss politics show more coherent attitudes and are more likely to participate in politics.[64] One study finds the most important factor associated with young adults' sense of efficacy and views of politics is the extent to which parents discuss politics with their children.[65]

There is an ongoing debate within political science about the effect of political heterogeneity on discussions of politics. Although interacting with people who are different from us tends to contribute to tolerance and understanding of opposing views and perspectives, the downside of these encounters is that people are uncomfortable with them and are less likely to put themselves in positions to have them.[66] Individuals typically try to avoid having political discussions with those with whom they believe they disagree.[67] When avoidance is impossible, individuals typically proceed carefully. The public expression of one's opinions, especially in settings where people disagree, can entail the real likelihood of being scrutinized, criticized, or ostracized.[68] One of the most common reactions is simply to remain silent or to engage only superficially.[69] People often do not participate actively in political discussions in environments where they worry about alienating themselves from friends.[70] Given adolescents' serious concerns about fitting in, this may be especially powerful for young people. Much of this work looks at heterogeneous political viewpoints, not ethnic or racial diversity. However, to the extent that ethnic diversity is associated with political diversity, we may see less frequent discussion in ethnically diverse communities than in predominantly White, Anglo communities where there is less opportunity for students to encounter people with different life experiences and viewpoints.

The vast majority of respondents, 80 percent, said they intend to vote when they are eligible (see Table 4.1). Students were also fairly active in their schools. On average, students participated in about two types of activities, although the range includes some students who engaged in as many as nine separate types of activities. It is important to note that students were asked whether they participated in *types* of activities, such as athletics and service clubs. This, then, is a conservative estimate of participation in school activities. Many students play on several different sports teams or participate in a variety of service or vocational clubs, but they would have been able to designate this as only one type of activity.

Finally, in the fall of 2001, students were big talkers: they discussed politics with others an average of two and a half days per week. Considering all of the other things on their minds, and the fact that they cannot legally participate in politics in many ways, this seems to be a high level of political discussion. Many students told us that they enjoy discussing political issues with their parents, friends, and extended families. There were, of course, many students who said they never discuss politics and that their parents are not involved in politics. But most students commented that they enjoy discussing politics because they get to hear others' opinions and because it is "fun." Importantly, not all political discussion is equal, and when we look at the frequency of discussion as the main indicator, we do not know much about the content of the discussions, which could be intolerant, uninformed, and shallow in nature.[71]

Ethnic Diversity and Civic Outcomes

Comparing Immigrant-Receiving Towns with Anglo Towns

Table 4.2 examines difference of means tests for each of the civic outcomes, comparing the two towns with ethnic diversity with those without it. Like the results in the previous chapter, most of the remaining analyses in this chapter examine only native-born American students whose parents were also born in the United States. This chapter also looks only at the 2001 cross-section. These results show that levels of political knowledge and generalized trust were lower among young people in the two ethnically diverse towns compared with their counterparts in the predominantly White, Anglo towns. Respondents in Storm Lake and Perry scored about four points lower on the political knowledge test

TABLE 4.2 Difference of Means Tests between Ethnically Diverse and Homogeneous Communities in Iowa

	Diverse towns	Homogeneous towns
Political knowledge	.63	.66**
Internal efficacy	.50	.52
External efficacy	.40	.41
Generalized trust	.30	.39**
Intention to vote	.82	.82
Participation in school activities	.27	.21***
Political discussion	.35	.34

Note: Values are means within each category. Foreign-born respondents and those with foreign-born parents are excluded.

*p < .05; **p < .01; ***p < .001.

than did those in the other three communities. And they were about 9 percent less trusting of others than were those in Boone, Carroll, and Harlan. The other outcomes—internal and external efficacy, intention to vote, and political discussion—showed no significant differences between these two types of communities. Students in the diverse towns were, however, *more* active in their schools than those in the homogeneous communities. The next set of analyses examine whether these differences are sustained when controlling for individual factors.

Individual Factors and Civic Outcomes

Each of the outcomes examined here varies across subpopulations; thus, multivariate models are necessary. There are significant differences according to gender, race/ethnicity, and socioeconomic status. Racial and ethnic minorities, girls, and low-income young people have significantly lower levels of civic knowledge and engagement than their counterparts.[72] One study indicates, for example, that Latino children, even controlling for whether they were born in the United States, typically have lower levels of political knowledge than Anglo children.[73]

The "resource model" of engagement attributes these differences to disadvantages among these groups in resources, particularly money and civic skills.[74] High-status parents are typically more knowledgeable themselves and can explicitly teach their children about politics, as well as provide a role model of a politically active, informed citizen. This contributes not only to higher knowledge, but also to higher levels of efficacy, trust, and participation. In addition, higher-status families are more likely to set high expectations for their children generally, not just with regard to political knowledge and engagement.[75] Schools are more likely to push higher-status or White, non-Hispanic children into classes and activities that promote high achievement, including advanced placement courses, some of which are civics courses.[76] Socioeconomic status and

TABLE 4.3   Regression Results of the Influence of Ethnic Diversity on Civic Outcomes

	Political knowledge	Internal efficacy	External efficacy	General-ized trust	Intention to vote	Participa-tion in school activities	Political discussion
Diverse towns	−.08***	−.02	−.03	−.08*	.01	.05**	.01
	(.02)	(.02)	(.02)	(.04)	(.03)	(.02)	(.03)
Measures of socio-economic status							
Family income	.01	.01*	.002	−.02	−.01	.02**	.02*
	(.01)	(.01)	(.01)	(.02)	(.01)	(.01)	(.01)
Planning to attend a four-year college	.08***	.05**	.05**	.17***	.17***	.09***	.06*
	(.02)	(.02)	(.02)	(.05)	(.03)	(.02)	(.03)
Rootedness							
Parents are farmers	−.02	−.02	.03*	.02	.02	.002	.002
	(.01)	(.01)	(.01)	(.03)	(.03)	(.01)	(.02)
Grandparents live in the state	−.02	−.04	.01	−.07	−.05	−.05**	−.06
	(.02)	(.02)	(.03)	(.07)	(.05)	(.02)	(.04)
Length of residence in the town	.01	−.002	−.001	−.01	−.004	.01*	−.01
	(.01)	(.01)	(.01)	(.01)	(.01)	(.01)	(.01)
Demographics							
Grade level	.03***	−.02**	.02	.04	−.01	.03***	−.002
	(.01)	(.01)	(.01)	(.02)	(.01)	(.01)	(.01)
Female	−.04**	−.07***	.02	−.03	.02	.10***	.01
	(.02)	(.01)	(.02)	(.04)	(.03)	(.02)	(.02)
Amount of civics coursework	.01*	.01*	.001	−.01	.02*	−.003	.01
	(.004)	(.004)	(.01)	(.01)	(.01)	(.01)	(.01)
Parents are married	.02	.003	.05**	.05	.01	−.03	.003
	(.02)	(.02)	(.02)	(.05)	(.03)	(.02)	(.03)
Constant	.28**	.73***	.15	.06	.89***	−.33**	.33*
	(.09)	(.08)	(.10)	(.25)	(.17)	(.09)	(.14)
	N = 666	N = 661	N = 664	N = 556	N = 666	N = 472	N = 661
	R² = .12	R² = .09	R² = .05	R² = .04	R² = .06	R² = .24	R² = .03

Note: Values are ordinary least squares unstandardized regression coefficients. Standard errors are in parentheses. Respondents include only those who were native born and those who had at least one parent who is native-born.

*p < .05; **p < .01; ***p < .001.

educational aspirations are also strongly correlated, suggesting that differences are likely to exist in political knowledge and civic engagement between students who plan to go to college and those who do not.[77] Judith Torney-Purta finds educational aspirations to be important for predicting political knowledge.[78]

A few other factors may contribute to differences in these civic outcomes. We should expect that older students and those who have taken more civics coursework will have higher levels of knowledge and other indicators of civic engagement. Further, it is possible that the young people who are more strongly "rooted" to the community will be more engaged within it. The same measures as those used in the models in the previous chapter are used here.

Even controlling for all of these individual factors, the differences and similarities between the diverse and homogeneous communities on political knowledge, trust, and participation in school activities remain strong (Table 4.3). Young people in the immigrant-receiving towns were less politically knowledgeable and less trusting of others than were their native-born counterparts in the predominantly White, Anglo communities. But students in the diverse towns were more participatory in their schools than those in the all-White towns. This will be examined in greater depth in the next section. Diversity had no effect on the other outcomes.

It is worth highlighting some of the individual factors that are significantly related to civic engagement. The one indicator that is significant in each model is whether the young person plans to attend a four-year college. Aspiring to attend college is positively related to each of these indicators of knowledge and engagement.[79] Parental income is related to internal efficacy, political discussion, and participation in school activities but not political knowledge, external efficacy, trust, or intention to vote. Given the high cost of some school activities (for uniforms, instruments, and so on), it is not surprising that parental income is significantly related to school activities.

Civic education is important in fostering political knowledge, internal efficacy, and intention to vote. For educators, this is obviously a comforting finding. Most of the "rootedness" measures are not significant. Farming kids are slightly more likely than others to believe that the government cares about their views, but longer-term town residents and those with multiple generations in the community are generally no different from newcomers with no extended family in the area.

In summary, ethnic diversity does not dampen all indicators of civic engagement. In fact, it is negatively related only to political knowledge and generalized trust. Participation in school activities is higher in the ethnically diverse communities than in homogeneous towns. The next section addresses this question by separating the two heterogeneous communities to examine potential similarities and differences.

Comparing the Effects of Ethnic Diversity in Storm Lake and Perry

Storm Lake and Perry are very similar communities, but they differ in the timing of the initial waves of immigration. Whereas there were nearly no immigrants in Perry until the early 1990s, Storm Lake's ethnic transformation began in the 1970s and continued through the 1980s with the arrival of Laotian refugees. This ethnic group still made up only a small fraction of the community's population, but it was a more gradual introduction to diversity for Storm Lake's residents than what was to occur later. As we saw in Chapter 3, there were significant differences between these two communities with regard to attitudes about immigrants. It is possible that because Perry was in the early stages of rapid ethnic diversification in 2001 when the surveys were conducted, there are similar differences in the effects of diversity on civic outcomes.

This section disaggregates Perry and Storm Lake to examine differences between the communities. Table 4.4 shows the differences of means between Perry and Storm Lake and between Perry and the White, Anglo communities. There are substantial differences between Perry and Storm Lake on four of the seven indicators. Storm Lake kids were more knowledgeable (by about five points), more likely to say they would vote (by 13 points), more active in their schools, and they more frequently discussed politics than did those in Perry.

In fact, comparisons of Perry and Storm Lake to the Anglo towns suggest that on most indicators, Storm Lake students compared favorably to those in homogeneous communities. Youth in Storm Lake, for example, were just as politically knowledgeable as those in the Anglo communities (p > .10). In Storm Lake, young people had similar levels of generalized trust as those in the homogeneous communities (p > .10). Storm Lake students were more likely to say they would vote (p < .10), to participate in their schools (p < .001), and to discuss politics (p < .05) than the native-born students in the predominantly White towns. Thus, the reason we see (in the previous set of results) the ethnically diverse towns' students participating more actively in school is because of the high level of participation in Storm Lake. Perry's students were just as participatory and discussed politics as often as the students in the Anglo communities, but the young people in Storm Lake dramatically surpassed the students in the other communities in terms of participation and political discussion. In contrast, Perry's young people were significantly less knowledgeable, slightly less likely to believe the government is responsive to them (p < .10), less trusting of other people, and less likely to say they would vote than were youth in the homogeneous communities.

These results hold up when we control for individual factors. The results in Table 4.5 demonstrate that Storm Lake students compared negatively to their counterparts in the predominantly White towns only on political knowledge.

TABLE 4.4 Difference of Means Tests between Perry and Storm Lake

	Perry	Storm Lake	White, Anglo towns
Political knowledge	.60	.65*	.66***
Internal efficacy	.51	.50	.52
External efficacy	.38	.41	.41
Generalized trust	.25	.34	.39**
Intention to vote	.75	.88**	.82*
Participation in school activities	.22	.30**	.21
Political discussion	.30	.40**	.34

Note: Values are means within each category. Significance levels correspond to comparisons between Perry and Storm Lake and Perry and the predominantly White towns.
*p < .05; **p < .01; ***p < .001.

TABLE 4.5 Regression Results for Civic Outcomes Comparing Perry and Storm Lake

	Political knowledge	Internal efficacy	External efficacy	General-ized trust	Intention to vote	Participa-tion in school activities	Political discussion
Perry High School	−.10***	−.02	−.06*	−.13*	−.06	.02	−.05
	(.02)	(.02)	(.02)	(.06)	(.04)	(.02)	(.03)
Storm Lake High School	−.06**	−.01	−.01	−.06	.06	.07***	.05
	(.02)	(.02)	(.02)	(.05)	(.04)	(.02)	(.03)
Measures of socio-economic status							
Family income	.01	.01*	.003	−.02	−.01	.02**	.02*
	(.01)	(.01)	(.01)	(.02)	(.01)	(.01)	(.01)
Planning to attend a four-year college	.08***	.05**	.05**	.16***	.17***	.09***	.06*
	(.02)	(.02)	(.02)	(.05)	(.03)	(.02)	(.03)
Rootedness							
Parents are farmers	−.02	−.02	.03*	.02	.02	−.002	.001
	(.01)	(.01)	(.01)	(.03)	(.03)	(.01)	(.02)
Grandparents live in the state	−.02	−.04	.01	−.07	−.06	−.05**	−.07
	(.02)	(.02)	(.03)	(.07)	(.05)	(.02)	(.04)
Length of residence in the town	.01	−.002	−.002	−.01	−.01	.01*	−.01
	(.01)	(.01)	(.01)	(.02)	(.01)	(.01)	(.01)
Demographics							
Grade level	.03***	−.02**	.01	.03	−.02	.03**	−.01
	(.01)	(.118)	(.01)	(.02)	(.02)	(.01)	(.01)
Female	−.04**	−.07***	.02	−.03	.01	.10***	.01
	(.02)	(.01)	(.02)	(.04)	(.03)	(.02)	(.02)
Amount of civics coursework	.01*	.01*	.002	−.01	.02**	−.002	.01*
	(.004)	(.004)	(.01)	(.01)	(.01)	(.01)	(.01)
Parents are married	.02	.004	.05**	.05	.01	.03	−.0003
	(.02)	(.02)	(.02)	(.05)	(.03)	(.02)	(.03)
Constant	.29**	.74***	.16	.10	.92***	−.31**	.36**
	(.09)	(.08)	(.10)	(.25)	(.17)	(.09)	(.14)
	N = 667	N = 662	N = 665	N = 557	N = 667	N = 473	N = 662
	R^2 = .13	R^2 = .09	R^2 = .06	R^2 = .04	R^2 = .07	R^2 = .25	R^2 = .04

Note: Values are ordinary least squares regression coefficients. Standard errors are in parentheses. Respondents include only those who were native born and those who had at least one parent who is native-born.
*p < .05; **p < .01; ***p < .001.

Even so, their scores were not as low as those of Perry students. The average native-born Perry student scored an entire letter grade lower than the average student in the Anglo communities; the average Storm Lake student scored about six points lower on this test than did those in the Anglo towns. Perry students were also less trusting and less likely to believe public officials care about people like them. Further, in Storm Lake, native-born students were considerably more active in their schools than were the students in any of the other communities.

By 2001, not only did young people in Storm Lake have more experience with diversification than those in Perry, but, as we will see in the next chapter, Storm Lake began an official response earlier than Perry and other communities undergoing rapid diversification. The "hunkering down" that we see in Perry has passed in Storm Lake. These young people have grown up in diverse elementary and middle schools. They have been friends with and known students with different ethnic backgrounds for most of their lives. It is not something that strikes fear or suspicion, whereas in Perry, where teens had not gone to elementary school with immigrants, diversity was still rather new in 2001. There was a higher degree of disengagement among the native population in Perry. Importantly, the disengagement was not spread across all of these indicators—only external efficacy, trust, and political knowledge. The next section compares the immigrant youth in Perry and Storm Lake with their native peers.

Immigrants' Attitudes about Civic Engagement

Where political socialization is thought by most to be largely unidirectional—from parent, school, or community to child—this may not always be the case for immigrant children.[80] Children of immigrant parents learn U.S. history and culture in school and often find themselves helping their parents communicate with a variety of political institutions and local agencies. Janelle S. Wong and Vivian Tseng find, in fact, that it is more common for children with immigrant parents to explain U.S. political concepts to their parents than it is for parents to explain concepts to their children.[81] The research is mixed as to the influence immigrant parents have on their children. Some suggest that immigrants are preoccupied with their new lives and are uninterested in U.S. politics and therefore do not teach their children much about politics.[82] Others contend that parents who were politically active in their countries of origin are likely to become active in their host country.[83] Tom W. Rice and Jan L. Feldman find that civic attitudes are very durable; they show that "American descendants of European immigrants retain at least a portion of the culture from their home country despite living outside that country, often for generations."[84]

Parent-to-child transmission is mediated by the length of residence in the United States and the social standing of the family. The preponderance of the evidence suggests that immigrant youth are less civically engaged than are children born in the United States, including those born to immigrants.[85] Young immigrants who have resided in the United States the longest are more politically active than newcomers.[86] Second- and third-generation immigrants are not only more active but have stronger identification with the United States.[87] A great deal of the research on immigrants' attitudes toward government examines Latinos. Some research has found that Latinos have higher external efficacy than Anglos.[88] Shaun Bowler, Francisco Pedraza, and Gary Segura show that Latino immigrants have a very positive view of the U.S. government that translates into greater confidence in the worthiness of direct political action.[89] At

TABLE 4.6 Regression Results for Civic Outcomes among Native- and Foreign-Born Students in Storm Lake and Perry

	Political knowledge	Internal efficacy	External efficacy	General-ized trust	Intention to vote	Partici-pation in school activities	Political discussion
Foreign born	−.07*	.02	.14***	.02	−.11	.04	.04
	(.04)	(.03)	(.04)	(.10)	(.08)	(.04)	(.06)
Measures of socio-economic status							
Family income	.02*	.02*	−.003	−.01	−.01	.03**	.03*
	(.01)	(.01)	(.01)	(.02)	(.02)	(.01)	(.01)
Planning to attend a four-year college	.08**	.03	.01	.23***	.14**	.11***	.04
	(.02)	(.02)	(.02)	(.06)	(.05)	(.03)	(.04)
Rootedness							
Parents are farmers	−.03	−.01	.04*	.02	−.01	−.003	−.03
	(.02)	(.01)	(.02)	(.04)	(.03)	(.02)	(.03)
Grandparents live in the state	.01	−.04	.02	−.05	.002	−.06*	−.02
	(.03)	(.03)	(.03)	(.08)	(.06)	(.02)	(.05)
Length of residence in the town	.01	−.002	.01	.001	.02	.02	−.001
	(.01)	(.01)	(.01)	(.02)	(.02)	(.01)	(.01)
Demographics							
Grade level	.04**	−.02	−.003	.03	−.02	.05***	−.01
	(.01)	(.01)	(.01)	(.03)	(.03)	(.02)	(.02)
Female	−.02	−.06**	.04	−.03	.07	.09**	.04
	(.02)	(.02)	(.02)	(.06)	(.05)	(.02)	(.03)
Amount of civics coursework	−.004	.02**	−.01	−.01	.003	.001	.02
	(.01)	(.01)	(.01)	(.02)	(.01)	(.01)	(.01)
Parents are married	.001	.01	.03	−.05	.002	.01	.07
	(.02)	(.02)	(.02)	(.06)	(.05)	(.03)	(.04)
Constant	.01	.66***	.33*	−.07	.86**	−.59	.22
	(.14)	(.13)	(.14)	(.37)	(.29)	(.16)	(.22)
	N = 336	N = 331	N = 335	N = 282	N = 336	N = 235	N = 331
	$R^2 = .19$	$R^2 = .09$	$R^2 = .09$	$R^2 = .05$	$R^2 = .08$	$R^2 = .32$	$R^2 = .06$

Note: Values are ordinary least squares regression coefficients. Standard errors are in parentheses. Respondents include only those in Storm Lake and Perry.
*p < .05; **p < .01; ***p < .001.

least one study shows that Latinos have low levels of both internal and external efficacy; further, third-generation Latinos are more likely than earlier generations of immigrants to agree that they have no say in government.[90] Although certainly not all of the foreign-born children in the study are Latino, the majority (53.4 percent) are.

Table 4.6 shows that the native- and foreign-born youth in Storm Lake and Perry differed significantly only with regard to political knowledge and external efficacy.[91] Immigrants had significantly lower levels of political knowledge than native-born young people. It is not surprising that immigrant youth continued to struggle with facts about American government. Unlike for American children brought up surrounded by information about their history and governmental structure, there is a steep learning curve for immigrants.

However, immigrants had more positive attitudes about public officials than did native-born youth. A cynic might say that it is precisely because of their lack of knowledge that they remain positive about their ability to influence politics. However, more realistically, these positive attitudes were likely born out of either their own experiences in their countries of origin or stories from their parents. Immigrant youth today, like those in the past, believe that their voices matter and public officials will listen to them.[92]

Summary

This chapter has shown that although ethnic diversity dampens some measures of civic engagement, it is unrelated to many others and actually enhances participation in school activities. The most consistently negative relationship with ethnic diversity is political knowledge. Native-born young people growing up in Perry and Storm Lake are less knowledgeable than their counterparts in more traditional, all-White Iowa small towns. The effects of diversity on political knowledge have gone largely unexamined in much of the literature on heterogeneity and social capital.[93] It is surprising that so little research on this topic looks at political knowledge, considering it is so critically important and highly related to nearly every other indicator of civic engagement. Two related explanations are potentially responsible for the lower levels of knowledge in the heterogeneous communities.

First, to the extent that adults hunker down in response to diversity, they may abdicate their responsibilities with regard to political socialization. They may gather less information about politics, withdraw from community activities, and discuss politics (even with their children) less often. As parents withdraw, they are less able to impart information to their children because they are picking up less information through their normal channels. This is especially true if parents discontinue political conversations. Political discussion with parents is one of the most significant ways young people learn about politics. When adults dampen their involvement, they are not only harming their own levels of social capital, but they are failing to educate their children about politics and government.

In talking with residents, I did not see much evidence that adults have pulled back on their civic responsibilities. Thus, the main explanation for the differences between political knowledge in the diverse towns and the homogeneous ones is due more to the decisions of schools. In heterogeneous communities, administrators and teachers make many decisions as they respond to diversity. The results show that taking civics courses is associated with higher levels of political knowledge. It is, of course, possible that some self-selection has occurred, such that the youth who are politically knowledgeable are more likely to be interested in and to take civics courses. However, given that Iowa requires civic education of all students in public high schools, the degree of self-selection is limited. Communities that must respond to rapid demographic changes may have to reallocate resources away from certain programs toward others. In diverse schools, teachers may focus their time and energy on creating a positive climate and making sure that young people are getting along with one another. Cultural competency programs do not typically include basic instruction in U.S. government and current affairs. Learning about tolerance and different cultures is most likely to occur in social studies classes. In math or science, there is little opportunity to discuss these issues, but in social studies classes, teachers may decide to focus on cultural competency at the expense of learning basic facts about the American system. The all-White schools may not believe they need to devote as much time to these issues and may, then, have more time devoted to the curriculum that would improve general political knowledge.

It could certainly be argued that ensuring that students from different backgrounds get along and interact positively with one another is an appropriate tradeoff for political knowledge. However, if young people leave high school with low levels of political knowledge, they will find it harder to pick up these facts later on. Yes, many students learn about politics on their own by watching the news and through life experience. But many obtain their knowledge about foundational elements of American government in school, and if schools fail to ensure that young people leave knowing the basic facts about their governmental structure, the likelihood increases that these young people will not become as engaged and interested in political affairs as they could or should. Further, we cannot rely on college curricula to make up this gap. Most young people do not graduate from college, and many of those who do never take courses in American government.

Some researchers would continue by highlighting the other areas in which ethnic diversity is associated with negative outcomes. In Perry, native-born young people are less trusting and have lower levels of external efficacy than their counterparts in the predominantly White communities. But importantly, this is not the case in the similarly diverse Storm Lake. Considering the growing literature on diversity's depressing effects on social capital, however, I think the null findings with regard to internal efficacy, intention to vote, and political discussion are at least as interesting as the negative findings with regard to a few of the indicators.

I believe the main rationale for these differences is that Storm Lake got a head start on Perry in coming to terms with the changes in their community. For 15 years before Latinos began to arrive in Storm Lake and Perry in large numbers, demographics changed gradually in Storm Lake. The level of diversity is not as important in predicting attitudes as is the rate of demographic change in a community. According to Daniel J. Hopkins, "It is those communities that have undergone sudden demographic changes, not communities that have long been diverse, where diversity's effects are pronounced."[94] Once local demographics stabilize, as they had begun to do in Storm Lake by the early 2000s, diverse places face no special barriers to social capital formation. In essence, by 2001, when the surveys were conducted, Perry was deep in the throes of responding to its diversification, while Storm Lake was beginning to stabilize. It is likely that as time passes, the lower levels of external efficacy and generalized trust in Perry may disappear, as they have in Storm Lake. The next chapter examines the effects of changes over time in these communities.

Finally, it is worth emphasizing the benefits of ethnic diversity. Storm Lake students were substantially more active in their school than were the young people in Perry and in the Anglo towns. It may be, as suggested by other scholars, that diversity alters individual incentives to participate. It is possible that ethnic diversity increases competition and the idea that one needs to protect one's interests by getting involved.[95] But this is doubtful because young people do not engage in school activities such as band, athletics, or science clubs to protect their interests. They get involved because they have a hobby or want to earn a scholarship for college or want to build a resume or do not want to go home after school. There are many reasons for this involvement, but they likely have little to do with the protection of interests.

More likely, heterogeneity gives young people opportunities to interact with people from varied backgrounds in informal settings where there are common goals—winning games, throwing a homecoming dance, or putting together the school yearbook, for example. Social psychology literature shows that in settings in which individuals must cooperate with one another, contact with diversity lessens prejudice.[96] Cooperative work can lead to close personal friendships with people that one might never have met otherwise.[97] It is also the case that as part of its efforts to instill cultural competency and tolerance in its students, Storm Lake High School aggressively promotes student activities.

In 2010, I asked Teresa Coenen, the principal of Storm Lake High School, to explain why the young people were so active in Storm Lake compared with the other communities. She responded that the school did not (and still does not) require participation, but that it has made a special effort over the years to promote the activities. The school has something she has been unable to explain to outsiders:

> I'm telling you, our school is remarkably different. . . . I call it the "it factor." I don't know what it is. I don't know how it happened. . . . We did enough work with cultural competency that I know it's bad to say that we're "color blind," that you don't see color. That's not what's going on here. It's not that we're color blind. It's that all of our colors blend together. It's more a mutation of colors. I always say, "Everyone here is green." Our school colors are green and white. . . . You might be Hmong, you might be Micronesian, you might be Asian, you might be

Sudanese or from the Congo, Ethiopia, El Salvador, or Guatemala. . . .
It doesn't really matter what your cultural heritage is. Here, you are
green.[98]

Coenen went on to explain how her predecessor, a principal who oversaw the
tumultuous 1990s in Storm Lake, made a point to encourage students to become
involved in the school's activities. He believed then, as she does now, that one
of the best ways to overcome some of the initial struggles with diversity was to
create an atmosphere where everyone works together and where everyone feels
he or she belongs. The school is not a major athletic powerhouse in Iowa, and
its test scores are not among the highest. The key to success for these students,
the school's administrators have long believed, is their connection to the school,
which can be strengthened only through participation in it.

These efforts early on had begun to show dividends by 2001–2002. In my
view, this high degree of integration and cooperation not only contributed to
Storm Lake High School's higher-than-average levels of involvement, but also
to the fact that its students' levels of civic engagement were the same as, or
higher than, those in homogeneous communities. For the students in this community, ethnic diversity had become the norm. They grew up living in a diverse
town, and their schools have been more heterogeneous than most suburban and
urban schools in the United States. By the early 2000s, diversity was nothing
new; thus, there was no reason to withdraw their trust in others or to feel
uncomfortable discussing politics. That the school was aggressive in promoting
activities and school pride also contributed to Storm Lake's outcomes, but it
should be said that if the students were distrustful of and hostile toward one
another, the school's efforts likely would have been in vain.

Native-born, Anglo young people in diverse small towns do not show many
signs of pulling into their shell, especially in the community that is further along
in its journey with immigration. Putnam writes, "To be sure, deconstructing
divisive racial and ethnic identities will not be so quick and simple, but an
extraordinary achievement of human civilization is our ability to redraw social
lines in ways that transcend ancestry."[99] It is likely that the drivers of this
redrawing of social lines are going to be young people. Just as parents in the past
have resisted rock music and interreligious dating, they are more likely than
their children to resist ethnic diversity. Young people, however, are more willing
to embrace change and are less likely to hunker down.

Much of the social-science scholarship on the relationship between ethnic
diversity and civic engagement reaches foreboding conclusions. As the country
becomes more ethnically diverse, much of the existing research predicts that
trust in others will decline, that participation in community and civic affairs
will wane, and that people will have less confidence in their public officials and
perceive their communities more negatively than when their communities
were more homogeneous. My research suggests that these conclusions may be

hasty—or, at a minimum, informed mainly by looking at diversity in particular types of (urban) environments. There are critical differences between large, highly dense urban neighborhoods and small towns. In small places, residents are practically forced to interact with one another. There may be only one or two grocery stores. There is likely to be on only one church of each denomination. There is only one school district and usually a single public high school for all young people. There are few private schools in small towns. Even in residential neighborhoods, the communities are not large enough to have a high level of segregation, so when immigrants decide to stay permanently, they end up living in ethnically mixed neighborhoods. The context for diversity is often very different in urban areas. Urban neighborhoods and schools are more segregated. There are more options in or near the neighborhood for shopping and other services, so that casual contact with "others" is limited. Even in urban communities that the census might define as diverse, it is possible for young people and adults alike to go about their lives without substantive interaction with anyone of a different racial or ethnic group. In small towns, the regular interaction between natives and immigrants has been a critical part of the reason there have not been dramatic declines in civic engagement.

Because so much of the social-science literature is focused on the urban experience, scholars miss this nuance. We can learn a great deal by testing social-science theories in rural environments. In this case, the civic futures of these diverse communities look bright, not bleak. Native-born, Anglo residents want to see the immigrants get more involved in civic affairs. Latino leaders are emerging who are beginning to become active in local politics. And the young people who have grown up in these diverse environments will at some point replace their older counterparts. They have years of experience with diversity, and it is very likely that differences in political knowledge and other civic indicators will decline over time. The next chapter examines this hypothesis in more detail.

5

Gradual Progress

I think the success stories you'll see are not with the adults who live here now, but with the children who go through our school systems and who are the next generation of leaders in our communities.
—Mark Prosser, Chief, Storm Lake Police

The preceding chapters have shown that native-born young people in these ethnically diverse small towns have responded to immigration with neither complete hostility nor hospitality. Young people in the diverse communities were less sympathetic to immigrants and less politically knowledgeable than those in the homogeneous towns. However, the results also demonstrate that there are important differences between the two diverse towns. In Perry, native-born young people were less tolerant of immigration than those in Storm Lake and those in the predominantly White, Anglo communities. There were no significant differences between the levels of tolerance in Storm Lake and those in the ethnically homogeneous towns. Further, Perry youth were not only less knowledgeable about politics but also less externally efficacious and less trusting than those in any of the other communities, including Storm Lake. And in Storm Lake, but not Perry, ethnic diversity was associated with increased participation in school activities. These results suggest there is more at play in these communities than merely the presence of immigrants and ethnic diversity.

These chapters have suggested that the reason Perry's young people lag behind their counterparts is that in 2001, the town had not yet come to terms with its identity as an ethnically diverse community. Storm Lake's native-born young people had grown up with immigrants for most of their lives. In Storm Lake, refugees from Laos began to settle in the mid-1970s. The size of this community grew throughout the 1980s. This diversification paved the way for the community to deal with the explosion in the number of Latino immigrants throughout the 1990s. To be sure, there were chaotic times in Storm Lake as the community learned to deal with rapid ethnic diversification. However, Perry had no smaller wave of immigration to help smooth the transition of diversification throughout this period. Perry's non-White population did not equal even 1 percent of the community's total population in 1990. In Storm Lake, 3.4 percent of its population in 1990 was Asian, and 1.1 percent was Latino. These small proportions were to grow dramatically in the next ten years, at rates that greatly exceeded the averages in the nation and in traditional gateway states such as California and Arizona. Importantly, in Storm Lake, there was at least a small foundation on which to build.

This chapter demonstrates, through the use of interviews, focus groups, and survey data, that by 2001–2002, Storm Lake had mostly accepted and come to terms with its diversity. Young people there had spent most of their lives in diverse schools, and this influenced their levels of tolerance and civic engagement in mostly positive ways. At the same time in Perry, however, the community was just beginning to deal more effectively with its demographic changes. The results suggest that the same pattern we saw in Storm Lake is likely to be played out in Perry. Young people there have grown more tolerant and engaged over time. The surveys show significant growth in Perry on the indicators of tolerance and most of the civic engagement measures. Focus group interviews in 2002 also suggest that young people in Perry believed that they were more progressive than their parents' generation and that they were beginning to consider integrated schools and diverse classrooms the "norm."

Why did Storm Lake move more quickly toward tolerance and accommodation? In addition to its early exposure to diversity in the 1970s and 1980s, other events converged that pushed the community to deal with the changes taking place instead of burying their heads in the sand. Storm Lake made national news during the '90s—and gained a mostly negative reputation, especially in Iowa. National media outlets wrote stories about the "new jungle" in Storm Lake referencing the undesirable conditions at the town's meatpacking plants, and in the 2000 presidential election, anti-immigrant groups ran negative advertisements using Storm Lake as a poster child for all the ills of unfettered immigration. These ads and the attention they brought with them galvanized the community to fight back against a distortion of its image. This united the community, and Storm Lake eventually became a model to which other ethnically diverse small towns look for guidance. No similar moment occurred in Perry; instead, acceptance and accommodation occurred gradually over the course of many years.

This chapter first examines the changes in attitudes and behavior among young people over a relatively short period of time—from the fall of 2001 to the end of the school year in 2002. In about eight months, young people in all of the communities showed increased support for immigrants and made gains on most of the indicators of civic engagement. The growth was most substantial, however, in Perry. In fact, by 2002, there were very few significant differences between Perry and Storm Lake, or between these diverse communities and the homogeneous ones.

The next sections examine Storm Lake and Perry in the 1990s and 2000s. It becomes clear that both diverse communities suffered through a chaotic and confusing period at the beginning of the rapid ethnic diversification. Storm Lake began to deal with these changes earlier than Perry did. Each community has moved on from this period. Both communities have elected Latino members to their City Councils, welcomed immigrant-owned businesses, and incorporated children of immigrants into school activities. Interviews with Hispanic leaders also indicate that interethnic relations are, today, mostly positive. By 2010, immigration had begun to stabilize in both of these towns, and much (although certainly not all) of the initial opposition had gone underground or had left the communities.

Short-Term Changes in Attitudes and Behavior among Youth

The results from the previous two chapters used surveys conducted in the fall of 2001. At the end of the school year in 2002, our team returned to each of the communities to examine changes over this short period of time. The reason for returning so soon was to capture as many of the original respondents as possible. Each year, at least one-quarter of the sample would graduate and scatter off to college, the military, and jobs. By even three years out, few of the original respondents would be available except through extraordinary efforts. Given that the time horizon is short, it would be surprising to see enormous changes on any of the indicators.

In all, 628 young people were surveyed in both waves, of which 582 (93 percent) were native-born and had native parents. There were slight changes in the survey to accommodate the schools' requests to reduce the time students would spend out of class at the end of the school year. At the end of the year, standardized tests increase in importance and can take many days outside regular class activities, so the survey instrument was shortened. Thus, among the civic engagement indicators, the generalized trust question was not included on the spring survey. Recall that the results reported in Chapter 4 for participation in school activities come from the spring 2002 survey because this question was not included on the fall survey. There were no reported changes, then, in generalized trust or participation in school activities. Changes in attitudes on all of the other questions from Chapters 3 and 4 will be examined here.

Change across Time in Homogeneous and Diverse Communities

The results of paired-samples differences of means tests demonstrate that there is significant growth on most of the civic engagement indicators—political knowledge, external efficacy, and intention to vote (see Table 5.1). The growth in political knowledge is highly significant in both homogeneous and diverse communities. Given that many students take social studies courses during the academic year that cover some of the factual questions asked on the survey, we would hope that basic political knowledge would increase. Both types of communities start with a D average (if we considered the 0–100 scale in letter grades) but end with about a B− or C+, suggesting a much more normal curve

TABLE 5.1 Change over Time in Civic Engagement in
Homogeneous and Diverse Towns

	2001	2002	Difference over time
Political knowledge			
Homogeneous towns	.69	.79	+.10***
Diverse towns	.66**	.81	+.15***
Internal efficacy			
Homogeneous towns	.53	.54	+.01
Diverse towns	.50	.51	+.01
External efficacy			
Homogeneous towns	.44	.59	+.15***
Diverse towns	.41	.55	+.14*
Intention to vote			
Homogeneous towns	.87	.91	+.03
Diverse towns	.87	.92	+.05*
Political discussion			
Homogeneous towns	.34	.14	−.20***
Diverse towns	.39	.21***	−.18***

Note: Values are the means within each category. The column farthest to the
right includes measures of significance for changes over time based on the paired
samples from 2001 and 2002. The differences reported in the 2001 and 2002
columns are within-sample t-tests from each year.

*$p < .05$; **$p < .01$; ***$p < .001$.

by the end of the school year. In fact, knowledge gains were so substantial in the
diverse communities that the gap that existed in the fall of 2001 has closed by
the end of the year. The fact that knowledge increased so significantly as to the
close the gaps between the predominantly White and ethnically diverse towns
suggests that any depressing effect of diversity on knowledge can be alleviated
in a relatively short period.

There was also significant growth in external efficacy across the school year.
Students in both types of communities became more likely to believe that public
officials are listening to people like them and that their voice can make a difference. There were no significant differences between the two types of communities in either the fall or the spring. Although there was a sense of frustration
about immigration among native- born kids in diverse towns, it still seemed that
they felt their concerns were being heard. Finally, young people were more likely
to say they would vote at the end of the school year, regardless of whether they
lived in a diverse or homogeneous community. The gains were statistically significant only in the diverse communities, however. There were no changes
across time with regard to internal efficacy.

There was a steep drop in the frequency of political discussion from the fall
of 2001 to the spring of 2002. The decline in political discussion may have been

due to a "9/11 effect." When our team arrived in late September 2001, students were still reeling from the terrorist attacks.[1] The shocking nature of this event, along with the continuous media coverage of it, likely contributed to increased political discussion, even among young people living a thousand miles from where the events occurred. Several months later, when the attention had died down and the shock had worn away, young people may have returned to "normal" levels of discussion of about one day per week. Although the difference between homogeneous and diverse communities in the frequency of discussion in the fall was not statistically significant, discussion was slightly more frequent in Perry and Storm Lake. In the spring, both types of communities experienced a drop, but the decline was slightly less extensive in the diverse communities and resulted in a significant difference in the amount of discussion between the two types of communities. Young people in the diverse towns discussed politics substantially more often than did those in the predominantly White towns.

Looking at the indicators of tolerance, there was significant growth in both types of communities on four of the seven measures (Table 5.2). Young people in both the diverse and homogeneous communities were more likely in the spring 2002 to say that immigrants do not take jobs from natives, that Asian people will improve life in their community, that their town would be better with more immigrants, and that there would not be fewer problems if there were more immigrants. There was no change in attitudes about whether immigrants should learn to speak English.

In the spring of 2002, nearly two-thirds of the respondents in all of the communities believed that immigrants had not taken jobs away from natives. There was also evidence of this in the focus groups, with young people seemingly blaming the native-born residents for not attempting to get the jobs at the meat-packing plants. The following conversation in Perry is indicative of many of these comments.

Interviewer: Some people I've talked to think that immigrants have taken jobs away from Iowans [who] would otherwise have those jobs.

Chris: They can get those jobs if they want.

David: I think it's a bunch of crap.

Jeff: If they want the job, they can get the job. That's all I can say.

Marcus: They could have come to Perry and got the jobs. The jobs were here. I didn't see a bunch of Iowans flocking to Perry to pick up the IBP jobs.

David: The Hispanics that have come—they are the ones—they want the jobs. They're the ones that want to start something fresh.

In the homogeneous communities, there were declines in support for the idea that Hispanics would improve life in one's community and for the idea that immigrants are harder workers than natives. In 2001, about 40 percent of young

TABLE 5.2 Change over Time in Support for Immigrants in Homogeneous and Diverse Small Towns

	2001	2002	Difference over time
Immigrants (do not) take jobs from natives.			
Homogeneous towns	.50	.63	+.13***
Diverse towns	.48	.60	+.12***
Hispanic people will improve life here.			
Homogeneous towns	.43	.33	−.10***
Diverse towns	.40	.37***	−.03
Asian people will improve life here.			
Homogeneous towns	.52	.54	+.02*
Diverse towns	.51	.56	+.05***
This town would be better with more immigrants.			
Homogeneous towns	.35	.39	+.04**
Diverse towns	.27**	.33	+.06***
Immigrants should (not have to) learn to speak English ASAP.			
Homogeneous towns	.19	.18	−.01
Diverse towns	.15	.15	0
Immigrants work harder than natives.			
Homogeneous towns	.46	.32	−.14***
Diverse towns	.41**	.33*	−.08***
There would not be fewer problems if there were (more) immigrants.			
Homogeneous towns	.48	.51	+.03*
Diverse towns	.41	.46	+.05*
Factor score			
Homogeneous towns	.41	.41	0
Diverse towns	.37	.39	+.02*

Note: Values are means within each category. The column farthest to the right includes measures of significance for changes over time based on the paired samples from 2001 and 2002. The differences reported in the 2001 and 2002 columns are within-sample t-tests from each year.

*p < .05; **p < .01; ***p < .001.

people in both types of communities said that Hispanic people would improve life in their community. This percentage remained the same in Storm Lake and Perry but dropped dramatically in the homogeneous towns. In the Harlan focus groups (see Chapter 3), many students made comments suggesting that they had no problem with immigration, as long as it was happening somewhere else. They did not believe that immigration would make their community better off.

An interesting "flip" in attitudes occurred with regard to beliefs about whether immigrants work harder than natives. In the fall semester, youth in the diverse communities were less likely than those in predominantly White towns to believe that immigrants work harder than natives. By the spring, however, young people in Perry and Storm Lake were *more* likely to believe that immigrants work harder than natives. Another male student in Harlan stated in a focus group discussion, "You know, [if] someone from Harlan wanted to get a job at IBP, they could do just as good as any of the other—any worker up there—and if they deserve the job, they'd get it. . . . If it's based off merit, anyone from Harlan would measure up to anyone from Mexico or, you know, China." It was seen as an insult to Anglo youth in Harlan to imply that immigrants worked harder than natives. In Perry, there was more support for the idea that immigrants are extremely hardworking, even more so than natives. Students told us often that they admired how hardworking the Latino immigrants were in Perry, even compared with natives.

On both of the indicators in which there were significant differences in 2002, respondents in the diverse towns were *more tolerant* than were those in homogeneous communities. In the fall of 2001, however, young people in the predominantly White towns were more likely than those in the diverse towns to say that immigrants would improve their communities. By 2002, these differences were no longer significant. The major finding is that there were no significant differences in 2002 in which teens in the homogeneous towns were significantly more sympathetic to immigrants than were those in the diverse towns. An across-time comparison of the factor score of each of these indicators demonstrates that there was no significant change in tolerance in the predominantly White communities but significant growth in tolerance in the diverse communities (p < .05).

The results suggest that on the whole, young people grow more supportive of immigrants and more civically engaged over the course of a school year. This growth is especially significant in ethnically diverse small towns compared with homogeneous ones. Further, by 2002, on every indicator on which there were significant differences between these two types of communities, the young people in diverse communities exceeded their counterparts in homogeneous towns. As shown in the previous two chapters, there are often significant differences between the two diverse communities, so the next section examines change over time in these two towns.

Changes in Attitudes in Perry and Storm Lake

In 2001, young people in Storm Lake were significantly more knowledgeable, more likely to say they would vote, and discussed politics with greater frequency than did those in Perry. By 2002, the differences in vote intention were no longer significant (Table 5.3). Native-born young people in both towns were substantially more knowledgeable in 2002 than in 2001, but the growth was more substantive in Storm Lake than in the Perry. The average grade on the knowledge test in Storm Lake in 2002 was B, compared with C– in Perry. Finally, youth in both schools discussed politics less frequently in 2002 than in 2001, but there continued to be more discussion in Storm Lake than in Perry.

TABLE 5.3   Change over Time in Civic Engagement in Perry and Storm Lake

	2001	2002	Difference over time
Political knowledge			
Perry	.61	.72	+.11***
Storm Lake	.67*	.85***	+.18***
Internal efficacy			
Perry	.51	.48	−.03
Storm Lake	.51	.53	−.02
External efficacy			
Perry	.40	.53	+.13***
Storm Lake	.43	.57	+.14***
Intention to vote			
Perry	.82	.93	+.11†
Storm Lake	.89**	.93	+.04
Political discussion			
Perry	.31	.16	−.15***
Storm Lake	.43**	.23**	−.20***

Note: Values are means within each category. The column farthest to the right includes measures of significance for changes over time based on the paired samples from 2001 and 2002. The differences reported in the 2001 and 2002 columns are within-sample t-tests from each year.

*p < .05; **p < .01; ***p < .001; †p < .10.

With regard to attitudes about immigrants (Table 5.4), in Perry there was growth on every indicator. This growth was statistically significant on four of the measures: Hispanic people would improve life in the community, Asians would improve life in their community, the town would be better with more immigrants, and there would not be fewer problems if there were more immigrants. Changes in tolerance in Storm Lake were less consistent. Native youth in Storm Lake were more likely in 2002 than in 2001 to say that immigrants did not take jobs from natives, that Asians would improve life in their community, and that their town would be better with more immigrants. However, there were significant declines related to beliefs about whether Hispanics would improve life in their communities and about whether immigrants work harder than natives.

In 2001, the differences between Storm Lake and Perry pointed to greater tolerance in Storm Lake. In 2002, there were some indicators in which Storm Lake's youth demonstrated greater tolerance than did those in Perry, but there were others in which the opposite was true. On two of the indicators where Perry's youth had lower levels of support for immigrants in 2001, there was substantial growth in Perry so that the differences between the two communities were no longer significant in 2002. The factor score demonstrates that in Storm Lake, there was no significant growth or decline in tolerance, but in Perry, toler-

TABLE 5.4 Change over Time in Support for Immigrants in Perry and Storm Lake

	2001	2002	Difference over time
Immigrants (do not) take jobs from natives.			
Perry	.50	.53	+.03
Storm Lake	.51*	.66***	+.15***
Hispanic people will improve life here.			
Perry	.36	.47	+.11***
Storm Lake	.47**	.34***	−.13***
Asian people will improve life here.			
Perry	.53	.58	+.05*
Storm Lake	.52	.56	+.04*
This town would be better with more immigrants.			
Perry	.27	.34	+.07**
Storm Lake	.31**	.35	+.04*
Immigrants should (not have to) learn to speak English ASAP.			
Perry	.15	.16	+.01
Storm Lake	.19*	.18	−.01
Immigrants work harder than natives.			
Perry	.42	.42	0
Storm Lake	.44	.33**	−.11***
There would not be fewer problems if there were (more) immigrants.			
Perry	.41	.48	+.07*
Storm Lake	.45**	.48	+.03
Factor score			
Perry	.37	.42	+.05***
Storm Lake	.41**	.41	0

Note: Values are means within each category. The column farthest to the right includes measures of significance for changes over time based on the paired samples from 2001 and 2002. The differences reported in the 2001 and 2002 columns are within-sample t-tests from each year.
*p < .05; **p < .01; ***p < .001.

ance grew significantly (p < .001). In fact, the gap that existed in 2001, when young people in Storm Lake had a significantly higher level of support for immigrants than did those in Perry, had closed. Tolerance had grown so much in Perry in just one academic year that there was no longer any difference between the two communities.

The next sections argue that Perry's comparatively faster growth in tolerance and engagement in the early 2000s was due to the fact that in Storm Lake, the community had already normalized its levels of tolerance and engagement. Tolerance and civic engagement grew among young people in Storm Lake throughout the late 1990s as the community began to cope with its population growth and cultural diversity. By 2002, these youth were already at least as supportive of immigration and as civically engaged as (and in some cases, more engaged than) those in ethnically homogeneous places. The results from 2001–2002 in Perry demonstrate that the community was beginning to mirror the Storm Lake experience, only about five to six years later.

Storm Lake in the 1990s and Today

"We were a bit chaotic in the mid-1990s for a while," stated Dale Carver, a long-time Storm Lake resident who is currently a community activist for the disabled and chairman of the Council of Ministers at his church. He was also, for more than 25 years, a human relations director at the turkey-processing plant in Storm Lake. He refers to the 1990s as a period of "turmoil." The rapid influx of foreign workers during this period, as well as the transience of the population, created hostility and fear in the community, and in the region Storm Lake obtained a negative reputation. According to Justin Yarosevich, assistant city manager and city clerk, "When I first started here [in 1995], the big thing was you couldn't—if you talked to somebody and said you were from Storm Lake, the first words off their lips were, 'Oh, can you walk at night there? That town's full of immigrants and [sotto voce] people from Mexico.'" Mark Prosser, Storm Lake's chief of police, believes the initial response from the community was mostly due to "fear of the unknown." He argues, "There is a touch of discrimination and prejudice in all of us, and I think we saw that."[2]

The mid-1990s were some of the most difficult years for the school system and other social service institutions. The sheer numbers of newcomers flooding into such a small community overwhelmed the system. Any rapid increase in population would be a burden on schools, hospitals, and law enforcement in small towns. The fact that so many were poor, uninsured, lacking in English skills, and transient added to the strain felt by teachers, medical personnel, and the city administration. From 1982 to 2007, enrollment in Storm Lake's public schools increased by 37 percent; the district went from nearly all White to 39 percent White.[3] The number of English Language Learner students increased dramatically. In 2003, the Storm Lake school district became the first in Iowa in which non-Hispanic Whites were a minority.[4]

Other public services were taxed, as well. Prior to the arrival of immigrants, the proportion of Storm Lake's hospital's care that went uncompensated was about 1 percent; by 1991, however, these costs increased to 13 percent of the budget.[5] Health insurance benefits at meatpacking plants typically do not begin until an employee has worked for several months, but this is often when many injuries take place because workers are still being trained. Hospitals also began to have the increased costs associated with full-time translators. In Storm Lake, this meant translators in both Lao and Spanish.

Crime increased in the first years after the community began to diversify. Storm Lake hired additional law enforcement officers, including community service officers to work specifically with the minority communities. Some residents attributed the increase in crime solely to the immigrants, but the police chief has long refuted the "myth of disproportionate crime rates." Since the early 1990s, the community has tracked arrests by ethnicity, and "in no time in that period has there ever been a disproportionate amount of minority arrests as compared to their presence in the community."[6]

Many native-born residents believed the quality of their services declined when the immigrants arrived and resented many of the changes in their town. A *New York Times* article in 1996 quoted residents who were annoyed that public signs and announcements were often written or spoken in multiple languages.[7] Some told reporters that immigrants were "ruining their town," even though others believed that the newcomers had added vitality to the community. Storm Lake had gained such a negative reputation in much of the region in the 1990s that residents in a neighboring town voted down efforts to open a meatpacking plant because they did "not want to become another Storm Lake."[8]

In 1994, members of the community, including Carver, initiated a Diversity Council. Its mission was to "be the vehicle used to promote and execute activities that will serve to educate, inform and bring together all parties involved in our diverse population. Its purpose would be to promote social and practical harmony to the betterment of the Storm Lake community." They conducted "Study Circles" where, according to Carver, for "our local Anglo-Saxons, it was the first time they ever sat down and talked with any [immigrants]. And you know what they found out? They're actually a lot more alike than they are different."[9] From the mid-1990s to the early 2000s, the task force accomplished many activities (see Table 5.5). Staff and students at Buena Vista University also played an active role on the town's Diversity Council. In 1998, the university's president formed a Diversity Task Force. The university created several multicultural student organizations, and in 2000 it hired a staff member whose primary job was to develop programs that help students learn to appreciate diversity.

In 1996, the Immigration and Naturalization Service raided Storm Lake's IBP plant, deporting 64 undocumented workers. According to Art Cullen, editor of the local *Storm Lake Times,* the raid was "complete with helicopters and dogs and a press conference for the benefit of *U.S. News and World Report.*"[10] The local police chief was actively involved in the raid due to his concerns about false identification and undocumented workers.[11] Cullen believes the raid was undertaken primarily because politicians "sensed the mood" in the rural areas; people were afraid that urban crime was moving to rural areas, and in Storm Lake people blamed the immigrants, despite statistics showing that "the Smiths do the same number of wrong things proportionately as the Sanchezes."[12] Also sensing the mood, the presidential candidate Patrick Buchanan held a rally in 1996 in Storm Lake to drive home his ideas about how immigrants are threatening American jobs.

Then in 2000, the community came to a crossroads. The Federation for American Immigration Reform (FAIR) ran a series of television ads using Storm

TABLE 5.5 Accomplishments of the Storm Lake Diversity Task Force in the 1990s and Early 2000s

- Established an international soccer league
- Southeast Asian church received a pastor
- All city employees received diversity training
- The city of Storm Lake solicited and received Spanish cable-television channel
- The Chamber of Commerce sponsored a customer-service training program about diversity
- Lutheran churches began to offer ESL classes and Hispanic information services
- Protestant church services in Spanish
- Expanded ESL classes offered at two largest employers
- Programs on immigration and diversity presented at all local service clubs
- Buena Vista University started a diversity committee
- The United Methodist Church and the Storm Lake Diversity Task Force co-sponsored Diversity Study Circle Program
- Hispanic radio program by La Amistad, Spanish-language religious programming
- Hosted a joint diversity committee meeting with Marshalltown, Iowa

Lake as its example of a small town overrun with illegal aliens. In these ads, chamber music played in the background of a rolling stream of black-and-white photos of Latinos in handcuffs and other stock photos of urban ghetto areas. A deep voice stated, "Welcome to Storm Lake, Iowa, where the meat packing industry replaced native Iowans with thousands of foreign workers and cut wages to half what they used to be. Where Medicaid costs rose 63 percent and four out of ten school kids don't speak English. Where jail costs have risen 62 percent and where quality of life is but a memory. Ask the candidates if they think one million immigrants a year are too many." Aired in conjunction with the 2000 Iowa presidential caucuses, the group wanted to draw attention to immigration to the Midwest. Local officials reacted with strong opposition. Governor Tom Vilsack and Lieutenant Governor Sally Pederson stated that they "deplored this propaganda campaign." Storm Lake's Mayor Jon Kruse demanded a "public apology to our community from the inconsiderate, uninformed, out-of-state political special interest group." The ads also galvanized the community. Carver explained,

> The mayor and some of the town leaders called me in, and we had a big meeting, a pow-wow, and we sent a police officer undercover to visit with the FAIR guys and . . . he came back and said, "They're just basically anti-Hispanic, anti-Mexican." "Fair" it isn't—they're anything but fair. And so we called a press conference, invited the news media, and cried foul. Those pictures are not Storm Lake. [Those ads] made the front page in the Sioux City paper, and [we] said, "That's it! We've been slapped in the face one time too many." And it really did ignite the community to stand up and say, "It's not as bad as people say it is. We're tired of being beat up on and being talked bad about because quality of

life is not bad here." . . . Some of the people that . . . were on the fence tolerance-[wise] . . . they had to get off the fence and decide which side they were going to be on. . . . Actually, FAIR sort of helped us, you know, by being over-the-top with their deceit, their betrayal of this community.

At that time, Assistant City Manager Justin Yarosevich explained, "This community was really struggling . . . with its image . . . you know, the older people wanted it to be like it was in 1978, [where they could] walk to mom-and-pop groceries and Ben Franklin [variety store] was there." Storm Lake's negative image challenged the older, more established residents and pushed them to make changes. Since that time, Storm Lake has redefined itself. For the past several years, the city has tried to build itself as a tourist destination through a $39 million economic development plan centered on its large eponymous glacial lake. A public–private investment in a new water park and resort hotel, the renovation of golf courses and beaches, and a dredging project has helped change the image of the community from the inside and the outside. More than 500 local individuals and companies donated to help fund the project, and nearly three-quarters of voters approved a $3.5 million bond measure.

Several examples illustrate the strides made by residents of Storm Lake since the FAIR ads. After several years of the schools' struggling with expanding enrollments, 81.5 percent of voters supported a bond for a new elementary school in 2007.[13] In 2000, the city elected its first Latino city councilor.[14] When his job was transferred and he resigned his post, Storm Lake elected a Latina to the council who had become a U.S. citizen only three years earlier. She was the top vote getter and was re-elected in 2007. In 2005, a delegation from Storm Lake visited the cities of Ayotlan and Santa Rita, Mexico, to establish a formal sister-city relationship. A year later, a delegation from Ayotlan came to Storm Lake.

The Ku Klux Klan (KKK) was planning a rally in Storm Lake in 2007, but the community's negative response led not only to its cancellation but to "a boisterous peace rally [that] replaced [the KKK rally]—Caucasians holding hands with African Americans, holding hands with Asian Americans, holding hands with Latino Americans."[15] According to Tony Talamantes, who immigrated to Storm Lake in the early 1990s, "Everywhere you go, you know, they welcome you and help you out. If you get a flat tire, more than one person will stop to give you a hand. If you go in a ditch, they pull you out. I cannot say nothing [sic] wrong about the people from here."[16] In 2010, the Storm Lake Police Department was identified as having "best practices" by the Vera Institute of Justice, a national organization.[17] Dana Larsen, editor of another local newspaper, summed up many of the attitudes of residents with whom I spoke in responding to a *New York Times* article in advance of the 2008 Iowa caucuses: "The *New York Times,* no less, has been back in Storm Lake, poking around as the national media periodically does in Storm Lake, mining for quaint Midwestern opinion on immigration. . . . Never mind that Storm Lake has adapted to diversity long ago, and almost all of its residents get along just fine. Election year is an ideal time for metro journalism to pay a courtesy call to mine up another eye-catching headline about how immigration 'shakes' rural Iowa."[18]

The results of the surveys in Storm Lake High School bear this out. In 2001 and 2002, ethnic diversity had no significant effect on sympathy for immigration among young people; those in Storm Lake were just as supportive of immigration as those in homogeneous communities. Further, compared with the predominantly White communities, the kids in Storm Lake were more active in their school. There were no significant differences in school participation between native- and foreign-born youth. By all accounts, very few non-Caucasian young people participated in school activities in the early 1990s, with the exception of soccer, but the results here indicate no significant differences in 2002.

Writing about Storm Lake in 2002, the commentator Dominic Pulera predicted that by 2010, media accounts of the town would "probably characterize it as yet another American success story, where people from heterogeneous backgrounds come together, learn to live side by side, and eventually create bonds of family and community that transcend race and ethnicity."[19] This research suggests that his description aptly fits the majority of residents' attitudes in Storm Lake. Although it has not happened overnight, Carver believes that interethnic relations in Storm Lake are significantly better today than they were in the 1990s. He said that the best place to see how well people of different cultures get along is in the high school, where "they're getting it figured out" even when "some of the parents don't."

Perry in the 1990s and Today

Immigrants began to arrive in Perry in the early 1990s. In many ways, the town had to catch up to Storm Lake in coming to terms with what ethnic diversity would mean to the community. According to Carver, Storm Lake was "way ahead of the curve for most communities. . . . Perry and Marshalltown and Denison have caught up, too. . . . We started in the early 1990s, while the rest of them didn't see changes until six or seven years later. We had an exchange with the Marshalltown [diversity] task force, and they came up here, and it was like looking at ourselves three years before that."[20] Until the late 1990s, longtime residents of Perry dealt with the growing population and increasing ethnic diversity only sporadically and with very little long-term planning. There seemed to be an assumption that the newcomers from Latin America would not be staying long. Letters to the editor in the early 1990s railed against IBP and its labor practices, as well as against the different cultural practices of the newcomers. An editorial in the *Perry Chief* in August 1990 encouraged residents to accept the new people coming to work at IBP, stating, "If the community were to be more accepting, perhaps these people could find a home here on a permanent basis. They are here to work and hold jobs, not to be vagrants and troublemakers."[21] In the next edition, Allie Schwarzen wrote, "Some say we should accept, I've lived in Perry all my life, and this is the first time in forty years I lock my doors. . . . And those of you who say I'm wrong, answer this, do you lock your doors, do you go out at night, do you rent out your extra rooms, and do you accept IBP?"[22]

Schwarzen did not speak for all residents. In the following edition, Ellen Hobbs Burton wrote, "I'm disgusted with the attitude of some of the people in this town and the lack of empathy for their fellow human beings."[23] According to the former mayor, Viivi Shirley, the opposition in the beginning was due not only to prejudice and fear, but also to the fact that the immigrants who arrived first were usually single men. Men arrived to work at the plant, and those who were married scouted things out before paying the expense to move wives and children. Shirley states, "You get a bunch of single men . . . or men who are alone (so they think they're single). . . . [N]o matter from where, you get single males together, and they work hard, [t]hey're going to probably drink and raise some hell and fight." Of course, small towns, like all communities, have experience with single men who get drunk and fight. According to Shirley, "I think on top of that, you had [differences in] the skin color (I mean, they cannot hide [in Perry] if they wanted to) and you have the language barrier."[24] Some native residents had trouble with what they saw as a disruptive group of single men who did not share their language or their values.

Throughout 1990 and 1991, the newspaper covered stories about the immigrants' arrival, both good and bad. It documented the need for an English as a Second Language (ESL) instructor in the schools; the increasing number of arrests, especially for public intoxication and driving while intoxicated; and church groups' efforts to help the Latino community with support groups, language instruction, translation services, and donations of furniture and clothing. In 1991, the Iowa Civil Rights Commission released a report about housing discrimination in Perry.[25] In its tests, people with various ethnic backgrounds and in a variety of conditions (such as single mothers on welfare, meatpacking workers, and more) attempted to obtain rental housing in Perry. They found substantial discrimination in the availability and pricing of rental property based on a subject's ethnicity, national origin, parental status, gender, employer, and economic circumstances. The availability of affordable housing in acceptable condition continued to be a problem in Perry for several years. The city eventually had to crack down on slumlords, including one who attempted to rent to new arrivals by the bunk (bed), leading to dangerous overcrowding in trailers and other homes.

In 1992, the *Perry Chief* ran a three-part series on the growing Hispanic population. The articles covered the numbers of Hispanic workers in Perry, their national origin, their legal status, and the immigrants' attitudes about their new home. At that time, the IBP plant manager stated that approximately 30 percent of the 690 employees were Hispanic.[26] Although this would have included more than 200 people, the schools reported very few Latino children due to the fact that few men had brought their families with them in these early days. At first, the Latino community was very small and was not yet visible to the majority of the community. In 1992, in the entire Perry public school system (grades K–12), there were 27 Hispanic students. The system employed one ESL teacher who traveled between the elementary, middle, and high schools.[27] School administrators dealt with the influx from year to year and were not making concrete plans for the future. When the current principal of Perry High School, Dan Marburger, began working there in 1995, there were only six Hispanic students, all of whom needed to learn English skills. During the academic year of 1995–1996, the number of Hispanic students increased dramatically. Marburger said that teachers began to panic, wondering how they could possibly teach their content to students who did not have English language skills. The school hired a full-time ESL teacher in 1996. Within the next five years, more families arrived, and the number of Latino students in the Perry schools jumped dramatically.

From the mid-1990s to the early 2000s, Perry began to realize slowly that the new neighbors were starting to settle in permanently. According to Juli Probasco-Sowers, the former editor of the local newspaper, the Latino population "sneaked up" on the Anglo community. It began with so few people, and in what seemed to many natives to be a very short period, Spanish-speaking foreign workers and, by the late 1990s, their families were everywhere. The mayor of Perry from 1994 to 2001, a local pharmacist, stated that during these years, "It was kind of like the 'us versus they' [sic] philosophy."[28] Rosa Morales de Gonzalez, an immigrant who moved to Perry in the 1990s, explained, "When we came here in the beginning, we felt like strangers."[29]

In addition to a lack of affordable housing, a significant concern was related to increases in crime. Just as in Storm Lake, the data indicated that the Hispanic population never committed a disproportionate amount of crime. However, several Anglo residents recalled a drive-by shooting in front a Latino night club in 1996. Although no one was hurt, the event likely reinforced some of the negative attitudes held by some of Perry's longtime residents.

By the late 1990s, a few Hispanic workers were beginning to buy homes, open businesses, and make plans to stay in Perry for the long term. In short, they were becoming much more visible in the community. In 1997, the police department added a bilingual officer to its ranks. According to Sandra Sanchez, director of the Project Voice/Immigrant Voices program at the Des Moines chapter of American Friends Service Committee, a few of Perry's foreign-born residents came together in the early 2000s to discuss their work at the plant and their lives in the community. Several of the churches in town developed a Hispanic Ministry, and a Diversity Council was created. In 2000, the Iowa State University's Extension program helped create Perry LINK to connect the established residents with Spanish-speaking newcomers and to help newcomers orient to Perry by connecting them to services.[30] This group conducted home visits, small-group educational meetings, and informational fairs.

By the mid-2000s, Perry had begun to respond more effectively to the needs of the Latino population, and much of the initial suspicion and hostility toward newcomers had died down. Although unlike in Storm Lake, there was no single moment when Perry's citizens decided to come to terms with their new composition and identity, by 2003 or so things were beginning to change. A longtime ESL teacher, Julie Walstrom, stated in 2010 that in her years in the Perry school system (1993–2010), the relationships between Anglo and Latino students changed for the better: "When I first came, the Hispanic students were very isolated. Sometimes they still are, but when you look at student groups, you see a lot more of a mix. I'm so proud of the way the school, teachers, and community have embraced all the changes. I don't think the kids in the high school even realize there are differences anymore."[31]

Other events demonstrated that the community was beginning to adapt to its new neighbors. Several residents commented on how significant it was when the Fareway grocery store began to carry specialty items targeted to the Latino community. In the early 2000s, Trinity Evangelical Lutheran Church in Perry offered a free medical clinic in which a translator was always available. Besides the meatpacking plants, other Anglo-owned businesses began to hire Latino employees, which to the immigrants was a sign that the community cared about Hispanic residents. In 2005, de Gonzalez said, "You go to the banks, to the school, and you will be receiving help in Spanish and also the hospital, the medical clinic, and that for me means a lot."[32] In 2004, Perry High School hired a bilingual home–school liaison, whose job includes getting instructions and information in Spanish to parents who do not read English.

In 2002, an emerging Latino leadership formed Hispanics United for Perry (HUP), a group that has actively promoted activities designed to bring the Anglo and Latino communities together. In 2006, a delegation of 22 Perry leaders traveled to Michoacán, Mexico, the hometown of many of Perry's newcomers. The trip was designed to help the Anglo community learn more about the lives of their Latino neighbors to facilitate understanding and empathy. Tyson Fresh Meats, the new owner of the meatpacking plant, helped fund scholarships so people could go, and according to Shirley, the trip sent dual messages to the people of Perry. For the natives, the fact that Tyson was chipping in indicated for the first time that the company understood it should play an important role in the town's transition. For the immigrants, the fact that the town's leadership was willing to go to Mexico meant that Latinos had finally become a real part of the local community. As a result of the trip, Mary Hillman, director of Perry's after-school program PACES, stated, "I started asking more questions of my Latino parents, and when I told them of the trip, they just opened up! Wow! This really opened doors to truly connecting with families."[33]

This transition, however, was not altogether smooth. In 2002, for instance, Perry amended its parking rules to prohibit parking in the front yard (ordinance 773). This had been a perennial complaint among native Iowans, who pride themselves on nice lawns and orderly looking neighborhoods. According to several residents, negative letters to the editor continued into the early 2000s. One report in 2000 in the *Chicago Tribune* quotes Vivian de Gonzalez, a U.S.

citizen who moved to Perry from Mexico in the mid-1990s, saying that she had heard people complaining about "those Mexicans" who were swimming in the same pool as their children.[34]

The responses from the young people in focus groups in 2002 indicated their ambivalence about immigration.[35] Several Anglo students commented about how they thought the meatpacking plant was good for the community because it brought diversity. One young girl, Laura, stated, "I think diversity is good . . . because we have a lot of people that have a lot of different backgrounds here . . . and we always have stuff downtown that's Hispanic and stuff. I think it's kind of neat." An Anglo male stated, "I think diversity is good because, like, they learn about our stuff, our culture, and we get to learn about them." Chris, another Anglo male, seemed to recognize the economic benefits of the meatpacking plant for Perry: "Oh, I think the plant's good for Perry. I think diversity is a good thing in the community. I think you accept people for who they are, and I never really hear of any problems with IBP or anything, like, with the people here. . . . It's a lot of jobs, and it keeps this town going."

Many Anglo students in Perry attempted to put themselves in the shoes of their new neighbors. One young man explained that he had mixed feelings about the plant, suggesting that it might not be a good place to work, not just for him, but for the immigrants who were employed there. Another young girl, Jennifer, argued, "If I lived in another country, I'd want to come here." Her friend, Julie, said, "Yeah, they deserve to come here if they want to." When one student mentioned that crime is a bigger problem with immigrants, her friend jumped in to say, "There's way more good Hispanic people than not." However, some comments demonstrated that young people in Perry had mixed feelings about the new arrivals. Laura, who thought diversity was "good" and the "Hispanic stuff" downtown was "neat," later showed more ambivalence. About five minutes after she made the comment about diversity, she stated, "I mean, there are a lot of them [immigrants]. They're kind of taking over. I mean, they have so many restaurants in this town, and . . . there's like four for Americans. You go downtown and, like, sometimes you don't even feel safe 'cause you walk by and they just start talking about you and laughing and you don't know what they're saying. I don't go down there very far."

Laura was not alone in her level of uncertainty. Young Anglos said they appreciated the influx of new people who were helping their community thrive and that they were learning about other cultures from their new neighbors. Some commented that they liked the new restaurants and that their soccer team, composed mostly of Latinos, was good for the first time in history. They also said, however, that the school was overcrowded, and they now had to share lockers. Many stated that any additional immigrants would pose a burden because there would not be enough room for everyone, and immigrant families already had to live together in homes with multiple families.

Interviews in 2010 suggested that some of this ambivalence had subsided and that interethnic relations were mostly positive. Angelica Diaz-Cardenas, the home–school liaison at Perry High School, told me that when HUP executes programs to bring Anglos and Latinos together, the activities are widely supported. For example, enrollment in the classes on Latino cooking must be capped because the demand from Anglo residents exceeds the capacity. Further, the group's largest activity—a Latino heritage festival held each September—draws nearly 1,000 participants to Perry, and in 2009 the majority of attendees were Anglo. The city moved the festival from an outlying park where it was held for a few years to the center of the downtown area.

Diaz-Cardenas and Guadalupe Duarte, the director of an immigrant advocacy center, stated that they have had mostly positive experiences with the Anglo citizens in Perry. Diaz-Cardenas arrived in Perry in the mid-1990s as a high school student who spoke very little English. She told me, "It would be understandable if everyone [in the Anglo community] was not completely welcoming and accepting of newcomers [in the early years]. . . . I have been to other places where people are not hostile [to immigrants], but you can see when you are not being welcomed just by the looks, the way they stare at you, or the way they look at you, and I haven't had that in Perry."[36] Duarte agreed, stating, "Perry makes you feel at home. Whoever comes here feels at home because we tend to have a welcoming community." Using the town's motto to "make yourself at home in Perry," Duarte stated, "Even if you're passing through, we'll make yourself at home."[37]

Duarte's use of pronoun—"we" instead of "they"—is important, a sign that he considers himself part of the Perry community. He feels this way despite a couple of stories he told about negative incidents that had taken place when he first moved to town in the early 2000s. He disclosed that when he first moved to Perry, he noticed that several of his Anglo neighbors had sold their homes and left. He said, "I don't know, I don't want to call it racist, you know . . . but that was probably the case." He was quick to add, "I don't see [this] much." Diaz-Cardenas had had no negative experiences and added that she returned to Perry after graduating from college—something she would not have done if the community had not been so welcoming. Duarte said, "I've been receiving offers from other states, but I don't want to leave."

For many immigrants who came to Perry after living in urban areas of California or New York, Perry was an oasis even back in the difficult period of the late 1990s. One young Mexican American girl explained in 2002 that her family had moved there from New York in 1996. When asked whether she believed Perry was a better place to grow up, she stated, "Oh, yeah. Sometimes, I think, like, what would it be like if I was in New York? Would I be a gang banger or be on drugs? Things like that. But right here, it's peaceful." Another young man had the following exchange in the focus groups.

> *Marco:* In, like, California, it's kind of bad over there, you know. They have, like, different—say, like, there's the African Americans, the Mexicans, the Whites. . . .

Interviewer: Like, distinct neighborhoods, you mean?

Marco: Yeah, they don't . . . like, right here in Perry, you know, we're all together.

Interviewer: Right

Marco: So, I'm coming from California and so, like, it's nice over here. I like it. There's peace. There's nothing . . .

Interviewer: No violence or gangs?

Marco: Like, in California, like, every little five minutes you would hear a cop car passing by, like, at 70, you know. High speed chases or something, you know. But here you don't hear that. When I came here the first time, I was like, "Wow, this is a big change for me." It's different.

Interviewer: Some people might think, "Oh, it's really boring in small-town Iowa."

Marco: I came here thinking that it was boring, but after the time passed, it's awesome. I like it here.

Jeff: . . . I think in big cities, the problem is when minorities or whoever go there, they wanna get to people that are like them, like, for security.

Chris: I think that happened at first [here].

David: Yeah, here that's what happened first, but when things—everyone kind of started to mix. . . . I mean, there are still groups. Hispanics usually hang out with Hispanics. But, I mean, there's still, if you pass them in the hall, I mean, everybody knows them. One of the kids will say, "Hey, there's one of your friends. Hey!"

In 2002, these students acknowledged that there was still separation between Latino and Anglo students. But they believed that because the town is small, everyone knew everyone else, including the immigrants or children of immigrants. In small communities with small schools, young people can be friendly with one another and know what is going on with one another without being close friends. This is common among Anglo youth, and it speaks volumes that immigrant youth were considered just as much a part of this sort of social network.

Most of the Anglo adults with whom I spoke echoed these sentiments. Today, much of the initially vocal opposition has died down. Mayor Jay Pattee and City Councilor Eddie Diaz, who migrated from California to Perry when he was in high school in the 1990s, suggested that much of the opposition to immigration, especially today, is underground. Opponents are unorganized and may make derogatory comments to one another but rarely speak out in public. Pattee believes there is more of "this kind of thing in the smaller towns around here than in Perry itself. People will . . . ask, 'How do you get along with all those *other* people?'"[38] In focus groups in Harlan, for example, several young people made comments about not wanting to turn into Denison, another immigrant-receiving community in Iowa.

In 2010, the only major negative comments about immigrants were related to frustration that the Latino community does not get more involved in community affairs. Doug Bruce, a local business owner, for example, stated that his only problem with the Latino community is that its members are reluctant to join civic groups or take part in activities:

> They've got great families. But in turn, they also have that—"Do you want to run for office"—[They say] "No." "Do you want to volunteer?" [They say] "No." "Do you want to help on this?" [They say] "No." My son was junior class president [in 2008], the one who chairs prom. So obviously the parents are the co-chairs. We got one Hispanic mom to show up to the prom committee.... [Native] people really don't *not* like the plant or *not* like the immigrants. They don't like the nonparticipation. Most people try to spin it that people don't like [the immigrants]. I don't like that. I don't think people care one way or the other. If you live in a small town, you're just trying to survive.[39]

Bruce's statements echo those of other residents, including many of the Latinos with whom I spoke. They, too, are frustrated with other Latinos' lack of involvement in civic affairs. Both Duarte and Diaz talked to me about getting more parents involved in the Parent–Teacher Association and getting more Latinos to vote. It seems, then, that this concern is widespread and could be alleviated with one generation. The children of immigrants—those who spent most of their lives in Perry—are significantly more likely to become actively involved in the community. Not only has turnover slowed down at the plant—thereby bringing in fewer new immigrants on a regular basis—but many immigrants have permanently settled down in these communities. This should lead to increased participation over the next five or ten years.

Both Perry and Storm Lake have some naysayers, people who continue to be unhappy about the immigrants in their community. When asked about whether the changes in Perry were for the better or the worse, one longtime resident told me, under the condition of anonymity, "I could get crucified for this, but I'd say worse." Art Cullen, editor of the local *Storm Lake Times,* told me about the "rednecks" who say, "You ought to just shoot them when they're coming across the border." These are often older residents and are today a significant minority.

Generational Differences and Optimism about the Future

In the focus groups, it became very clear that most of the adolescents in Perry believed that interethnic relations were better in 2002 than they had been in the 1990s. And they were very optimistic about the future of the community. One of the most common themes repeated by young Anglo students in Perry was that their attitudes diverged from their parents' and grandparents' beliefs. Chris believed that adults who have opposed the immigration into Perry are motivated primarily out of fear.

> *Chris:* I think . . . the problem is . . . the people of Perry was set for so many years just to how it was, and then, when, you know, a lot of Hispanics started moving here and they're just . . . um . . . you know . . .
>
> *Interviewer:* Uneasy with it?
>
> *Chris:* Yeah, it's just, it's not a big deal at all. Like, a person's a person. Like, if we're talking about racism or whatever, it's just the people are scared. . . . A lot of people will say stuff like, "They need to speak English" and stuff. It's things like that. It bugs me. Like, I don't have a problem at all.

Later, Chris and his friends discussed the divisions between them and their parents:

> *David:* I mean, I think the kids that really develop this city . . . I think the schools have really shaped the town.
>
> *Jeff:* 'Cause it's the parents that are still—
>
> *David:* Yeah, the older people that don't understand—like, they weren't ever around people of other cultures.
>
> *Jeff:* I think when we go home and you, like, hear your parents saying something bad about it. I don't speak out. I [ought to] speak out against people that are racist against something like that.
>
> *Interviewer:* So you're saying you guys have more progressive views than even your parents do?
>
> *Chris:* Yeah, immigration and things like that in this town.
>
> *Jeff:* It's simply 'cause they don't know.
>
> *David:* Right, I think we've learned to grow to understand.

In addition to believing that their attitudes were more progressive than those of the older generations, the young people were optimistic about changes on the horizon. The interviewer asked a mixed group of Anglo and Latino students whether attitudes toward Hispanics were better in 2002 than in the past:

> *Rosalinda:* I think [people are] opposed still.
>
> *Interviewer:* That's interesting. You think she's right about that?
>
> *Keith:* I think most people are opposed.
>
> *Interviewer:* Opposed to the new population that has come in?
>
> *Keith:* I think they're opposed, but there's a lot that are accepting it, and there's, like, programs around town that brings the culture.

Robert: It's brought a lot to our town, too, like restaurants, and I guess there's been a good cultural impact.
Interviewer: So, do you think people are getting used to it?
Keith: Starting, yeah.
Rosalinda: Starting to, yeah.

The young people were optimistic about the future in part because they saw greater tolerance among young people like them. As the older generations are replaced by younger folks who have grown more comfortable with being around people from other cultures and with different backgrounds, it is likely that these communities will continue to grow, physically, intellectually, and culturally.

Summary

This chapter argues that Perry was slightly behind Storm Lake in coming to terms with its new character as a multiethnic community. Perry's kids made substantial gains in support for immigrants between 2001 and 2002. These gains were greater than those in Storm Lake and in the homogeneous communities. In fact, only in Perry was the growth in support for immigration over this short period of time statistically significant. Perry also made significant gains in many of the civic engagement measures, especially political knowledge. The young people in Perry still lagged behind the others in terms of political knowledge and discussion, but in general the changes were in the positive direction.

The qualitative data from interviews and focus groups tells us why the young people in Perry and Storm Lake had differences in their levels of engagement and tolerance, despite the fact that immigrants began to arrive in large numbers at about the same time in communities that were similar in most other respects. There was great consensus that the early, much smaller migration of Tai Dam refugees to Storm Lake in the 1970s and 1980s helped to cultivate the soil for understanding and acceptance, especially among young people. This earlier wave of refugees also meant that by the mid-1990s, some of the non-Caucasian youth were second-generation Storm Lakers; in Perry, however, all of the non-Caucasian kids were newcomers. Further, because of its higher profile in national news and its status as a target of anti-immigrant groups, Storm Lake was pushed into reconciliation. The Anglo community had already slowly begun to adapt to its newcomers, but after 2000, the community began to fight back against its negative portrayal in the media.

In Perry, the same type of reconciliation has occurred, but it has taken a bit more time. If one examines some of the markers of change, for example, Storm Lake met them before Perry in each case. Storm Lake elected a Latino to its City Council in 2000; Perry appointed a Latino council member in 2010. Storm Lake began a Diversity Committee in the early 1990s; Perry's began to meet in the late 1990s. In 2002, Perry bought software to translate public documents into

Spanish; Storm Lake had long employed translators to provide public notices and other documents into Spanish and Lao.[40] In 2005, Perry participated in a public dialogue about immigration, led by the Study Circles Resource Center.[41] According to Dale Carver in Storm Lake, these types of discussions took place there in the late 1990s. Storm Lake sent a delegation to towns in Mexico from which many of its residents hail in 2005; Perry did the same thing one year later. And the results of the surveys show that Storm Lake students, both native- and foreign-born, were very active in school in 2002; in Perry, it was not until much later that school activities became more diversified and even then, not to the level found in Storm Lake. Principal Marburger told me in 2010, "I think . . . in our mind, we've made progress [with getting Latino children involved in school activities]. We've got data that shows that. We're trying to get our Hispanic kids involved in non-traditional activities. Soccer is still 80 percent Hispanic kids. Our purpose there is trying to get more Anglo kids in that. Girls' basketball, we had 12 Hispanic girls go out for the . . . team, which is a high for us. . . . We've made inroads in band and choir."

The epigraph for this chapter quotes Storm Lake's police chief describing the future successes of the children who grow up in his community and stick around to become leaders. This was a common refrain among residents in both Perry and Storm Lake. Art Cullen said that rural areas have seen much loss in population in recent years, and he is excited about the future of his community. In a few years, when "Raul is elected to the local farm bureau," old-timers will be shocked, but it will be an interesting experience. We can only speculate about the future, but the pattern over the past twenty years indicates that, barring a catastrophe, this confidence in the future may be justified.

6

What Happened to My Town?

Many opponents of immigration are old stock Americans who have all but forgotten their immigrant ancestors. They often live in small towns . . . and have relatively little contact with immigrant families in their neighborhoods, churches, and friendship networks.
—Charles Hirschman

In the 2008–2009 academic year, first-, second-, and third-generation immigrant students from around the world together made up a majority of the student body at Storm Lake High School. Forty-one percent of the students were non-Hispanic White. For many Americans, this is exactly the future they do not want to see: small communities taken over by immigrants and their children. Charles Hirschman's statement likely fits well with most people's notions of small-town America. We are unsurprised to read a newspaper story such as the *Chicago Tribune* piece from 2008 about "a sense of unrest familiar in small towns and suburbs across America," where the integration of immigrants "into small-town America is marked . . . by a language of fear, resentment and anger."[1] This book has demonstrated that these characterizations of small-town America are not borne out in reality, particularly when we examine the process of adaptation over time. The initial wave of immigration brought fear and resentment, but these feelings dissipated over a relatively short period of time.

Throughout history, the most virulent anti-immigration rhetoric in the United States has played on the fears many Americans have about outsiders. These fears are supposedly most pronounced in small towns, where change happens more slowly. White residents of ethnically homogeneous communities like those examined here tend to have many reservations about the impact immigrants will have on their communities, especially during the initial period of diversification or in anticipation of immigration. This chapter examines whether the major concerns people had about immigration in small towns have been realized in Perry and Storm Lake. Where do these communities stand today? What are the lessons other homogeneous small towns (and even suburbs and urban neighborhoods) can learn about immigration and rapid demographic change?

Small Towns and the Immigration Debate

In American politics, there are few more hot-button contemporary political issues than immigration. If one watches the cable news networks, listens to talk radio, or reads political blogs, one would think that everyone in the United States has a strong opinion about immigration reform. A recent study finds that 70 percent of the episodes of *Lou Dobbs Tonight* in 2007 contained discussion of illegal immigration, as did 56 percent of *The O'Reilly Factor* and 28 percent of *Glenn Beck*.[2] In April 2010, the issue shot again to the top of the nation's agenda when Arizona passed a controversial law that makes the failure to carry immigration documents a crime and gives police broad power to detain anyone suspected of being in the country illegally.[3] Under the law, state residents can sue the local government if they believe federal or state immigration law is not being enforced. Officials in Arizona argued that because federal immigration policy is failing to curb illegal immigration, states and localities must act to protect their citizens. A federal judge issued a preliminary injunction that blocked the law's most controversial provisions, and as of this writing the future of the law is pending in the U.S. Supreme Court. Nonetheless, the law put immigration policy back on the national agenda.

Arizona is not alone. In June 2011, Alabama passed the nation's new "toughest" anti-immigration bill. The law has many similarities to its Arizona predecessor, but among other provisions, it also requires public school officials to ascertain whether students are in the country without documentation and to report annual tallies to state education officials. Further, in the first quarter of 2011, state legislatures introduced 1,538 bills and resolutions related to immigration reform.[4] Only 9 percent of these became law, and not all of these laws were anti-immigrant. But many of them give law enforcement and other state agencies broader power to enforce federal law, prohibit landlords from renting to anyone who cannot provide documentation of his or her legal status, and punish employers—and in some cases, those seeking work—who do not verify the status of their employees.

In addition to new state laws, hundreds of local ordinances have passed since 2005 seeking to make life more difficult for undocumented immigrants. In Farmers Branch, Texas (pop. 26,000), ordinances were passed in 2006 that fine landlords who rent to illegal aliens, allow local authorities to screen illegal aliens in police custody, and make English the official language of the city. The city has a substantial foreign-born population: 26.7 percent of all residents were born outside the United States. The ordinances have been challenged and are part of an ongoing, expensive legal battle. The city filed another appeal, this time with the Fifth Circuit Court of Appeals, in January 2011, and has spent nearly $4 million to defend itself in state and federal courts.[5]

Hazleton, Pennsylvania (pop. 23,000), and Fremont, Nebraska (pop. 25,000), have also been in the news because of their anti-immigrant ordinances. These laws have also passed in small towns with fairly small immigrant populations, including Valley Park, Missouri (pop. 6,500); Taneytown, Maryland (pop. 5,100); and Bridgeport, Pennsylvania (pop. 4,300). Even tiny communities with almost no immigrants have gotten on board. In Oklahoma, Inola (pop. 1,589) and Oologah (pop. 883) both passed anti-immigrant ordinances, even though more than 99 percent of their residents were born in the United States.

During the first few years of the immigrants' arrivals in Perry and Storm Lake, longtime residents had many of the same concerns about immigrants as do those in these other towns. Many of these fears and early feelings of suspicion have dissipated, but this chapter focuses not on attitudes about immigration but, instead, on whether the early fears about the negative effects of immigration have eventually been reflected in reality by looking at where Perry and Storm Lake stand today. In particular, this chapter examines three of the biggest fears about negative effects of immigrants: a sense that immigrants will overrun the town; the belief that immigrants cost communities too much, especially compared with what they give back; and the perception that immigrants do not want to assimilate or become full members of the communities in which they live.

Expectations about the Effects of Immigrants in Small Towns

Americans concerned about increasing numbers of immigrants are worried about the potential changes to their communities. Some media accounts suggest that these fears are heightened in small towns, where residents are unaccustomed to diversity. In most cases, the expectations about dramatically negative outcomes in Perry and Storm Lake were not substantiated.

"Immigrants Will Overrun the Town"

One of the major concerns people in small towns have about immigration is a fear of being "overrun." We hear this when people express concerns about immigrants taking over the town or the country, or when people say that in time, "they" (the immigrants) will be the majority. In 2004, Mauricia Ann Proper wrote in a letter to the editor of the *Storm Lake Pilot Tribune*: "I am seriously concerned that it will not be long before the illegals (I will not refer to them as 'immigrants,' as they are not here legally) outnumber the citizens of this country."[6] The sense of being overrun, of course, is a subjective feeling. One person may feel swamped if even 1 percent of his or her community is composed of immigrants, while another may not have any problem if a third or more of the community is foreign born. Assuming that overrun in absolute terms indicates that the White, Anglo population becomes a minority, this is certainly not the case today in Perry, where a still substantial majority, 61 percent, of residents are non-Hispanic White (Table 6.1). In Storm Lake, this proportion has fallen to slightly less than 50 percent, and no racial or ethnic group composes a majority. Non-Hispanic Whites remain the clear plurality in Storm

TABLE 6.1   Post-treatment (2010) Comparisons of Iowa Communities across Population, Ethnicity, and Socioeconomic Status

	Iowa	Boone	Carroll	Harlan	Perry	Storm Lake
Population[a]	3.05 mil[c]	12,661	10,103	5,106	7,702	10,600
Ethnic composition						
Percent non-Hispanic White[a]	88.7	95.5	95.2	95.8	61.1	48.2
Percent Latino[a]	5.0	2.0	2.4	1.9	35.0	36.1
Percent foreign born[b]	3.8	1.2	1.2	0.9	21.8	23.8
Socioeconomic status						
Percentage with bachelor's degree or higher[b]	24.2	17.5	19.3	18.6	10.8	24.2
Percentage of individuals below the poverty line[b]	11.5	15.0	11.0	9.5	15.1	15.8
Median household income[b]	$48,052	$43,256	$43,710	$38,881	$35,881	$39,510
Per capita income[b]	$25,060	$22,611	$24,310	$22,496	$16,885	$17,083

[a] *Source:* 2010 U.S. Census.
[b] *Source:* American Community Survey Estimates, 2005–2009.
[c] mil, million.

Lake but are no longer the majority. A look at the public schools indicates that non-Hispanic White students have become a much smaller proportion of the schools since immigrants began to arrive. At Storm Lake High School, Latinos represent the largest ethnic group (Table 6.2). In Perry, non-Hispanic Whites still compose a majority of students in the high school. Without a refugee population, Latinos make up the only real minority group in Perry, composing 40 percent of students.

There are three potential reasons for the growth of the non-White population. First, it could simply be that new migrants have come at continuingly high

TABLE 6.2   Post-treatment Comparison of Public High Schools in Iowa Study Towns, 2008–2009

	Boone High School	Carroll High School	Harlan High School	Perry High School	Storm Lake High School
School size/enrollment	726	578	597	566	682
Percentage on free/ reduced lunch	23.8	24.6	25.1	54.1	47.8
Percent non-Hispanic White	95.9	96.7	96.8	57.8	41.3
Percent Latino	2.0	1.9	1.5	40.4	43.5
Percent Black	1.3	0.9	1.1	0.9	3.5
Percent Asian	1.1	0.5	0.3	0.7	11.6

Source: National Center for Education Statistics in the Common Core of Data for 1990–1991 academic year.

TABLE 6.3 Asian and Hispanic Population Change in Perry and Storm Lake, 1990–2010

	Perry	Storm Lake
Percent change in Asian population (1990–2000)	+317	+160
Percent change in Asian population (2000–2010)	+14	+26
Percent change in Hispanic population (1990–2000)	+3,885	+1,979
Percent change in Hispanic population (2000–2010)	+43	+71

Source: 1990, 2000, and 2010 Decennial Census.

levels. However, the non-White population in these towns today is mostly native-born. Fewer than a quarter of all of the residents were born outside the United States: 23.8 percent in Storm Lake and 21.8 percent in Perry. Thus, a majority (about 54 percent) of those who are Hispanic or Asian (a group composing a substantial 9.8 percent of Storm Lake's population) were born in the United States, and many of them were born in these communities.[7] Further, in both Perry and Storm Lake, immigration has leveled off significantly since 2000 (Table 6.3). In both towns,, the continued growth in these populations is significant but nowhere near the size of the growth during the 1990s. Residents believe that the populations in these towns are stabilizing after a very turbulent 20 year period. According to Dale Carver, the longtime Storm Lake resident, "The workforce has stabilized. Turnover is down. The transient population is going. . . . We have business owners of all different ethnic backgrounds now and have had for several years."

Another reason the non-White population is shrinking is that some of the immigrant groups, particularly Latinos, have higher fertility rates than Anglos. According to the U.S. National Center for Health Statistics, the average fertility rates for Hispanics from 1990–2007 was consistently higher than that of any other racial/ethnic group—that is, 2.88 children for Hispanics, compared with 1.93 for Asians, 2.15 for African Americans, and 2.06 for non-Hispanic Whites.

Finally, it is also possible that the Anglo community has left the diverse towns. In other meatpacking towns, there has been some concern about "white flight," especially from the public schools. An article in the *Omaha World Herald* from 2004 quotes White, Anglo families in Schuyler, Nebraska, home of an Excel plant, who had switched their children to a nearby school with fewer Hispanic students.[8] The sociologist Lourdes Gouveia argues that merely looking at the drops in Anglo enrollment may not indicate significant white flight. The Whites who make up these communities are often older and have fewer children than the Latino immigrants who move in. Across Iowa and other rural states, enrollment had been declining among Whites for many years preceding the arrival of immigrants. In Harlan, for example, the enrollment in the high school did not grow at all between 1990 and 2008. Thus, had immigrants never moved into Perry and Storm Lake, enrollment would likely have stagnated or declined.

There is little concern among the community leaders with whom I spoke about a mass exodus of the White population. There is recognition that some unknown—but likely small—proportion of the population has left because they did not like what was happening. Councilman Eddie Diaz of Perry said, "I think it's just reasonable to assume that some people have [left], just going through the history of our country. . . . I wouldn't doubt it for a minute. [But] I don't think it's a huge percentage." Michael Hanna, a former principal at Storm Lake High School, stated in 2003, "Storm Lake has not experienced White flight; the district has an open enrollment policy, and more families are choosing to join the school community than to leave it."[9]

For many of those most concerned about being overrun by Latinos or Asians, the source of the demographic change does not matter. They do not particularly care whether the Anglo population is moving away or the number of immigrant children has exploded. They believe that as Whites decrease in number relative to non-Whites, their communities and schools are worse off. They would look with alarm at the data in Table 6.2 showing that the two schools in the immigrant-receiving communities have the highest poverty levels, as measured by the percentage of students on the free/reduced lunch program. It is worth noting, then, that Table 6.1 demonstrates that even as Perry and Storm Lake have become more ethnically diverse, their economic profiles are not substantially different from those of Boone, Carroll, and Harlan. They have higher poverty rates than Carroll or Harlan but a similar rate to that of Boone. Perry has a smaller percentage of residents with bachelor's degrees than the other communities; Storm Lake's high rate is likely attributable its being the home of Buena Vista University. Median household incomes in Perry and Storm Lake are similar to those in Harlan. Thus, despite increasing diversity, the communities' economic profiles remain comparable.

In addition to dropping rates of immigration into Storm Lake, the Iowa Bureau of Refugee Services and the nonprofit Lutheran Services in Iowa, agencies that have brought many refugees to the state, announced in 2010 that they would be closing their doors because of lack of funding.[10] Their closing is expected to lead to a significant decline in the number of refugees resettling in Iowa over the next several years. Unless significant changes take place in the economy or in public policy, the growth in the Latino population over the next several years will be primarily due to differences in fertility rates among the families who already live in Iowa. Congressman Steve King has suggested that the country adopt a "fertility plan" to encourage Whites to have more babies as a way to counter Iowa's population losses and potential labor shortages, but his plan has not gained much attention or support.[11]

Nostalgia for the Past

These statistics are unlikely to reassure many of those who feel their community is being flooded with immigrants. This feeling is less about the real numbers of immigrants compared with longtime residents than about a sense of loss or dislocation on the part of the natives. Even if Latinos and other ethnic groups continue to be a minority, the community is not the same place as the one old-timers remember. The idyllic places they remember from childhood, where everyone knew everyone else and where everyone felt a sense of kinship with others, is gone. "Nothing holds the town together anymore," one septuagenarian resident of Perry told me, capturing the feeling that the town he has long known has disappeared.

It is hard to know how many of these sentiments are due to the demographic changes in the community and how many are simply a product of an older population that looks back on the past with rose-colored glasses. John Mueller writes that people have a "tendency to look backward with misty eyes, to see the past as much more benign, simple, and innocent than it really was. No matter how much better the present gets, the past gets better with reflection, and we are, accordingly, always notably worse off than we used to be."[12] A nationwide poll taken in 1996 showed that a majority of adults of all ages think things were better in the past than they are today and that this tendency rises with age and declines with income and education.[13] The older and relatively lower-status residents who make up a significant portion of these small towns likely would have longed for the "good old days" even if not one single immigrant had ever settled in the towns, only now they have a group to hold responsible for the changes they perceive as negative.

Some older long-term residents of small towns remember only the good things about their communities, despite the fact that rural communities have always had divisions and problems. There have always been those who do not feel they fully belong. One longtime resident of a small community in Michigan summed up this sentiment with this statement: "I've only been here in Mapleville for 23 years. I've raised four children here. So I'm not really from here. You have to live here for five generations for people to say you're from here."[14] There have always also been class divisions and social stratification in small towns. It is different in many ways from the stratification seen in urban areas, but we must remember that small towns have never been utopian communities where literally everyone knows and cares for everyone else.[15] For those who look back wistfully, the disputes and divisions that existed prior to the immigrants' arrival, as well as the economic problems of the 1970s and 1980s, are forgotten. No data will persuade these folks that things are not worse today than they used to be. In Perry and Storm Lake, this population is a small and shrinking minority.

Social and Political Displacement

Finally, in addition to the demographic profiles of the communities, an underlying and often unspoken part of the fear of being overrun is a concern that immigrants and their children will displace longtime residents politically and socially. People may be concerned about the numbers of immigrants themselves, but more problematic is the idea that once there is a critical mass, this group could wield considerable power in these small communities. It is possible that some of the concerns about being overrun with immigrants could be assuaged if natives knew that immigrants would continue to have very little real power or influence in their communities.

The immigrants in both Perry and Storm Lake have for the most part shied away from community affairs and have little interest in displacing the Anglo population. Voter turnout among Hispanics in elections has started to grow but is still minuscule compared with their proportions of the population. Some of this is no doubt due to ineligibility of non-citizens to vote, but many believe there is a more significant problem than simply legal status. For example, Perry's mayor identified about 300 registered voters in 2008 who had Hispanic surnames. In total, about 2,700 people voted in 2008 in Perry. If every Latino who was registered to vote did so, this population would have totaled no more than 11 percent of the electorate, even though this group makes up a third of the town's overall population. The mayor believes there is no way that the remaining Latinos are not legally eligible to vote. Instead, there are two related problems. Many of the Latino residents lack interest in and knowledge about politics, and there is not enough formal mobilization of Latinos.

General civic involvement within the Latino community is also lacking. Several members of the Perry Rotary and Lions Clubs told me they do not have any Latino members. Again, some believed there is little interest on the part of immigrants to join these organizations. Others admitted that the meetings often occur in the middle of the day, which is prohibitive for many hourly workers or small business owners. Although no one admitted this was the case, historically it has also been common for newcomers to be excluded from civic organizations.[16] According to several leaders in the immigrant community, the Latinos in Perry are just starting to become aware of these opportunities. As the director of an immigrant advocacy center, Guadalupe Duarte has given a few well-received presentations to the local Kiwanis group but is not a member himself.

Some Anglo community leaders also discussed their concerns about so-called tokenism and burnout among the Latinos who do participate. In each of these communities, any non-White person who gets involves may suddenly find himself or herself being asked to participate in numerous activities. According to one person who spoke off the record, these people are "getting pulled in thirty different directions" and will soon burn out. There are not enough Latinos or Asians who show high levels of interest and have the time, resources, or political skills to get involved. When they do step up, they may find themselves sitting on every board in town.

Ironically, one of the biggest complaints among longtime Anglo residents about the Latino and Asian communities was their lack of involvement in community activities. Justin Yarosevich of Storm Lake described these sentiments. "There are people in the community who want it to happen like that," he said, snapping his fingers. They think, "If 30 percent of the community is Laotian, then 30 percent should be on every board and commission." Some residents seem to take it personally when immigrants do not participate in community activities, viewing this as a sign that immigrants do not care about the communities in which they have settled. They see it as just one more sign of immigrants' unwillingness to accept American social norms.

The irony is that when immigrants do get involved, they run the risk of being seen as too aggressive; as pushing too hard and demanding change too fast; and as stepping out of their prescribed place in society. On the one hand, some people seem to be concerned about being displaced by immigrants, but on the other, native residents resent it when newcomers do not jump at the chance to be involved in community activities. Immigrants are in a Catch-22 and sometimes find they have to walk a fine line.

"Immigrants Reduce Opportunities for Natives"

Another concern expressed by some long-time residents of small towns is related to the effect of immigrants on the opportunities available for native-born workers and their children. In particular, some rural residents are upset about the effect of cheap immigrant labor on local job opportunities. Based on political rhetoric, one might assume most people—especially those in rural areas—believe that immigrants take jobs from natives; however, this group is actually a minority. The Iowa Poll conducted in 2007 showed that only 36 percent of Iowans believed that immigrants "take jobs from legal residents," and a majority, 54 percent, believed that immigrants "take jobs that legal residents don't want."[17] Further, Iowans do not hold immigrants—even undocumented immigrants—responsible for the immigration situation. The same poll showed that 83 percent of Iowans believed employers who hire undocumented immigrants are to blame when undocumented immigrants are found working in Iowa. Only 9 percent blamed the immigrants.

Although most economists agree that immigrants help economic growth and expand the demand for goods and services, much of this work is not focused on the effects of immigrants on small-town America. The dilemma for small towns today is that there seems to be a choice: these towns can choose between inviting low-skilled immigrant labor and dealing with the resulting influx of Latino, Asian, or African families, or they can risk becoming ghost towns. Describing the situation in many rural areas, Mark Grey and his colleagues write, "Over the last two decades, there have been three kinds of Iowa communities: urban areas such as Des Moines that have grown with relatively diverse economies and burgeoning suburbs; rural communities that are shrinking and aging rapidly; and towns that have grown with immigration."[18]

Numerous small towns across the United States are either teetering on the edge or have already lost their populations. Patrick Carr and Maria Kefalas point out, "For every thriving metropolis now, there are dozens of agroindustrial brain-drain areas where economic growth has stalled."[19] Examples are not hard to find: the local aluminum plant in Ravenswood, West Virginia (pop. 4,000), closed in 2009, leaving nearly 700 people unemployed. Although it has since reopened, residents of Georgetown, South Carolina (pop. 9,000), were worried when the local steel mill closed in 2009. Newton, Iowa (pop. 15,000), lost the Maytag Corporation and its 2,500 jobs when, in 2006, it was acquired by Whirlpool.[20] Since then, many other businesses in Newton have either boarded up or had to lay off many workers, an elementary school closed, and the city budget has been cut dramatically. A report by *60 Minutes* stated, "Even the local chapter of the Optimists Club has closed."[21]

According to Kate Bronfenbrenner, a labor relations professor, "We had ghost towns in the past. We could have them again."[22] In his book about the effects of globalization on the Midwest, the journalist and Pulitzer Prize nominee Richard Longworth (also native of Boone) disagrees and argues that, unlike those in the Great Plains, the towns will not die. Instead, "They'll keep their schools and hospitals, government offices, gas stations and Wal-Marts, which are the biggest private-sector employer in many of them. Some will be cheap places to live for people who work in the nearest city."[23] Postindustrial ghost towns, then, will have a "zero-sum economy" where people work in service jobs and essentially pay one another.[24]

So residents of small towns have only a few models in their efforts to survive. They can refuse to allow factories or plants because they want to keep out immigrants, or they can embrace these changes. When Oscar Mayer's Perry plant sold out to IBP in 1988, it was just another in a long line of old line packers to close or sell. Even so, most people agree that Perry was much better off than the communities whose plants closed for good. Some residents were displaced, but as immigrants poured into the community, instead of boarding up, local businesses grew. New ones opened. Instead of consolidating with other small-town schools, enrollment in Perry and Storm Lake climbed, eventually creating more jobs for teachers and school staff. As of 2010, Perry's population had grown by 16 percent since 1990 and Storm Lake's, by 21 percent. In the non-immigrant-receiving communities in this study, Boone and Carroll managed basically to maintain their numbers, but Harlan's population declined by nearly 1 percent since 1990. Boone has been helped because of its proximity to Iowa State University in Ames. Carroll has maintained its population by becoming a retail hub for much of southwestern Iowa. Harlan has suffered from the same fate as most other small towns that continue to rely heavily on agriculture and that lack a manufacturing or retail base.

Although a few longtime residents argue that Perry would be better off if Tyson shut its doors and left town, most recognize that the community depends mightily on these plants. One does not need to imagine what might happen if Tyson closes its Perry or Storm Lake facilities. In Garden City, Kansas, one of the nation's largest beef-packing plants burned down in 2000, putting 2,300 people out of work. After the fire, public school enrollment declined by 300 students, and crime in the town increased.[25] More recently, the hog slaughtering plant in Sioux City, Iowa, closed in April 2010, citing a bad economy, aging infrastructure at the plant, and reduced consumer demand. After leaving 1,400 workers out of a job, this community's jobless rate rose steadily for months. In March 2011, the city purchased the plant and received a federal grant to raze the facility to build a business park. Another pork processor, Global Foods Processing, committed to constructing a new facility that would employ about 200 workers, a far cry from the number left out of work when the other plant closed.[26] Smithfield Foods also closed six other pork plants in 2009 in small towns in North Carolina, Virginia, Florida, Kansas, Ohio, and Nebraska.

Immigration and Customs Enforcement (ICE) raids have also led to significant changes in many meatpacking plants and the towns that host them. A raid by ICE at a poultry-processing plant in Stillmore, Georgia, in 2006 led to 120 arrests, the loss of a third of the town's population, and substantial drops in local business activity.[27] Following the raid, the plant recruited and hired local African Americans and paid increased wages as a way to attract workers. The plant even hired homeless people from a nearby mission and transported convicted felons from a local halfway house. But high turnover among the new workers, along with lower productivity and labor disputes, has left the company unsure about the future.[28] In Cactus, Texas, an ICE raid in 2006 left "the streets of this small, isolated city in the Texas panhandle ... virtually empty."[29] Similar stories have emerged from Lauren, Mississippi; Greeley, Colorado; Grand Island, Nebraska; and Worthington, Minnesota, among other small towns whose factories were raided as part of the Bush administration's policies in 2006 and 2007. In Alabama, farmers have had a very difficult time finding workers since the state's anti-immigration measures took effect, forcing them to leave crops to die on the vine in some cases.[30] In Albertville, Alabama, 123 children withdrew from the public schools within days of the measures' effective date.[31] In some places, such as Grand Island, the plants have hired refugees to replace the immigrants who were either arrested or fled after the raid.

In most other places, such as Postville, Iowa, the immigration raids have devastated the community. Postville (pop. 2,200) has become the quintessential example of many things, both positive and negative: the effects of globalization on small towns and, in particular, the meatpacking industry's reliance on a global market and labor force; a homogeneous small town's initial suspicion about and eventual acceptance of outsiders (in this case, a group Hasidic Jews from New York); and the devastating effects of ineffective immigration policies, especially the use of high-profile raids. Postville—or "Hometown to the World," as it now calls itself—became the home of a kosher slaughterhouse and meatpacking facility in the late 1980s, prompting hundreds of Hasidic Jews to move to a community that, like Perry and Storm Lake, had been composed of White, Anglo, Christian residents.[32] As the plant became more productive and successful, immigrants and refugees from around the world settled in Postville to work in the plant.

After a decade, Postville was seen as a huge success. A story on National Public Radio in 1998 described Postville as "an experiment that has worked and has shown that if people want to, they can do it."[33] By "it," the reporter meant acceptance of diversity. Examples of diversity's success in Postville look much like what has occurred in Perry and Storm Lake, including the election of an ethnic-minority member to the City Council, an official rebuke of white-supremacist hate literature, and an exchange trip of community leaders to Mexico. In 2008, the plant, Agriprocessors, was raided; nearly 400 undocumented workers were arrested, and many eventually deported. Its owner has been prosecuted for financial fraud and money laundering and sentenced to 27 years in prison. The plant closed until July 2009, when it was purchased and renamed. As of April 2010, the plant was slaughtering only about 18 percent of the cows it had killed prior to the raid.[34] The town's population has shrunk by at least 40 percent. The local economy is in shambles, leading to steep losses in tax and utility revenue and higher rates for those who stayed. Several businesses closed, especially those that were Latino-owned and other businesses that served the immigrant community. Ripple effects continue outside the town: local farmers who provided livestock have had to find a new market, and the country's kosher meat supply has taken a devastating blow.[35]

Thus, although some residents of ethnically diverse small towns may wish to "go back to the good old days," most recognize that the experience in Postville could very well be their own. When the Postville plant was raided, Viivi Shirley, then the mayor of Perry, stated, "Thank God it wasn't Perry."[36] It is certainly true that millions of Americans who worked in the manufacturing sector in the 1960s and 1970s have lost out with the new economy. Whether factories have moved overseas or have brought in workers from other countries, one cannot deny that some Americans have borne the brunt of these changes. It is important, however, to remember that change in the manufacturing sector is only one of many economic factors that have contributed to the demographic changes that were to take place in towns like Perry and Storm Lake. Shirley said that when she moved to town in 1963, Perry was thriving, but "then the railroad closed and that was pretty devastating. And then the farm crisis." And, then, of course, came the years of labor concessions and the eventual sale of Oscar Mayer. It is impossible to isolate any one of these events as the culprit in the displacement of so many formerly middle-class Anglo Americans.

For their part, the native-born adolescents were not very concerned about immigrants' taking jobs or reducing their economic opportunities. There were no significant differences in opinion about whether immigrants take jobs from natives between those in the diverse communities and those in the homogeneous ones. Further, the focus groups in Perry in 2002 indicated that many students believed the meatpacking plant had contributed positively to the health of the community. The main negative comment about the plant was that it smelled bad, causing the towns to be "dirtier" or "stinky." When asked whether Perry would be a better place without the plant, students said:

Kyle: It's OK to have [the plant] because it provides jobs for people.

Caitlin: I think [the plant] is good. I think we could use something else besides the plant, like some other work job, you know. But I think it's good.

Josh: I think [if the plant left], it would make a huge difference. IBP is more or less running this town, and before it was Oscar Mayer running the town. . . . Things have happened—some of the money comes from there. They sponsor a lot of things, so they're keeping this town going, actually. So if they're, like, done, this town would slump.

On the subject of an additional 300 jobs and more immigrants moving to town, students said:

Brent: I guess it'd be an alright thing if it was just gonna be a whole bunch of honest work, hardworking people coming in. I guess if they were coming to get the job done, it'd be fine. . . .

Jason: It'd be alright. More jobs for more people to help the economy.

These sentiments might be chalked up to naiveté, to young people who simply lack understanding of the local economy or the effects of immigration. Taking the comments at face value, they indicate an underlying lack of concern about any threat to their opportunities. Like many Americans, these young people see their success as an individual matter and unrelated to structural changes in the economy. Considering that so many native-born rural youth leave the communities of their birth and never return, it is not unrealistic for them to believe that the newcomers in their towns are unlikely to have a significant effect on their life chances.

Costs to Public Services

In the initial years after diversification began, there were substantial increases in costs to local public schools, hospitals, and law enforcement. Katherine Fennelly and Christopher Federico demonstrate that rural residents are especially concerned about the costs of immigration, particularly beliefs that immigrants are a burden to the country.[37] Native residents concerned about public spending on immigrants worry not only about budgetary issues but also about their own access to these services and about sharing the burden of paying for them. When hundreds of people migrate into towns with fewer than 10,000 people, there is a significant effect on the availability of housing, school resources, public health, and crime. In Perry and Storm Lake, this was exacerbated by the fact that the influx consisted of so many who did not speak English and had low-income jobs with no health benefits (at least at first). These increases led some natives to believe that immigrants are merely a sponge, soaking up the community's free public services.

A report by the nonpartisan Congressional Budget Office in 2007 found that in the aggregate and over time, tax revenues from immigrants exceed costs of services. However, the report also states, "Many estimates also show that the cost of providing public services to unauthorized immigrants at the state and local levels exceeds what the population pays in state and local taxes."[38] Local and state governments are mandated to provide services related to law enforcement, education, and health care, regardless of residents' legal or income status. Thus, localities bear the brunt of many of the costs associated with rapid ethnic diversification.

The increase in costs is often reported, but what gets less attention is that many of these costs dissipate over time. First, immigrants to rural America had made substantial gains by the early 2000s. In just a decade, fewer rural immigrants were living in poverty, and the median household income had risen. Meatpacking plants and other work in rural manufacturing had given many immigrants in small towns a foothold on economic stability and the working or middle class.[39] As the rates of immigration slow down, some of the early concerns about costs associated with crime, housing, uncompensated medical care, and additional school instruction have subsided. Once employees at the meatpacking plants stay on for several months, they become eligible for health insurance, reducing the uncompensated medical costs at local public hospitals. Concerns about crime have always been outsized compared with the statistics. Although police forces still find the need to use translators and liaisons within the immigrant communities, some of these costs have declined and will continue to do so.

At the schools, according to Angelica Diaz-Cardenas, an alumna and current staff member at Perry High School, one of the most significant changes in the past ten years has been the declining use of ESL services. When she arrived as a high school student in Perry in the mid-1990s, she says,

> There were five or six of us in ESL, and then you saw the numbers increase [quickly]. Then [there were], like, two or three different ESL teachers just at the high school level to keep up with all the newcomers that were coming in with no English. I mean, [these were] just new students. And right now, we're seeing that decreasing, our number of Hispanic or Latino students who are coming into the school not knowing English. I mean, we have only a few.

In addition to decreasing numbers of ESL students, housing problems have eased, according to government officials, as the communities have stabilized and immigrants have become permanent residents in town. In Storm Lake, Justin Yarosevich explained that the community would like to see more renters become homeowners, but there several mitigating problems with that goal in this economic period. The more serious issue the community has suffered through since the early 1990s is a lack of housing, and this problem has been reduced significantly.

It is also important to remember that small towns and rural areas have long been notoriously underserved. Rural areas, just like inner cities, have problems recruiting doctors, nurses, teachers, school administrators, and law enforcement officers.[40] They also have small tax bases from which to work, so budgets are often difficult to balance, even without rapid demographic change. It is not as if these communities went from being financially safe and secure, with all their needs easily met, to having huge shortfalls and unmet needs. This does not downplay the significant burden of population growth to public services in the early years. But we must remember that not only were things never easy in rural towns, but the runaway costs have declined significantly over time.

Finally, not only have costs associated with immigrants dissipated, but these groups have contributed significantly by helping to revitalize other economic sectors. Retail establishments that might have been on the verge of collapse in dying rural areas have been brought back to life by immigrant shoppers. Smaller local manufacturing companies in small towns, as well as farmers in the area, also benefit from the continued presence of the food processing plants. Farmers take their livestock to the plants; others grow food for the livestock to eat. Many local industries produce and sell implements and other necessary equipment to the farmers. Each of these businesses employs many residents across rural America. Communities also have had to hire new people in professional occupations, such as health care workers and teachers. As Sandra Madsen, a former mayor of Storm Lake, told the *Nation* magazine in an interview in 1997, the locally owned banks were thriving, and unlike the blight in other regional small towns, Storm Lake had a stable downtown with no vacancies. Madsen then stated, "Five years from now I think this town will realize we are all better off for the change we have gone through."[41]

There is also a great deal of upward mobility for the immigrant population. After a few years, some immigrants leave their backbreaking jobs at the plants and open small businesses of their own, contributing to the local economy and tax base more directly. Some immigrants open businesses that cater primarily to other migrants, but over time some of these companies begin to serve the Anglo community, as well. Other immigrants leave the plants to take less dangerous jobs at smaller manufacturing firms, and some obtain white-collar jobs in banks, schools, and other industries that now demand bilingual services.

Quality of Schools

One last factor in the concern about a reduction in opportunities, particularly for young people, is that immigrants will cause the quality of the schools to suffer. As discussed earlier, some of the issue concerns increasing costs, but there is more to this fear than simply worry about public budgets. Parents worry that immigrant students will pull down the average test scores, which could jeopardize school funding in today's educational environment. For example, the increasing diversity of the pool of test takers has been blamed for the drops in national average SAT scores in 2010.[42] Some also may worry that immigrant students lead to a reallocation of school resources—away from advanced placement and other honors curricula, for example, toward ESL and other remedial education that targets children of immigrants.[43] Finally, some parents may worry that because immigrant children tend to require more time and energy from teachers, good teachers will not be attracted to schools with high proportions of immigrants.

In Chapter 2 we saw that, before the immigrants arrived, the five schools in the study started off at roughly the same place in available measures of school quality. The data indicate there have been some changes in Perry and Storm Lake since 1990. At that time, the five schools paid teachers roughly the same salaries, and teachers had similar levels of education and years of experience. Now, teachers in each of the five communities are still paid roughly the same, but the teachers at Perry High School and Storm Lake High School differ from the others in their average years of work experience and percentage who hold master's degrees (Table 6.4). The principals at these schools discussed the problems associated with keeping their best teachers. They both told me that urban districts can afford to pay more; this is a problem especially in Perry, located only 50 miles from Des Moines. Dan Marburger, the principal of Perry High School, explains:

> One thing we've found is that because of our staff development, and initiatives on how to teach reading and how to overcome poverty and all the things we do, we turn out some pretty good teachers who then get hired away from us. A few years ago, the elementary school lost six teachers just to Ankeny [a nearby town]. . . . We train pretty good teachers. When they come here, they don't have those skills, but when they're here 5–6 years and they're starting to become that master teacher, they go out and interview and people say, "You've got a lot of experience with diversity and a lot of things."

Teresa Coenen, Storm Lake High School's principal at the time, concurred: "The minute [we] send a teacher off to a national training, we realize that we are very potentially training them to leave us. But yet you want them to have the training." So the problem is not that good teachers do not go to or want to stay in Perry and Storm Lake. Rather, they obtain training and experience that makes them attractive to other districts, and they are essentially stolen away.

Principal Marburger told me that one of the main ways Perry High School has found success attracting Latino teachers and keeping others of its best teachers is by "growing [its] own." The school tries to attract former students to come back to Perry as teachers. Other small towns with large proportions of immigrants have also tried this strategy. The school district in Garden City, Kansas, offered college scholarships to students who agreed to return to the

TABLE 6.4   Teacher Quality and Student Test Scores in Public High Schools in Iowa Towns, 2008–2009

	Boone High School	Carroll High School	Harlan High School	Perry High School	Storm Lake High School
Average teacher salary[a]	$48,664	$46,922	$44,168	$45,913	$47,510[d]
Average teacher years of experience[a]	13.4	13.7	10.5	5.9	6.0
Percentage of teachers with master's degree[a]	32	26	24	20	15
Percentage of students scoring proficient or higher on Iowa state test[b]	77.4	72.0	83.2	73.0	69.4
Graduation rate[c] (%)	89.1	90.7	94.5	88.9	60.2

[a] *Source:* "Teacher Pay in Iowa," searchable database of 30,000 full- and part-time public schoolteachers licensed by the State of Iowa for the 2008–2009 school year, available online at http://data.desmoinesregister.com/teachersalaries/iowa-teacher-salaries.php.

[b] *Source:* Iowa Public K–12 School Rankings, based on data from the Iowa School Profiles provided by the Iowa Department of Education for the 2008–2009 year, available online at http://www.psk12.com/rating/USindexphp/STATE_IA.html.

[c] *Source:* Data from the Iowa Department of Education based on the 2008–2009 academic year.

[d] This is the average salary at Storm Lake High School after eliminating one teacher who earned $82,000 per year. The next-highest salary was $58,000.

community as instructors.[44] Of course, this takes many years and is not a viable solution to the immediate problem of losing a district's best teachers to higher-paying jobs in other communities. Because of the differences in skills required by and taught to teachers in Perry and Storm Lake, these districts need to be able to increase their teachers' salaries and other benefits dramatically to stay competitive. This has not happened, unfortunately, and has led to lower levels of experience and education among teachers.

Although the school administrators admit that keeping their best teachers is an ongoing problem, it does not seem to have universally harmed the quality of the education the young people are getting, at least as measured by scores on state-mandated tests and by graduation rates. Perry High School has scores similar to Boone's and slightly higher scores than Carroll. Storm Lake's scores are lower than those in the other towns, but not substantially so. Nearly 70 percent of students in Storm Lake score proficient or higher on the Iowa Tests of Educational Development. Perry's graduation rate is similar to that of the homogeneous schools. Storm Lake's is considerably lower, which at first glance has led many people to believe the problem is the high level of diversity at the school. Coenen, however, explained what is really going on:

> [Storm Lake High School] has a program by which our students can go on to a fifth year of instruction at the high school's expense to finish up and get an associate's degree before [they] ever get out of high school.

We are the only charter school like that in the state. . . . The charter now has become such that out of 158 graduates [in 2010], 74 signed up for the charter school, which means they're going to go one more year at the community college. Most will be on the Fort Dodge campus [of Iowa Central Community College]. We bus them back and forth every day. At our expense. So that's half the class. That's huge.

Each student who chooses to go for a fifth year is seen statistically as a non-graduate, thereby dragging the graduation rate of the school down. In reality, of course, the students taking advantage of this program not only graduate from high school, but they get a foothold in higher education and earn an associate's degree.

Another problem contributing to the low graduation rates is that Storm Lake has a policy of educating any student who shows up at the door, even those who are older than 18 and will not be able to graduate because of their age. In Iowa, as long as a student enrolls before age 21, he or she has a right to attend a public school. At 21, however, he or she cannot attend public school any longer. Some schools push students like this into a general equivalency diploma (GED) program, but Storm Lake High School does not. She used the following as an example:

We had a cluster of students this year who came from Vietnam . . . in the 18–20 year range. One was over 21, and we couldn't take the student. Their goal was language acquisition and a high school diploma. The only way that's going to happen is here. We could send them to get a GED, but we could tell them they can only be here for two years and they'll never get a diploma, and they still want to be here. They know they're going to learn more English and learn more educational things than if they just prepared for a GED.

These two factors, she believes, account for the substantially lower graduation rates at Storm Lake High School. She views both of these programs positively and believes that they are worth the school's taking a hit in statewide rankings on graduation rates.

The evidence is mixed, then, about whether the schools have suffered as a result of the arrival of immigrants. Test scores and graduation rates, especially in Storm Lake, are lower than the other schools. Experienced and more highly educated teachers do not stay in Perry or Storm Lake as long as they do in the other schools. To some people, these data indicate a problem associated with immigrants. To others, however, they indicate that there is a problem with the measurement, especially with regard to graduation rates. They tend to see the problem not with the immigrant students, but with the lack of resources that highly diverse schools need, compared with economically and ethnically homogeneous populations.

"Immigrants Will Not Assimilate"

Finally, a significant concern for many small-town residents is the notion that immigrants do not wish to "assimilate." There are multiple definitions and conceptions of this term, but in general, people with this concern are worried that immigrants today do not wish to shed their native ethnic identities in favor of becoming "real Americans." Some natives believe that immigrants do not want to share American experiences or history and be incorporated into a common cultural life.[45] As evidence for these beliefs, people point out that migrants do not become active in the community, cannot speak English, and keep to themselves.[46] This belief is perhaps most clearly expressed by former the U.S. representative and presidential candidate Thomas Tancredo:

> Today's immigrants have a much different attitude than immigrants who settled here one hundred years ago. This newer, post-modern wave of immigrants isn't assimilating into our culture because, unlike their predecessors, they have adopted a kind of parasitic approach to the United States. They aren't interested in becoming citizens; they simply want to attach themselves to their American host and feed off of it while maintaining their native identities and cultures.[47]

When immigrants cannot speak English, many natives perceive this as a sign that they do not *want* to learn English and that they therefore do not *want* to become an American. Similarly, if immigrants live in ethnic enclaves and befriend other immigrants, it is seen as a sign that they are segregating themselves because they do not *want* to be friends with natives or join in community-wide activities. There is also resistance and resentment when immigrants celebrate their heritage through festivals or parades, activities some see as anti-American.

When political scientists think about assimilation, they often consider Robert Dahl's model in which immigrant groups gradually (in about three generations) become assimilated into mainstream society.[48] His study of the Irish and Italian immigrants to New Haven, Connecticut, in the early and mid-twentieth century suggested that immigrants came to behave—socially, economically, and politically—like native-born Americans once they rose out of the lower class. There are, of course, many problems with this and other similar notions of assimilation that presume immigrants must, at some level, give up their ethnic heritages in favor of a dominant American culture. This chapter does not intend to pass judgment about whether immigrants should have to assimilate or whether fears about under-assimilation are ethnocentric and xenophobic in nature. Instead, this section acknowledges that this is a serious concern among some native-born residents of small communities and examines whether their concerns have a basis in reality. In essence, it leaves the normative judgments about assimilation to others.

I am certainly not the first to point out the difficulty of learning a new language as an adult, especially without classes or time to devote to honing this skill.[49] By all accounts, when employers or religious groups have provided opportunities for immigrants to learn English, the classes usually fill to capacity. Others have also called attention to the aspect of human nature that causes people to seek out others who are most like them, people with whom they feel kinship or a sense of security.[50] Ethnic enclaves in these Iowa communities are often trailer parks or apartment complexes on the outskirts of town—places where many immigrants come to live when they first arrive, primarily due to social networks and affordability. When they are able, immigrants leave these places in favor of ethnically mixed residential neighborhoods within town. Given the physical layout of these communities, once one leaves the trailer parks, it is nearly impossible to find anywhere else to live besides ethnically integrated neighborhoods. With the exception of the most affluent neighborhoods, there is relatively little ethnic segregation. Longtime Anglo residents live side by side with Hispanic and Asian newcomers, regardless of their wishes.

Finally, history demonstrates that there really is nothing new under the sun. With every wave of immigration to the United States, first-generation immigrants are believed not to Americanize quickly enough for natives.[51] In the early twentieth century, first-generation Italians, Eastern Europeans, and Germans continued to use their native languages throughout their lives. In many Iowa towns, it was not uncommon for churches to hold services in German, Swedish, or even Latvian until well into the twentieth century. To this day, several Iowa communities celebrate their German heritage; annual German festivals take place in the Amana Colonies and in the towns of Manning and Davenport. In 2011, the 31st annual Tivoli Fest in Elk Horn, Iowa, celebrated the town's Danish heritage, complete with a flag ceremony in which both the American and Danish flags were raised.

Richard Alba and Victor Nee have suggested a new definition of assimilation that moves beyond the normative debate and gets at the underlying idea of what it means in today's society for immigrants to be fully incorporated.[52] They define this as the state when one's life chances are at parity with those of mainstream groups, without regard to racial or ethnic background. Helen Marrow points out that this type of assimilation is easier for immigrants in rural America than in urban areas. The local economic norm in rural areas and small towns is usually more achievable than that in urban areas, where costs of living are higher and opportunities for social and economic mobility are reduced. Marrow states, "Indeed, rural and small-town Americans often take great pride in their working- or lower-middle class identity, whereas urban natives' ideas of what constitutes the local economic mainstream may both imply and require a higher level of educational or occupational attainment."[53] She finds in the rural South, as I do in the Midwest, that the low-wage jobs in meatpacking often allow (some) immigrants to achieve a measure of economic stability and sometimes even upward mobility. In Perry and Storm Lake, as in other similar communities, some immigrants leave meatpacking in favor of less dangerous jobs that offer great upward mobility for them and their children.[54]

An important but often overlooked aspect of immigration into rural areas is that the migrants who choose to move to and reside in small towns are often different from those who choose to live in urban areas. People who choose to live in small communities appreciate the benefits of this lifestyle. A significant majority of immigrants come from rural backgrounds in the countries of their birth and so towns like Perry or Storm Lake feel much more like home than New York City or Chicago. They value the tranquility, strong social networks, and opportunities for their children to remain in small, safe schools where the temptations of the big city—drugs, gangs, and dropping out of school—are more remote. In essence, the migrants to small towns are not only economically closer to natives than those in urban America, but they have important cultural similarities.

The experiences of immigrants in Perry and Storm Lake should allay some of the fears about a lack of incorporation or assimilation into mainstream American culture and values. The results of the surveys in Perry and Storm Lake demonstrate that immigrant children, just like native Anglo youth, believe that people should learn to speak English immediately. Second- and third-generation immigrant young people in Perry and Storm Lake speak English just as well as native students, some even with the same accents and dialects. The principal at Perry High School, Dan Marburger, put the issue very succinctly in 2010: "Our Hispanic families have adjusted and really become a part of the melting pot. I hate to say that they've lost part of their culture, but I think that is so. I think their kids have kind of lost the old ways of Mexico and El Salvador and adopted this way. I don't know if that's right or wrong but it is what it is."[55]

Further, the results reported in Chapter 4 indicate that immigrant youth do not differ from their native counterparts with respect to most civic values. Immigrant students intend to vote, they discuss politics as often, and they participate in school activities at the same rates as native-born young people. Their rates of civic engagement have certainly only increased since the early 2000s. In 2010, the Storm Lake High School choir, for example, consisted of more than 150 young people representing eight native languages. Twenty-five years earlier, the choir had only 38 members.[56] Thus, although first-generation immigrants lag behind natives with regard to civic involvement and English-language skills, their children catch up fairly quickly.

Another sign of acculturation is interethnic dating. When the Irish and Italians first came to the United States, many people were staunchly anti-Catholic, and there was very little interfaith dating or marriage. Some believe that intermarriage is the culmination of the assimilation process.[57] In Perry and Storm Lake, interethnic dating is more common today than it was ten years ago. Even in the focus groups conducted in Perry in 2002, students said that there were a few interethnic couples, but they did not believe anyone had a problem with that. In recent years, the homecoming kings and queens have often been from different ethnic backgrounds. Few appear ready to classify interethnic dating as the norm, but neither is it completely taboo or even frowned on, especially by young people.

Finally, another sign of the second generation's acceptance of American mainstream ideas is the increasing tendency of Latinos and other immigrants to go away to college. In 2002, 63 percent of high school graduates went to college immediately after high school.[58] It is not only believed to be an economic necessity; it has also become part of American mainstream culture to go on to higher education after high school. In the early years of the demographic transformations in Perry and Storm Lake, very few immigrant children went on to higher education; in fact, graduating from high school was hardly a given among this population. In just a few short years, however, this has changed. When Councilman Eddie Diaz graduated from Perry High School in 1997, he was the only one of his Latino friends who went to college. But in 2010 he said, "If you look at the number of Latino students going on to higher education [today], it's pretty impressive. I think that's one of the benefits of living in a smaller community. At least our school district is very good. So we've produced some pretty good students who've gone off to do some pretty good things." The principal at Perry High explained that he and his staff work very hard to inculcate the value of higher education and try to make it possible by helping students—even undocumented immigrant youth—earn scholarships, grants, and loans for higher education.

Summary

We have already seen that over time, the attitudes of native-born residents—both youth and adults—in Perry and Storm Lake became increasingly tolerant and more understanding of newcomers from other countries. This chapter shows that the initial fears some residents had about the negative influence of immigrants have not been borne out in reality. The public schools have become very diverse, especially in Storm Lake, and yet by all accounts the quality of the schools has not suffered, especially once we learn the context behind some negative statistics. Those concerned with losing power to an increasingly large Latino minority have little reason to be concerned. Although Latinos have joined the City Councils in both Perry and Storm Lake, native-born residents still hold nearly all of the significant positions of power in these communities. In fact, Anglo residents often complain about the lack of involvement on the part of ethnic minorities. The initial dramatic increase in local costs for public services has started to wane. As migration has slowed and many of those who have come in the past 15 years have settled into the community, there is a declining need for ESL and remedial education, two very costly services for public schools.

Finally, the children and grandchildren of first-generation immigrants have followed the path of most immigrant groups before them and have adopted many of the same styles and tendencies as native-born Americans. Not only have the immigrants and their children learned about and adapted to the local cultures of these Iowa small towns, but the communities themselves have changed. In his work on the effects of diversity on civic engagement, Robert Putnam concludes, "My hunch is that at the end we shall see that the challenge [of diversity] is best met not by making 'them' like 'us,' but rather by creating a new, more capacious sense of 'we,' a reconstruction of diversity that does not bleach out ethnic specificities, but creates overarching identities."[59] Some may think a "capacious sense of 'we'" is an impossibility, especially in small, rural communities with long histories of ethnic homogeneity.

However, Putnam's hunch has begun to be realized in these communities. To be sure, there are still residents who resent the changes. For the most part, however, they are older residents whose memories of these towns in the 1950s and 1960s are their own golden-age periods. There are many elderly residents who support the changes and appreciate seeing their communities revitalized instead of experiencing the depressing fates of neighboring small towns. For the majority, the idea of community has grown larger and much more inclusive. In Storm Lake, for example, Teresa Coenen, the principal of the high school and a native resident of the predominantly White town of Harlan, told the following anecdote that she believed illustrates the benefits of the diversity and the inclusiveness of Storm Lake:

> [My husband and I] are both from big families, and [my daughter] is related to everybody [in Harlan]. Everybody knew her parents. . . . So she left Harlan and came to Storm Lake for her senior year and had a great experience here. . . . I can tell you without a doubt in my mind, [if the reverse had occurred] it would not have been a successful experience for her. . . . The community expectation is different [in Harlan]. It's about who you know and how long you've known them. It's about those relationships. . . . [In Storm Lake], you just accept that your neighbors are going to change. . . . There's so much migration here that you can come in and find a group of students that's like you, and they're very accepting of you. It was a great experience for her, and it allowed her to be able to go away to college, whereas we thought she'd probably live with us for the rest of her life.

Given the rhetoric around the immigration debate, many would be surprised to hear that a 17-year-old girl would choose to leave the comfort of the small, homogeneous community in which she had lived her entire life during her senior year of high school and attend an ethnically diverse school 80 miles away. That her mother was the principal at the school likely gave her not only the idea to do it but also some comfort as she embarked on the journey. Even so, as we can all probably remember, parents can provide only so much comfort to teens as they deal with cliques, dating, and the pressures of school. Coenen was quite adamant that if a student had transferred to Harlan during his or her senior year, the experience would not be nearly as successful because of the premium people there place on longstanding relationships.

Storm Lake High School's sense of community, however, made the transition relatively seamless for Coenen's daughter. She was welcomed and quickly found a group of friends and by the end of the school year, when she tried to tell her parents who had asked her to the prom, she could only remember his first name, "John." After some discussion about how they knew each other, Coenen figured out the boy's identity. She said, "I told her that she could have just told me it was the Asian 'John' in her comp class, but she said she didn't think about him like that. There's a girl who had been raised in a very Caucasian [community] and . . . by April, she 'doesn't think like that' because, [to her] he's just 'John.'" Coenen went on to explain that this is very normal for the kids at Storm Lake High School. When an incident occurs and students are asked to describe the people involved, they say, "I don't know. He had dark hair." She said that dark hair can describe the vast majority of students at the school, and students have to be prodded to say a race or ethnicity, not because they are being politically correct, she insisted, but because they just do not think in those terms.

The problem that many scholars have with traditional notions of assimilation is that they imply a one-way transformation of attitudes and acculturation on the part of newcomers. It can demand that minorities bend to the dominant culture. To be sure, in the early years of immigration in Perry and Storm Lake, both communities attempted to force assimilation. Local ordinances were passed to prohibit multi-car parking at private residences and parking on yards. Others mandated home and yard maintenance, as well as car maintenance, such as prohibitions on junk cars or cars with flat tires. There are ordinances in these communities related to multifamily dwellings, with limits on the number of people per room. None of the ordinances directly target immigrants, but according to former Mayor Viivi Shirley, "It [was] direct. It's a response that 'you've got to do things our way. We cannot possibly think about another way [of doing things]." When her husband became mayor of Perry in 2002, and when she later succeeded him, they explicitly chose not to pursue these types of policies.[60] The current mayor continues their policy and even actively recruited a Latino to join the City Council.

These communities have become much more inclusive, not only through attitude changes, but also via more formal policies. The Storm Lake Police Department has community service officers who speak Spanish or Lao. The front door of City Hall has "Welcome" posted in English, Spanish, and Lao. In 2002, after the Iowa legislature voted to make English the state's official language, it took only a few days for Perry city officials to purchase computer software that translates city documents into Spanish.[61] In accommodating some of the needs of their new neighbors, these communities have come to realize that their initial concerns were unfounded. Natives began to realize, for example, that when newcomers broke seemingly obvious rules, such as allowing grass to grow higher than six inches or parking in the yard, it was not because they were purposely flouting the rules; they just were not aware of such policies. By giving a little, the people of these towns became more understanding, and the newcomers could begin to become full members of the community. In the process, attitudes shifted on both sides. In essence, Putnam's hunch became reality.

Several residents in these communities discussed the benefits—personally and collectively—of their towns' diversity. Yarosevich pointed out that, although the young immigrants of the second generation fit right into local culture in Storm Lake, they have also "kept enough" of their native culture that it really benefits the community. He said that he loves that he is raising his children in a community where the Fourth of July parade has the usual patriotic displays, but also includes blocks of residents wearing traditional garb from many backgrounds, including Irish, German, Mexican, and Laotian. Other native-born residents commented that the young people growing up in these communities had more exposure to different cultures and languages that would make them more comfortable in the so-called real world.

Dale Carver of Storm Lake told the following story that he believes demonstrates how being surrounded by diversity has benefited his life. This account also shows how far the community has come in adapting to the changes over the past two decades:

> I grew up in an all-White community, all-White school, you know, 35 miles from here. My wife and I were recently at a Boy Scout quarterly meeting. . . . The entertainment was the folk dances, Hispanic folk dances. I saw boys no older than Cub Scouts. It was just, you know, hilarious, just wonderful entertainment. And that same night we went to the Southeast Asian Christian New Year at the Knights of Columbus Hall and danced to Asian music and ate some Asian food. And both of us [grew] up in the part of the country [that] never would have dreamt this possible. You know? We have friends in these different cultures, and we shared and we danced and enjoyed. It was really quite enlightening, if you stop and think. . . . But it was good, it was really good.

For all those who are afraid of the potentially catastrophic changes to their community as a result of immigration, Carver's story should provide some comfort. He has not just accommodated the new members of his community. He does not just tolerate their presence; nor does he secretly resent the changes they represent. Rather, Carver and most other native residents in Perry and Storm Lake appreciate how immigrants have revived their towns and how they have expanded the experiences and viewpoints of what had been a fairly exclusive and parochial group.

CONCLUSION

The Implications of a New Normal

I wish we could bottle this and take it everywhere. I wish the world could experience life through the eyes of these students here.
—Teresa Coenen, Principal, Storm Lake High School

In 2009, a recent Perry High School graduate and his family were in a horrific car accident. The boy's parents and sister died, and he was paralyzed. As many would expect of small towns, people came out in a big way to help. The community helped pay to bury the family. Several residents went in together to buy the boy a computer so he could keep in contact with his classmates and friends during his recovery. That everyone knew the boy and his family were undocumented immigrants did not stop them from helping him in his time of need.

In 2010, another boy from Perry perished. Lance Corporal Joshua Davis, a 2009 graduate of Perry High School, died in Helmand Province in Afghanistan. The entire community came out for the funeral. Afterward, "Mr. Perez," a Perry resident, mentioned to the high school principal that he had been at the service. "My boys played with Josh," he said. "I didn't know the family, but I thought [attending] it was the right thing to do." In small communities, this may not be a particularly uncommon courtesy. However, when immigrants first began to arrive in Perry, few would have anticipated that within 20 years Hispanic and Anglo families would treat one another as relative equals or that immigrants would be incorporated so deeply into the life of this small community.

This study shows that over time, people in small, formerly ethnically homogeneous towns adapt fairly well to rapid ethnic diversification. In the first few years, young native-born residents of small towns in Iowa, like their elders, were somewhat ambivalent about their new neighbors. It took a while for the people of small towns—both young and old—to come to grips with the changes taking place in their communities. Although the two diverse towns in this study followed different paths to acceptance and incorporation of immigrants, the outcomes have been similar. The doomsday predictions about the destruction of small-town culture have not been realized. Both the official responses and natives' attitudes toward immigrants changed. Young people—both native and immigrant—have helped to drive this change. Since the early 2000s, children in Perry and Storm Lake have become accustomed to life in a diverse community. Today, by the time they reach high school, diversity is "no big deal" anymore. This chapter discusses the book's major findings and their implications.

Rural Research

It is my hope that this book not only addresses an interesting practical and political question about the response to immigration in rural America but pushes others to recognize that there are interesting phenomena outside major urban areas. Scholars and pundits alike commit serious errors when they paint "red America" with a broad brush. It does not matter if the painting depicts rural people as patriotic, God-fearing, apple-pie-baking, hospitable, hardworking "real" Americans or whether it depicts them as homophobic, racist, uneducated, unsophisticated, voting-against-their-own-interests, coverall-wearing hicks. Although some researchers find it easy to believe such sloppy notions about rural people, the main problem on this front for scholars has been indifference to people who live outside metropolitan areas. In spite of the power of rural Americans in national politics, there are very few recent publications within political science analyzing rural areas. There simply has not been much scholarly interest in developing a complex understanding of people living or growing up in small towns. In the absence of systematic research, stereotypes prevail, and journalistic accounts dominate our knowledge of these areas. The problem is that the media's quest for a juicy story translates into reports of conflict, even when the overriding story is one of calm. Thus, some are surprised when they hear about Anglo families in a small town coming together to help an undocumented immigrant who has been in a tragic accident.

Many assume that theories designed to explain and predict national or urban phenomena are also appropriate for understanding rural areas. There are cases when this proves to be correct. For example, Chapter 3 shows support for the ideas of symbolic politics in explaining native youths' attitudes about immigrants. In Perry, negative attitudes related to African Americans are indirectly associated with sympathy toward immigrants. This theory, designed around and primarily studied in national and urban contexts, helps to explain some of what is going on with regard to small-town native-born youths' attitudes about immigrants. Moreover, the evidence suggests that even though local communities are vitally important contexts in shaping political socialization, localities exist within larger contexts that also have important roles to play in adolescent development.

In other respects, however, these types of theories do little to explain life and behavior in rural areas and small towns. For example, although the evidence indicates that negative attitudes related to African Americans among Anglo youth in Perry are related to their support for immigrants, the results show this is not the case in Storm Lake. This theory gives no indication about why this phenomenon exists in one small, diverse community but not in the other. For that, we need to understand more about the towns' histories, particularly the fact that Storm Lake had a bit more experience with diversity than did Perry. Further, the idea that diversity contributes to a general pulling back or hunkering down fails to recognize the importance of the civic arena or the density of social networks in small towns. Strong social networks are not frayed so easily. According to Nicholas A. Christakis and James H. Fowler, these networks "have a memory of their own structure (staying intact even if people come and go) and their own function (preserving a culture when people come and go)."[1] There was very little evidence of a general drawback of civic and social activity as a consequence of diversity. In fact, in Storm Lake young people were much more participatory in school activities than in other communities. For adults, too, the same coffee klatches, Bible studies, Rotary clubs, and lunch bunches that had existed in these communities for years continued after immigrants began to arrive. In fact, the chief complaint among native residents was that immigrants did not participate in these activities and thus missed out on a critical defining element of small-town life.

Another example of the undertheorizing about small towns and rural areas is with regard to the expectations of power threat theory. In a somewhat simplified form, this theory predicts that hostility toward minority groups will increase as communities become more diverse. This idea fails to recognize that the adjustment process that takes place is influenced not only by changes to natives' underlying beliefs and fears about immigrants, but also by material and social incentives.[2] In small towns today, residents and community leaders understand they are on a precipice. People in these towns repeatedly used the word "survival" as they discussed responses to immigrants. Many people lamented the economic displacement of so many of their friends and neighbors as jobs were transferred overseas or replaced by low-skilled laborers who accepted relatively poor conditions and mediocre pay. Even so, with few exceptions, residents of these communities recognized that immigrants had helped save their towns. Fears about the negative consequences of immigration were balanced by the realization that the growth occurring in their communities was due primarily to the arrival of immigrants. Rural people are sophisticated enough to deal with these nuances, but hardly any of our existing theories anticipate this response, because few urban or suburban places have to worry about their very survival.

A small proportion of the vast literature on immigration in the United States considers its effects in small towns. Political science is especially guilty in this regard, as most of the existing studies have been conducted by scholars in other disciplines. Researching immigration and other social phenomena in small towns offers many advantages. One can actually talk to a significant portion of the community in interviews or through surveys, for instance. Because diverse towns exist next door to predominantly White towns of similar size and with similar histories and cultures, valuable comparisons can be made. Further, there are several small towns like Perry and Storm Lake throughout the Midwest and South. A comprehensive study of their experiences would be a constructive addition to the literature.

Perhaps the most valuable aspect of conducting research in small towns is that in many ways these communities are microcosms of American society. In many suburbs or central cities, class stratification is rigid. In suburban and urban areas, there are communities where nearly everyone is highly educated and affluent and others where half of the adult men are unemployed. In contrast, small towns typically include the entire range of the economic and social spectrum. The upper class in small towns typically includes doctors, lawyers, and businesspeople; there are middle-class teachers, accountants, and nurses; there are folks scraping by on minimum wage and with seasonal work; and there are the destitute. Even the immigrant experience is well represented in some of these communities. There are refugees from all over the world, legal migrants with green cards and working papers, and undocumented immigrants. Small towns do not have a significant portion of highly educated or high-skilled immigrants, but most other types of immigrants can be found in dozens of small communities in the Midwest. These folks represent a wide spectrum of U.S. society, and studying these communities allows us to project some of what we learn onto the larger population. Nationwide samples also have this power but do not allow for in-depth analysis, such as interviews and focus groups, that help scholars gain a better understanding of the mechanisms at work behind statistical associations.

The main lesson from the experiences of Perry and Storm Lake for the larger society is that the increasing ethnic diversity in the United States is no cause for alarm. In some ways, this is a hard test of the ability of Americans to adapt to changing demographics. Many stereotypes of rural people expect us to find this population to be particularly closed-minded or even overtly hostile to change. The small communities that have undergone significant demographic change due to immigration have been forever changed, but not for the worse. The Anglo Americans who were born and raised in ethnically homogeneous small towns have been able, over time, to become accustomed to living in diverse communities. This is particularly the case with young people, many of whom by this point have been raised in schools and communities in which diversity is the norm. In a single generation, the people of Perry and Storm Lake have dealt with some of their initial suspicions and fears about outsiders. Suppositions about allegedly provincial and insular rural people were put to the test in these towns, and the communities managed to turn these notions on their heads.

Given that this study takes an in-depth look at only two diversifying small communities in the Midwest, it is reasonable to wonder whether we might see similar outcomes in other places. It is important to reiterate the assumption that lies at the heart of this research: context matters. The local context makes a difference in how residents respond to demographic changes. That means we should be cautious in assuming that every community, particularly communities that look very different from those examined here, would respond in the same way to rapid diversification. Due to residential segregation in urban or suburban communities, for example, it is easier for people to have limited contact with others in different racial, ethnic, or class-based groups. As such, the type of transformation we see in Perry and Storm Lake may take much longer in larger, more densely populated places. Further, because class stratification is less pronounced there than in many urban areas, there is "more contact among the various social classes through public schools," according to Cynthia B. Struthers and Janet L. Bokemeier, which "has a positive affect [sic] on social relations."³ The dramatic inequalities of wealth and income in urban environments may make it more difficult for those residents to see themselves as members of a single community in the way people often do in small towns.

In his book *Remaking the Heartland,* Robert Wuthnow points out that small towns in the Midwest have survived because of the social institutions that were set in place before the 1950s. Midwestern residents "inherited an effective system of local government that had been worked out in earlier decades along the eastern seaboard."⁴ Other institutions put in place well before immigrants from Latin America began to arrive were important foundations for small towns coping with the changes in agribusiness in the second half of the twentieth century. Wuthnow argues that Midwesterners have long had to adapt to changing conditions, and the strong social and economic ties to one another laid the groundwork that led meatpackers to choose small towns like Perry and Storm Lake in the 1980s and led residents to accept the demographic changes that followed. This history and culture, then, is essential to keep in mind as we consider whether diversity is likely to have the same impact in places outside this region.

At the same time, the preponderance of the scholarly evidence strongly indicates that small-town residents across the country learn to adjust to the changes in their communities. The towns selected for this study are not much different from Lexington, Nebraska; Austin, Minnesota; Sparta, North Carolina; Fort Morgan, Colorado; or the dozens of other towns across the Midwest, the Plains, and the South that within the past two decades have become more ethnically diverse because of the arrival of immigrants. My results demonstrate that each place is unique, and this distinctiveness is particularly important in understanding the process of native residents' learning to accommodate change. However, the major finding with regard to the outcome of diversification is likely to be similar across these and other small towns: people adjust, and over time natives and immigrants create a new normal in these small communities.

The Importance of Time

That it takes time for people in these suddenly ethnically diverse small towns to come to terms with a new normal is, of course, no revelation. The vast literature on the history of immigration into the United States shows that change takes time. Newcomers need time to learn about and adopt aspects of the culture in which they are now living. Natives go through an adjustment process as they get to know their new neighbors and work through their initial fears and suspicions. Adjusting to changes like those seen in these communities is lifelong process. It is often accompanied by intense internal strife as people evaluate their own beliefs, which have been structured by the social and political world, and contemplate making changes in their thinking.[5] It is possible for people to alter even deeply ingrained beliefs and values, but it can take a long time. As this process takes place, cultural change materializes at the community level. New norms and values are formed, and a new normal eventually emerges.

Although not surprising, the importance of time is worth highlighting because people in both the scholarly and journalistic communities make errors when they do not embrace its real significance. Numerous scholarly studies examine the effects of diversity at one point in time. In the cases examined here, a single cross-sectional study conducted at the beginning of the diversification process would likely lead to overly pessimistic conclusions about the possibility of immigrant incorporation. Alternatively, a single study at a later point in time might be too rosy in its predictions, missing the important period of difficulty and tension that often follows the initial years. In terms of public policy, a failure to recognize the importance of time leads some to believe that immigrants take too long to assimilate or to expect native-born, Anglo residents of small towns (and other communities) to smoothly adapt to the rapid changes in their towns. Mark Grey, an activist and scholar, succinctly states about the adjustment process in diversifying small communities: "The problem is, it takes a while to make it work. People look for overnight solutions and we tell them, over and over again, there isn't one."[6]

We should be wary about the rhetoric about parasitical immigrants who do not want to become part of American society. In 2001, Tom Vilsack, then the governor of Iowa, told the *Washington Post* that the meatpacking industry had "become the poster child for immigration problems."[7] In 1999, as a result of his study of the "Hog Pride" plant, Grey wrote, "Many Latinos refused to become a new working class in rural Iowa. . . . They used the wages available at Hog Pride (or some other packer) to simultaneously escape permanent membership in the Iowa working class and raise their economic status back home."[8] Today, turnover rates are still higher in the meatpacking plants than in other industries, but in Perry and Storm Lake, most residents said turnover rates at the plants had declined since Tyson bought out IBP. According to Tyson, the turnover rate among hourly employees declined by 30 percent from 2008 to 2009 and that as of 2010, more than 50 percent of its U.S. workforce had five or more years of experience.[9]

Some of the early sentiments about the negative role of meatpacking plants may have changed due to declining turnover rates along with the growth in the population of immigrants who have settled permanently in the communities. Although the work is hard and dirty and the companies continue to have serious problems, the meatpacking industry today seems to offer many newcomers a chance to make a decent living, giving their children opportunities for future upward incorporation into small-town life. According to this and other recent studies, immigrants have begun to become part of the rural working class.[10] Immigrants believe that life is better in these small towns than it was in their native countries or would be in U.S. urban environments. Many newcomers have purchased homes and moved beyond the meatpacking plant for employment. Their children have finished high school at higher rates than they might have in major cities, and when possible they have sought higher education. In Storm Lake and Perry and other towns like them, Latinos are serving in local government and now have some role in local decision making. There are still social, cultural, and political distinctions between immigrants and natives, and their life chances are far from equal, but the economic gulf between the two groups is not as wide as it is in urban areas, making it easier for the chasms in other areas to begin to close. Without a study spanning multiple years, these processes would have been missed.

As for the native responses, some learn to appreciate aspects of the newcomers' cultures. Like Dale Carver in Storm Lake or Jay Pattee in Perry, they take opportunities to learn more about these other cultures and actively work toward reconciling differences between the two groups. Even those who have not embraced newcomers in this way have come to understand that their initial fears and concerns have not been realized and that life has gone on much as it did before the immigrants arrived. Young people have played an important role in this endeavor, helping their elders come to understand they are not so different from immigrants and giving them an opportunity to interact via their children or grandchildren. This is not to say that everyone gets along or that there are no interethnic tensions. It does indicate, however, that theories predicting increasing ethnic hostility and reduced civic engagement or social capital on the part of the White/Anglo majority have not been borne out in reality. Once again, we can only witness this process by examining change over time.

Social change has always taken time. Periods of immigration have always been met with skepticism, paranoia, and nativist sentiments. But when we allow enough time to pass, most immigrant groups become full members of their communities, and natives come to accept members of what were once considered out-groups. We are an impatient people, however. Many expect native-born Americans to adapt to demographic changes without any resentment, with no questions about their new neighbors and devoid of conflict—even internal conflict. Similarly, others expect immigrants to assimilate immediately. They should be able to speak English right away. They should know both the written and the unwritten rules of community life. And they should adopt the behavior and preferences of their surroundings without delay. Many are uncomfortable with the fact that learning to adapt to change is a lifelong process for individuals and communities.

Public Policy Implications

As outlined at the outset of this study, governmental policies play a crucial role in determining migration patterns to and within the United States. Immigration policy is one of the most contentious areas of American politics today. But much of what passes for debate about the policy overlooks the reality of immigration in small towns and rural areas. Most people continue to think immigration is a serious issue only in major cities or along the U.S.–Mexican border. As such, most policy discussions fail to capture how immigration has played out in small towns or to consider the effects of national policy on these communities.

Recent policies have exacerbated some problems for small towns. At the end of the Bush administration, immigration policy focused on, among other things, high-profile raids at factories, many of which were located in small towns. In Iowa, raids in Postville and Marshalltown led to hundreds of arrests, several deportations, the destruction of many families, and the devastation of local communities.[11] Furthermore, it did little to accomplish its purported goal: to stop undocumented workers from entering or staying in the United States. The Obama administration has replaced high-profile raids with threats of serious fines to employers unless they fire or refuse to hire undocumented employees, leading many employers to lay off workers who lack appropriate documentation. Although the number of undocumented immigrants has decreased in recent years, deportations have skyrocketed during the Obama administration.[12] Though perhaps more humane than the raids, Obama's policy also does little to solve the broader problems with the undocumented immigrants who have lived in the United States for decades.

If the federal government honestly intends to make significant reforms to immigration policies, it should consider the effects of reforms not only on U.S. cities and border towns but also on rural communities. To do so would take into account the views of small-town residents, as well as the experiences they have had with immigration over the past 20 years. Reformers need to understand that small towns have already suffered great population losses due to economic restructuring. Some have managed to survive primarily by embracing immigration. Native-born Americans in small towns have come to accept change and adapt accordingly. Young people, many of whom have fled small towns in droves over the past 30 years, have positive things to say about their experiences growing up in these diverse places. They feel better prepared for the "real world" because they have been exposed to ethnic and cultural diversity. Those who have gone away to college often say that campus life is actually less ethnically, culturally, and economically diverse than life in the communities in which they were raised. As a result, some have expressed interest in returning to their hometowns, if only there were more economic opportunities.[13]

Many immigrants intend to stay in these towns permanently. What many Anglos viewed as horrible work in the meatpacking plants, Latinos "saw as a golden chance at a new beginning."[14] They want to stay near their families and they believe the native townspeople have been good to them. So after years of transience among the immigrant population and economic woes, these communities have stabilized. While most small towns watch their best and brightest move away to attend college and to get jobs in urban or suburban places, these communities have a burgeoning number of family-oriented, hardworking young people who want to stay in or return to small towns to raise their own families. Immigration reform must not stop this momentum and undo years of adaptation and adjustment.

One of the most difficult aspects of immigration reform is the question about what to do with the approximately 11 million undocumented immigrants in the United States. Surprisingly perhaps, natives in these communities had very little concern about immigrants' legal status. Some, such as school personnel, legally cannot discriminate on the basis of legal status. But the lack of concern spread beyond those who were legally bound to provide services to everyone, regardless of their immigration status. Nearly everyone acknowledged that some portion of the non-native community had entered illegally or otherwise did not have legal papers to stay. But it did not seem to matter much to anyone. Many native-born young people were empathetic, commenting, "I would do it, too," and "Who wouldn't want to come here?" Adults admittedly looked the other way because they understood the importance of the immigrants to the survival of their towns. Especially now, since demographic changes have slowed and immigrants have begun to settle in the community, very few people support rounding up undocumented workers at the expense of the local economy. Many also told me that given their experiences, they understand that it would be a logistical nightmare to attempt to remove undocumented immigrants and that doing so would break up families and destroy communities.[15] They also believed that the foreign workers in their communities were hardworking, law-abiding, family-oriented folks who were simply trying to create better lives. The blue-collar, working-class backgrounds that are prevalent in small towns have helped to create a lot of empathy for the immigrants, regardless of their legal status.

This is not to say that people would not prefer that immigrants come here legally and have legitimate opportunities to stay. It means only that if ensuring that every foreign-born resident has legal papers means risking the loss of all of the hard work communities have done to survive economic restructuring and adapt to immigration, few native residents would take that risk. Policies should be amended to make it easier for immigrants to enter the United States legally and to allow them a means to stay here legitimately—to pay taxes and earn benefits in their own names, abide by laws and customs, and give their children, whether born in this country or not, opportunities for economic and social advancement.

The recent move among some local and state governments to enforce federal immigration laws are only likely to aggravate tensions and, like the raids, are unlikely to make a real dent in the number of undocumented immigrants.

Some small towns that have passed harsh anti-immigrant provisions have later seen them as a mistake. Legislation in Riverside, New Jersey, penalizing anyone who employed or rented to an illegal immigrant led thousands of recent immigrants to leave and several businesses to close before the Town Council eventually rescinded the law.[16] Perry and Storm Lake residents, especially community leaders, stated that they had worked hard to develop trust between local law enforcement and the immigrant community. They believe the enforcement of such laws would destroy all they have built and ultimately do a poor job in protecting the border. Many community leaders also argued that such policies are an expensive burden for cash-strapped local governments. In fact, in at least one case, Storm Lake chose not to enforce a policy because it did not make sense for residents: when the English-only law passed in Iowa in 2002, Storm Lake ignored it. The police chief stated, "When the legislation passed, it didn't make a bit of difference to us, and if it is repealed, it also will not change the way we provide service to all people."[17]

Nearly everyone with whom I spoke argued that the children of immigrants, whether born in the United States or not, deserve our understanding and compassion. Even though their congressional representative introduced legislation to revoke so-called birth-right citizenship, most residents rejected the idea. There was a strong sense that even if the parents had come to the country illegally, the children had done nothing wrong and deserved the opportunities to earn an education and rise up the economic ladder. Most of these kids were highly Americanized: they spoke English fluently; many had never been to their countries of origin and had no allegiance to or identity with them; and most were indistinguishable from their native-born counterparts.

Many residents told me they believe young people who have lived in the country for many years and meet the academic requirements should have real access to higher education, including in-state tuition and access to financial aid. The principals divulged that they worked hard to help any student who had the grades and wanted to go to college. They were repeatedly disappointed when a good student's immigration status was the only thing standing in the way. In Perry and Storm Lake, some people support these policies because they believe it is a moral or civil rights issue; others have instrumental reasons. One man cited the fact that it would be better for the community for these young people to receive college educations because so many were staying permanently in "his" town. He said that otherwise there would be a large number of young people who could never rise out of poverty or obtain well-paying jobs. And, he admitted, providing an opportunity for higher education might mean that some would move away to obtain good jobs, a fact he believed was not necessarily all bad for the children of the immigrants or for the community itself.

This study also highlights a tremendous lack of financial support for rural areas and small towns. Historically, rural policy has been synonymous with agricultural policy. This is part of the ongoing myth that rural areas are composed only of farms and the open countryside.[18] However, as of 2002, less than

2 percent of the U.S. population was employed in agriculture, and only 20 percent of all non-metropolitan counties were considered farming-dependent.[19] Farmers make up a small proportion even in rural areas and small towns. These communities are unlikely ever to receive the attention and funding they need as long as the federal government assumes "If ag [does] well, rural [will] do well."[20] For example, an analysis by the Center for Rural Affairs in 2007 demonstrated that across the 13 leading farm states with Department of Agriculture investment in rural development, the federal government spent "nearly twice as much to subsidize 260 big farms as it spent to create genuine opportunity for millions of rural people."[21] President Obama seems to recognize this problem; by executive order he established the first White House Rural Council in June 2011. The council's first report highlights the broad needs in rural communities, not only in agriculture, but also in the lack of access to high-quality health care, low rates of educational attainment, high rates of poverty and unemployment, needs of returning military veterans, and necessity for more investment in rural businesses. The report does not, however, contend with the issues of rapid ethnic diversification in rural communities; nor does it mention immigration.

In the early years of rapid ethnic diversification, Perry and Storm Lake bore an enormous burden in costs for social services. State and federal government agencies should step up their support so local governments have what they need. In recent years, however, rural-focused legislation, such as the New Homestead Act, has failed to gain necessary support from non-rural legislators.[22] The private sector can play an important role, as well. Many residents of Perry and Storm Lake told me that Tyson Fresh Meats has been a much better corporate citizen than its predecessors. For example, Tyson helped pay some of the travel costs associated with the Perry officials' trip to Mexico in 2006. However, almost everyone agrees that the company could do more.

Chapter 6 also demonstrated that some of initial costs associated with rapid ethnic diversification dissipate over time. Schools' expenses for ESL and other targeted services are no longer needed to the extent that they were in the early days. The children of first-generation immigrants have excellent English skills, making these programs a small component of the school curriculum. Costs associated with law enforcement, hospitals, and other social services have also diminished, especially over the past few years.

There continue to be difficulties with a lack of resources in some areas. The schools in Perry and Storm Lake, for example, have more trouble with teacher turnover than do ethnically homogeneous communities. This is not because teachers do not like their jobs and move on but because they develop marketable skills in learning to teach and administer programs in a high-poverty, diverse setting. Urban school districts can afford to pay more and poach many of the best staff. The same is true in the medical field, in law enforcement, and in many private sector jobs. Thus, rural areas have great difficulty keeping those who could be instrumental in establishing a bright future for these towns. Ironically, meatpacking plants and immigrants were drawn to rural areas because they have lower costs. As newcomers begin to settle down and the next generation becomes fully incorporated into community life, these are the very things that might drive out the best and brightest. States should recognize the value of these small towns and help them stay competitive with urban areas.

Some argue that small towns that cannot keep up with the global economic situation deserve to wither on the vine. Others maintain that most investments in rural communities are wasteful. These critics contend that when the government gives loans or grants to rural communities to help attract business by building roads, updating sewer systems and utilities, and installing broadband Internet, the economic benefits do not outweigh the costs.[23] There are, however, many reasons to care about and help support Midwestern small towns. Most of our food comes from this region, and few people understand how it is produced or the consequences of environmental degradation or of cheap meat and corn. Rural states remain politically powerful due to equal representation in the Senate and the Electoral College, so understanding their beliefs and values should be important to everyone. Predominantly rural states have the highest rates of military enlistment; even though they make up only 17 percent of the nation's population, rural Americans compose 44 percent of the men and women serving in uniform.[24] Those in urban areas are relying on rural young people to protect us abroad. There are serious economic and social problems that are not simply going to disappear if small communities die: rising rural poverty; increasing rates of divorce, welfare dependence, and obesity; and rising drug use, especially use of methamphetamines. Allowing these small communities to die is like allowing part of this country's past to waste away and be forgotten. Further, since so many Americans have small-town roots, there should be a willingness to preserve our past. In most cases, small communities are not waiting for the federal government to bail them out. They are doing whatever they can to save themselves and keeping their fingers crossed that the government will not pass policies that counteract their hard work.

Embracing immigration is one of the means of survival for small towns. Interethnic relations in the diverse communities have improved dramatically over the past 20 years. It would be good idea for these communities to become more vocal about their positive experiences with immigration. The negative perceptions and fears about immigration outlined in Chapter 6 are pervasive in predominantly White communities that have very few immigrants. Leaders in Perry and Storm Lake could help people in other communities learn that, even though there were difficult periods in the beginning, immigration has been a mostly positive experience for their towns.

Storm Lake High School also provides an excellent model of an innovative way to plug the brain drain and help prepare students—both immigrant and native—for the regional economy. The charter school program may cause some problems when graduation rates come out, but it is a program that has proved very effective for its students. In the creative and forward-thinking program, the high school spends its per-pupil revenue to pay tuition at a community college so students can attend a fifth year of instruction. The school recognizes that it has a high-poverty population that may not be able to afford a four-year degree. It also accepts that not everyone wants to, or has the ability to, go to a traditional college or university. In the charter program, students graduate with a high school diploma and an associate of arts degree.[25] The programs are geared toward jobs in the local or regional economy, thereby giving young people who want to stay in town an opportunity to do so without having to live in poverty or work at minimum-wage jobs with little opportunity for advancement.

Storm Lake High School also provides an interesting framework for helping other schools and communities cope effectively with demographic changes. Primarily because the community has always been a working-class place and has not had the resources to fund some of the infrastructure projects commonly found in more affluent towns, the schools are open to the public and host a variety of activities not related to education. For example, residents can have wedding receptions in the high school gym and first communion parties in the elementary school building. Anyone can use the playground. Most weekday mornings, several community members use the high school's weight room to exercise. "That's one of the things that makes the community take a great ownership of the school," according to the principal, Teresa Coenen. "When I need something, I just say, 'Hey, I have a need.'" Her needs have included providing meals and transportation to students who want to attend school-related concerts and sporting events out of town. Local residents pay for these programs, along with many other ones that otherwise would be available only to those students whose parents can afford them. These types of arrangements help unify the community, which in the long run may increase the incentives for young people to stay in town after graduation.

This chapter begins with an epigraph quoting Coenen, Storm Lake High School's principal in 2010. She told me she wants to "bottle" what is going on in her school, which she described as a place where young people from different ethnic backgrounds got along, where they participated in activities together, and where nearly every student had an opportunity to feel welcome and find a group of friends. Coenen believed that schools in other diverse small towns, as well as in urban areas, could learn a lot from the experiences in Storm Lake. Similarly, scholars, pundits, and politicians would do well not to ignore and stereotype the people living in these communities. There are valuable lessons to be learned across many different disciplines. These communities need all of the support and interest they can get.

APPENDIX

Samples, Survey Items, and Variables

TABLE A.1 Representativeness of Sample and Local Populations in Fall 2001

	Farm[a]	White	Black	Asian	Latino	Other
Boone sample	4.5	96.9	0.6	0.0	0.6	1.9
Boone population	4.7	97.9	0.3	0.2	0.8	0.7
Boone High School	—	98.5	0.1	0.8	0.3	0.2
Carroll sample	8.0	98.7	0.1	0.4	—	0.4
Carroll population	8.1	98.3	0.2	0.3	0.5	0.6
Carroll High School	—	98.4	0.5	0.2	0.9	—
Harlan sample	8.4	97.6	—	0.5	—	2.0
Harlan population	10.4	98.0	0.1	0.3	1.0	0.8
Harlan High School	—	98.4	—	0.2	1.3	0.2
Perry sample	13.6	66.7	2.3	2.3	22.4	5.5
Perry population	4.1	75.2	1.0	0.5	14.5	1.3
Perry High School	—	76.6	2.1	2.0	19.3	—
Storm Lake sample	10.6	72.0	—	13.0	12.6	2.3
Storm Lake population	8.2	78.2	0.3	3.9	11.1	1.4
Storm Lake High School	—	66.0	1.0	12.8	20.0	0.2

Source: Population figures are based on figures from the U.S. Census, 2000. School population figures are based on the 2001–2002 school year. Dashes indicate that schools do not collect or report the information.

Note: Values are percentages.

[a] Sample reflects percentage reporting that both parents are employed full time in farming.

TABLE A.2 Survey Items and Descriptive Statistics

Survey items	Range[a]	Mean[b]	Standard deviation[b]
Dependent variables for Chapter 3[c]			
Immigrants in Iowa take jobs away from Americans who want to work.	0–4	1.99	1.23
Hispanic people that move here from other countries will improve American life with new ideas and customs. (reversed)	0–4	1.71	1.10
Asian people that move here from other countries will improve American life with new ideas and customs. (reversed)	0–4	2.06	0.92
[Town name] would be a better place to live if more immigrants moved in from other countries. (reversed)	0–4	1.34	1.04
When people move here from other countries, they should learn to speak English as soon as possible.	0–4	0.77	0.92
Immigrants work much harder than the people born here in the United States. (reversed)	0–4	1.87	1.16
There would be fewer problems if there weren't as many immigrants allowed to move here.	0–4	1.82	1.28
Dependent variables for Chapter 4			
Political knowledge[d]	0–7	4.40	1.45
How many U.S. Senators does each state have?[e]	0–1	0.64	0.48
In the U.S. House of Representatives, the member who is elected to preside is called the:	0–1	0.28	0.45
Where can you find the Bill of Rights?	0–1	0.74	0.44
How often are U.S. presidential elections held?	0–1	0.91	0.28
Who is the current chief justice of the Supreme Court?	0–1	0.36	0.48
Who is the current vice president of the United States?	0–1	0.84	0.36
Which system of governance is defined by power divided between national, state, and local governments?	0–1	0.62	0.49
Internal efficacy[f]	0–12	6.00	2.00
I am as well informed about politics as others. (reversed)	0–4	1.93	1.01
Other people are better at understanding complicated political issues than I am.	0–4	1.79	1.04
I have a pretty good understanding of political issues. (reversed)	0–4	2.40	0.92
External efficacy[g]	0–8	3.00	2.00
Public officials don't care what people like me think.	0–4	1.68	0.96
People like me don't have any say in what government does.	0–4	1.60	1.10
Generalized trust: You can generally trust people to do the right thing.	0–1	0.34	0.47
Intention to vote: If you were 18 and eligible by 2004, would you vote in the next presidential election?	0–1	0.80	0.40
Participation in school activities:[h] Which of the following activities are you involved with at your high school? Please fill in as many as apply to you: band/choir, varsity sports, Honor Society, cheerleading/poms/flags, science/math/computer club, foreign language/international club, speech/debate or forensics, Future Farmers of America, Student Council/Student Government Association, school newspaper/yearbook, service club, other.	0–9	2.03	1.68
Frequency of political discussion: How many days in the past week did you talk about politics with your friends and family?	0–7	2.39	2.20

Survey items	Range[a]	Mean[b]	Standard deviation[b]
Independent variables for Chapter 3			
Slavery: The history of slavery and discrimination has made it difficult for Black people to work their way out of poverty.	0–4	2.03	1.04
Segregation: It is better for people of different races to lives apart from one another, in separate neighborhoods, than in the same neighborhood. (reversed)	0–4	1.10	1.11
Evaluation of African Americans[i]	1–10	4.82	2.80
Evaluation of Hispanics	1–10	4.89	2.90
Evaluation of Whites	1–10	9.09	1.88
Independent variables that are the same for Chapters 3 and 4			
Family income[j]	1–6	3.40	1.45
Planning to attend a four-year college: What are your plans for after high school graduation?	0–1	0.63	0.48
Parents are farmers: Are your mother and father employed as full-time farmers?[k]	0–2	0.31	0.63
Grandparents live in state: Do any of your grandparents live in Iowa?	0–1	0.81	0.39
Length of residence: How long have you lived in [town name]?[l]	1–6	4.70	1.60
Grade level: What grade are you in?	9–12	10.68	1.04
Female: What is your sex?	0–1	0.49	0.50
Amount of civics coursework: Since the beginning of the ninth grade, how much American government or civics classes have you completed up to now?[m]	0–5	1.86	1.92
Parents are married: Are your parents currently married to each other?	0–1	0.68	0.47

Note: All variables have been recoded 0–1 in the statistical analyses to standardize and be able to compare effects. These are their original values.

[a] For all items scaled 0–4, the response options were 0 = strongly agree; 1 = agree; 2 = neither agree nor disagree; 3 = disagree; 4 = strongly disagree. For all 0–1 variables that are yes or no, 0 = no; 1 = yes.

[b] The means and standard deviations are based on the entire sample. Where differences exist with results in the text, it is because many of the analyses in Chapters 3 and 4 exclude respondents who are foreign born and those who have at least one parent who is foreign born.

[c] All of these measures are scaled so the higher values indicate the more sympathetic response.

[d] The measure used in an additive index of the number of correct answers to the questions listed.

[e] Each knowledge question had four possible response options: three incorrect answers and one correct answer. There was no "don't know" option. They were recoded here so that 0 = incorrect answer; 1 = correct answer.

[f] The measure is an additive index. Cronbach's alpha (standardized) = .594.

[g] The measure is an additive index. Cronbach's alpha (standardized) = .523.

[h] The measure is an additive index. Cronbach's alpha (standardized) = .517.

[i] 1 = cold, 10 = warm.

[j] The measure is the estimated income (in 2001 dollars) of mothers' and fathers' income based on the occupations respondents identified for each parent.

[k] 0 = neither parent employed in farming; 1 = one parent employed in farming; 2 = both parents employed in farming.

[l] 1 = less than 1 year; 2 = 1–3 years; 3 = 4–6 years; 4 = 7–10 years; 5 = more than 10 years; 6 = all my life.

[m] 0 = none; 1 = less than six months; 2 = six months; 3 = between six months and one year; 4 = one year; 5 = more than one year.

TABLE A.3 Factor Analysis of Dependent Variables in Chapter 3

	Fall 2001
	Component 1
Immigrants (do not) take jobs away from natives.	.698
Hispanic people will improve life here.	.825
Asian people will improve life here.	.607
This town would be better with more immigrants.	.741
Immigrants should (not have to) learn to speak English ASAP.	.603
Immigrants work harder than natives.	.528
There would (not) be fewer problems if there were (more) immigrants.	.802

	Spring 2002	
	Component 1	Component 2
Immigrants (do not) take jobs away from natives.	.541	−.628
Hispanic people will improve life here.	.751	.442
Asian people will improve life here.	.574	.391
This town would be better with more immigrants.	.772	.004
Immigrants should (not have to) learn to speak English ASAP.	.593	−.413
Immigrants work harder than natives.	.475	.451
There would (not) be fewer problems if there were (more) immigrants.	.807	−.234

Note: All of these individual measures were scaled so the higher values indicate the more sympathetic response.

Extraction method: Principal components analysis. For Fall 2001, one component was extracted, explaining 48.2 percent of variance. For Spring 2002, two components were extracted. Component 1 explains 43.0 percent of variance, and Component 2 explains 16.7 percent of variance. The analyses in Chapter 5 use only the first of the extracted components to compare change from 2001 to 2002.

Notes

INTRODUCTION

1. Paul Allen Beck and M. Kent Jennings, "Pathways to Participation," *The American Political Science Review* 76 (1982): 94–108; Russell J. Dalton, "Reassessing Parental Socialization: Indicator Unreliability versus Generational Transfer," *American Political Science Review* 74 (1980): 421–431; M. Kent Jennings and Richard G. Niemi, "The Transmission of Political Values from Parent to Child," *American Political Science Review* 62 (1968): 169–184; Ken L. Tedin, "Assessing Peer and Parent Influence on Adolescent Political Attitudes," *American Journal of Political Science* 24 (1980): 136–153.

2. On peers, see Bruce A. Campbell, "A Theoretical Approach to Peer Influence in Adolescent Socialization," *American Journal of Political Science* 24 (1980): 324–344; Ada W. Finifter, "The Friendship Group as a Protective Environment for Social Deviants," *American Political Science Review* 68 (1974): 607–625. On schools, see David E. Campbell, *Why We Vote: How Schools and Communities Shape Our Civic Life* (Princeton, N.J.: Princeton University Press, 2006); Robert D. Hess and Judith V. Torney, *The Development of Political Attitudes in Children* (Chicago: Aldine, 1967); M. Kent Jennings and Richard G. Niemi, *The Political Character of Adolescence: The Influence of Families and Schools* (Princeton, N.J.: Princeton University Press, 1974); Richard Niemi and Jane Junn, *Civic Education: What Makes Students Learn* (New Haven, Conn.: Yale University Press, 1998).

3. Stephen E. Bennett, "Why Young Americans Hate Politics, and What We Should Do about It," *PS: Political Science and Politics* 30 (1997): 47–53; John Bynner and Sheena Ashford, "Politics and Participation: Some Antecedents of Young People's Attitudes to the Political System and Political Activity," *European Journal of Social Psychology* 24 (1994): 223–236; Cliff Zukin, Scott Keeter, Molly Andolina, Krista Jenkins, and Michael X. Delli Carpini, *A New Engagement? Political Participation, Civic Life, and the Changing American Citizen* (New York: Oxford University Press, 2006).

4. Several studies use the Jennings and Niemi socialization panel study. They are incredibly useful in allowing us to see change over time, but even these studies have not examined the effect of place on socialization: see, e.g., Paul Allen Beck and M. Kent Jennings, "Family Traditions, Political Periods, and the Development of Partisan Orientations," *Journal of Politics* 53 (1991): 742–763; M. Kent Jennings, "Generation Units and the Student Protest Movement in the United States: An Intra- and Intergenerational Analysis,"

Political Psychology 23 (2002): 303–324; M. Kent Jennings, "Political Knowledge over Time and across Generations," *Public Opinion Quarterly* 60 (1996): 228–252; M. Kent Jennings and Gregory B. Marcus, "Partisan Orientations over the Long Haul: Results from the Three-Wave Political Socialization Panel Study," *American Political Science Review* 78 (1984): 1000–1018; M. Kent Jennings and Richard G. Niemi, "Continuity and Change in Political Orientations: A Longitudinal Study of Two Generations," *American Political Science Review* 69 (1975): 1316–1335; M. Kent Jennings and Richard G. Niemi, *Generations and Politics* (Princeton, N.J.: Princeton University Press, 1981); Richard G. Niemi and M. Kent Jennings, "Issues and Inheritance in the Formation of Party Identification," *American Journal of Political Science* 35 (1991): 970–988; Eric Plutzer, "Becoming a Habitual Voter: Inertia, Resources, and Growth in Young Adulthood," *American Political Science Review* 96 (2002): 41–56; Ronald B. Rapoport, "Partisanship Change in a Candidate-Centered Era," *Journal of Politics* 59 (1997): 185–199.

5. These exceptions include Pamela J. Conover and Donald Searing, "A Political Socialization Perspective," in *Rediscovering the Democratic Purposes of Education*, ed. Lorraine M. McDonnell, P. Michael Timpane, and Roger Benjamin (Lawrence: University Press of Kansas, 2000), 91–126; Campbell, *Why We Vote*; James Gimpel, J. Celeste Lay, and Jason Schuknecht, *Cultivating Democracy: Civic Environments and Political Socialization in America* (Washington, D.C.: Brookings Institution Press, 2003); Julianna Sandell Pacheco, "Political Socialization in Context: The Effect of Political Competition on Youth Voter Turnout," *Political Behavior* 30 (2008): 415–436. Some studies examine the effects of time or period on socialization: see David O. Sears and Nicholas A. Valentino, "Politics Matters: Political Events as Catalysts for Preadult Socialization," *American Political Science Review* 91 (1997): 45–65; Nicholas Valentino and David O. Sears, "Event-Driven Political Socialization and the Preadult Socialization of Partisanship," *Political Behavior* 20 (1998): 127–154.

6. Herbert Blumer, *Symbolic Interactionism: Perspective and Method* (Englewood Cliffs, N.J.: Prentice Hall, 1969).

7. Charles H. Cooley, *Human Nature and the Social Order* (New York: Scribner's, 1902); David L. Miller, ed., *The Individual and the Social Self: Unpublished Essays by G. H. Mead* (Chicago: University of Chicago Press, 1982); Charles W. Morris, ed., *Mind, Self, and Society* (Chicago: University of Chicago Press, 1934).

8. See also Georg Simmel, *The Metropolis of Modern Life*, in *Simmel: On Individuality and Social Forms*, ed. Donald Levine (Chicago: University of Chicago Press, 1971), 324–339.

9. Urie Bronfenbrenner, *The Ecology of Human Development: Experiments by Nature and Design* (Cambridge, Mass.: Harvard University Press, 1979); Urie Bronfenbrenner, with P. A. Morris, "The Ecology of Developmental Processes," in *Handbook of Child Psychology: Volume 1: Theoretical Models of Human Development*, ed. William Damon and Richard M. Lerner (New York: John Wiley, 1998), 993–1028.

10. Angus Campbell, Philip E. Converse, Warren E. Miller, and Donald E. Stokes, *The American Voter* (New York: John Wiley, 1960).

11. For an excellent discussion of this turn away from the "social logic of politics," see Alan S. Zuckerman, ed., *The Social Logic of Politics: Personal Networks as Contexts for Political Behavior* (Philadelphia: Temple University Press, 2005), 11–16. Some notable scholars have argued that once we account for the political, social, and economic traits of those we survey, neighborhood or "community" effects are nonexistent: see Jonathan Kelley and Ian McAllister, "Social Context and Electoral Behavior in Britain," *American Journal of Political Science* 29 (1985): 564–586; Gary King, "Why Context Should Not Count," *Political Geography* 15 (1996): 159–164. John Zaller's theory suggests that mes-

sages flow from elites to masses pretty much unfiltered and unaltered by local political context. An information flow downward (or outward) from national media sources will penetrate all settings to a similar degree, affecting politically aware voters in much the same way: John Zaller, *The Nature and Origins of Mass Opinion* (New York: Cambridge University Press, 1992).

12. Bernard R. Berelson, Paul F. Lazarsfeld, and William N. McPhee, *Voting: A Study of Opinion Formation in a Presidential Campaign* (Chicago: University of Chicago Press, 1954); Paul F. Lazarsfeld, Bernard Berelson, and Hazel Gaudet, *The People's Choice: How the Voter Makes Up His Mind in a Presidential Campaign* (New York: Columbia University Press, 1968 [1944]).

13. Lazarsfeld et al., *The People's Choice*, 27.

14. Paul Allen Beck, Russell J. Dalton, Steven Greene, and Robert Huckfeldt, "The Social Calculus of Voting: Interpersonal, Media and Organizational Influences on Presidential Choices," *American Political Science Review* 96 (2002): 57–74.

15. Nancy Burns, Kay Lehman Schlozman, and Sidney Verba, *The Private Roots of Public Action: Gender, Equality, and Political Participation* (Cambridge, Mass.: Harvard University Press, 2001); Robert Huckfeldt, Paul E. Johnson, and John Sprague, "Individuals, Dyads and Networks: Autoregressive Patterns of Political Influence," in *The Social Logic of Politics: Personal Networks as Contexts for Political Behavior*, ed. Alan Zuckerman (Philadelphia: Temple University Press, 2005), 21–48; Robert Huckfeldt and John Sprague, *Citizens, Politics and Social Communication* (Cambridge: Cambridge University Press, 1995); Diana C. Mutz, "Cross-Cutting Social Networks: Testing Democratic Theory in Practice," *American Political Science Review* 96 (2002): 111–126; Diana C. Mutz, *Impersonal Influence: How Perceptions of Mass Collectives Affect Political Attitudes* (New York: Cambridge University Press, 1998); Diana C. Mutz and Jeffrey Mondak, "Dimensions of Sociotropic Behavior: Group-Based Judgments of Fairness and Well-Being," *American Journal of Political Science* 41 (1997): 284–308; Alan Zuckerman, Laurence Kotler-Berkowitz, and Lucas A. Swaine, "Anchoring Political Preferences: The Importance of Social and Political Contexts and Networks in Britain," *European Journal of Political Research* 33 (1998): 285–322.

16. Robert Huckfeldt, "Political Loyalties and Social Class Ties," *American Journal of Political Science* 28 (1984): 399–417; Robert Huckfeldt, "The Social Communication of Political Expertise," *American Journal of Political Science* 28 (2001): 425–479; Robert Huckfeldt, "Social Contexts, Social Networks, and Urban Neighborhoods: Environmental Constraints on Friendship Choice," *American Journal of Sociology* 89 (1983): 651–669; Huckfeldt and Sprague, *Citizens, Politics and Social Communication*; William N. McPhee, *Formal Theories of Mass Behavior* (New York: Macmillan, 1963).

17. Ronald S. Burt, "Social Contagion and Innovation: Cohesion versus Structural Equivalence." *American Journal of Sociology* 92 (1987): 1287–1335.

18. Chris B. Kenny, "Political Participation and Effects from the Social Environment," *American Journal of Political Science* 36 (1992): 259–267.

19. Mark Granovetter, "The Strength of Weak Ties," *American Journal of Sociology* 78 (1973): 1360–1380.

20. Robert Huckfeldt, Paul Allen Beck, Russell J. Dalton, and Jeffrey Levine, "Political Environments, Cohesive Social Groups, and the Communication of Public Opinion," *American Journal of Political Science* 39 (1995): 1025–1054.

21. Diana C. Mutz, *Hearing the Other Side: Deliberative versus Participatory Democracy* (Cambridge: Cambridge University Press, 2006).

22. John W. Books and Charles L. Prysby, *Political Behavior and the Local Context* (New York: Praeger, 1991).

23. Scott D. McClurg, "Social Networks and Political Participation: The Role of Social Interaction in Explaining Political Participation," *Political Research Quarterly* 56 (2003): 449.

24. Campbell, *Why We Vote*; Gimpel et al., *Cultivating Democracy*; Scott D. McClurg, "The Electoral Relevance of Political Talk: Examining Disagreement and Expertise Effects in Social Networks on Political Participation," *American Journal of Political Science* 50 (2006): 737–754; Mutz, *Hearing the Other Side*; J. Eric Oliver, *The Paradoxes of Integration: Race, Neighborhood, and Civic Life in Multiethnic America* (Chicago: University of Chicago Press, 2010).

25. Scott D. McClurg, "Political Disagreement in Context: The Conditional Effect of Neighborhood Context, Disagreement and Political Talk on Electoral Participation," *Political Behavior* 28 (2006): 349–366. See also Gimpel et al., *Cultivating Democracy*.

26. Matthew J. Burbank, "The Psychological Basis of Contextual Effects," *Political Geography* 14 (1995): 623.

27. William J. McGuire, "Personality and Attitude Change: An Information Processing Theory," in *Psychological Foundations of Attitudes*, ed. Anthony C. Greenwald, Timothy C. Brock, and Thomas M. Ostrom (San Diego, Calif.: Academic Press, 1968), 171–196.

28. Erik H. Erikson, *Childhood and Society*, 2d ed. (New York: W. W. Norton, 1963); James Youniss, Jeffrey A. McLellan, and Miranda Yates, "What We Know about Engendering a Civic Identity," *American Behavioralist Scientist* 40 (1997): 620–631.

29. Duane F. Alwin and Jon A. Krosnick, "Aging, Cohorts, and the Stability of Sociopolitical Orientations over the Life Span," *American Journal of Sociology* 97 (1991): 169–196; Beck and Jennings, "Family Traditions"; James Max Fendrich and Kenneth L. Lovoy, "Back to the Future: Adult Political Behavior of Former Student Activists," *American Sociological Review* 53 (1988): 780–784; Jennings and Marcus, "Partisan Orientations over the Long Haul"; Gerald Marwell, Michael T. Aiken, and N. J. Demerath III, "The Persistence of Political Attitudes among 1960s Civil Rights Activists," *Public Opinion Quarterly* 51 (1987): 359–375; Sidney Verba, Kay Lehman Schlozman, and Henry Brady, *Voice and Equality: Civic Voluntarism in American Politics* (Cambridge, Mass.: Harvard University Press, 1995).

30. Campbell, *Why We Vote*, 5.

31. Rosalyn George, "Urban Girls' 'Race' Friendship and School Choice: Changing Schools, Changing Friendships," *Race, Ethnicity, and Education* 10 (2007): 115–129.

32. Min Zhou, "Ethnicity as Social Capital: Community-based Institutions and Embedded Networks of Social Relations," in *Ethnicity, Social Mobility, and Public Policy: Comparing the U.S.A. and U.K.*, ed. Glenn C. Loury, Tariq Modood, and Steven Teles (New York: Cambridge University Press, 2005), 131–159.

33. Sonya Salamon, "Culture," in *Encyclopedia of Rural America: The Land and People*, ed. Gary A. Goreham (Santa Barbara, Calif.: ABC-Clio, 1997), 172.

34. William Freudenberg, "The Density of Acquaintanceship: An Overlooked Variable in Community Research?" *American Journal of Sociology* 92 (1986): 32.

CHAPTER 1

Epigraph: Harold Wilson, speech to the Consultative Assembly of the Council of Europe, Strasbourg, France, January 23, 1967, reprinted in *New York Times*, January 24, 1967, A12.

1. If you like meat, especially pork, Iowa is your state. This particular delicacy is definitely worth trying. This is just my opinion, but there just is not enough meat on a stick anymore.

2. Douglas S. Massey and Chiara Capoferro, "The Geographic Diversification of American Immigration," in *New Faces in New Places: The Changing Geography of American Immigration,* ed. Douglas Massey (New York: Russell Sage Foundation, 2008), 25–50.

3. Everett S. Lee, "A Theory of Migration," *Demography* 3 (1966): 47–57; Douglas S. Massey, "Why Does Immigration Occur? A Theoretical Synthesis," in *Handbook of International Migration,* ed. Charles Hirschman, Philip Kasinitz, and Joshua DeWind (New York: Russell Sage Foundation, 1999).

4. Jorge Durand, Douglas S. Massey, and Chiara Capoferro, "The New Geography of Mexican Immigration," in *New Destinations: Mexican Immigration in the United States,* ed. Víctor Zúniga and Rubén Hernández-León (New York: Russell Sage Foundation, 2005), 1–20.

5. Alejandro Portes and Rubén G. Rumbaut, *Immigrant America: A Portrait,* 3d ed. (Berkeley: University of California Press, 2006); Alejandro Portes and Rubén G. Rumbaut, *Legacies: The Story of the Immigrant Second Generation* (Berkeley: University of California Press, 2001).

6. Durand et al., "The New Geography of Mexican Immigration"; Douglas S. Massey, Jorge Durand, and Nolan J. Malone, *Beyond Smoke and Mirrors: Mexican Immigration in an Age of Economic Integration* (New York: Russell Sage Foundation, 2002); Pia M. Orrenius, "The Effect of U.S. Border Enforcement on the Crossing Behavior of Mexican Migrants," in *Crossing the Border: Research from the Mexican Migration Project,* ed. Jorge Durand and Douglas S. Massey (New York: Russell Sage Foundation, 2005), 281–290; Alejandro Portes and Robert L. Bach, *Latin Journey: Cuban and Mexican Immigrants in the United States* (Berkeley: University of California Press, 1985).

7. Katherine Fennelly and Helga Leitner, "How the Food Processing Industry Is Diversifying Rural Minnesota," working paper no. 59, Julian Samora Research Institute, Michigan State University, East Lansing, 2002; Roberto Suro and Audrey Singer, "Latino Growth in Metropolitan America: Changing Patterns, New Locations," Center on Urban and Metropolitan Policy of the Brookings Institution and the Pew Hispanic Center, Washington, D.C., 2002.

8. Michael J. Broadway and Terry Ward, "Recent Changes in the Structure and Location of the U.S. Meatpacking Industry," *Geography* 76 (1990): 76–79.

9. Michael J. Broadway, "Beef Stew: Cattle, Immigrants, and Established Residents in a Kansas Beefpacking Town," in *Newcomers in the Workplace: Immigrants and the Restructuring of the U.S. Economy,* ed. Louise Lamphere, Alex Stepick, and Guillermo Grenier (Philadelphia: Temple University Press, 1994), 25–43.

10. Wilson J. Warren, *Tied to the Great Packing Machine: The Midwest and Meatpacking* (Iowa City: University of Iowa Press, 2007), 41.

11. Karen D. Johnson-Webb, "Employer Recruitment and Hispanic Labor Migration: North Carolina Urban Areas at the End of the Millennium," *Professional Geographer* 54 (2002): 406–421; Fred Krissman, "Immigrant Labor Recruitment: U.S. Agribusiness and Undocumented Migration from Mexico," in *Immigration Research for a New Century,* ed. Nancy Foner, Ruben G. Rumbaut, and Steven J. Gold (New York: Russell Sage Foundation, 2000), 277–321.

12. Mark A. Grey and Anne C. Woodrick, "'Latinos Have Revitalized Our Community': Mexican Migration and Anglo Responses in Marshalltown, Iowa," in *New Destinations: Mexican Immigration in the United States,* ed. Víctor Zúniga and Rubén Hernández-León (New York: Russell Sage Foundation, 2005), 133–154.

13. Mark Friedberger, *Shake-Out: Iowa Farm Families in the 1980's* (Lexington: University of Kentucky Press, 1989).

14. David B. Danbom, *Born in the Country: A History of Rural America* (Baltimore: Johns Hopkins University Press, 1995), 267.

15. Paul Lasley, F. Larry Leistritz, Linda M. Lobao, and Katherine Meyer, *Beyond the Amber Waves of Grain: An Examination of Social and Economic Restructuring in the Heartland* (Boulder, Colo.: Westview Press, 1995).

16. Mark A. Grey, "Pork, Poultry and Newcomers in Storm Lake, Iowa," in *Any Way You Cut It: Meat Processing and Small-Town America,* ed. Donald D. Stull, Michael J. Broadway, and David Griffith (Lawrence: University of Kansas Press, 1995), 109–127.

17. Janet Benson, "Undocumented Immigrants and the Meatpacking Industry in the Midwest," in *Illegal Immigration in America: A Reference Handbook,* ed. David W. Haines and Karen E. Rosenblum (Westport, Conn.: Greenwood Press, 1999); Lionel Cantú, "The Peripheralization of Rural America: A Case Study of Latino Migrants in America's Heartland," *Sociological Perspectives* 38 (1995): 399–414; David Griffith, "Social and Cultural Bases for Undocumented Immigration into the US Poultry Industry," in *Illegal Immigration in America: A Reference Handbook,* ed. David W. Haines and Karen E. Rosenblum (Westport, Conn.: Greenwood Press, 1999), 157–171; Barry Yeoman, "Hispanic Diaspora," *Mother Jones,* July–August 2000, 36–77.

18. Grey, "Pork, Poultry and Newcomers."

19. Helen B. Marrow, *New Destination Dreaming: Immigration, Race, and Legal Status in the Rural American South* (Stanford, Calif.: Stanford University Press, 2011), 241.

20. Rochelle L. Dalla, Amy Ellis, and Sheran C. Cramer, "Immigration and Rural America: Latinos' Perceptions of Work and Residence in Three Meatpacking Communities," *Community, Work and Family* 8 (2005): 163–185; Carlos Garcia, "The Role of Quality of Life in the Rural Resettlement of Mexican Immigrants," *Hispanic Journal of Political Science* 31 (2009): 446–467.

21. Mark A. Leach and Frank D. Bean, "The Structure and Dynamics of Mexican Migration to New Destinations in the United States," in *New Faces in New Places: The Changing Geography of American Immigration,* ed. Douglas Massey (New York: Russell Sage Foundation, 2008), 53. See also Douglas S. Massey, Rafael Alarcon, Jorge Durand, and Humberto Gonzalez, *Return to Aztlan: The Social Process of International Migration from Western Mexico* (Berkeley: University of California Press, 1987); Douglas S. Massey, Luin Goldring, and Jorge Durand, "Continuities in Transnational Migration: An Analysis of Nineteen Mexican Communities," *American Journal of Sociology* 99 (1994): 1492–1533.

22. Rogelio Saenz, "The Changing Demography of Latinos in the Midwest," in *Latinos in the Midwest,* ed. Rubén O. Martinez (East Lansing: Michigan State University Press, 2011), 33–55.

23. William Kandel and John Cromartie, *New Patterns of Hispanic Settlement in Rural America,* Rural Development Research Report, no. 99, Economic Research Service, U.S. Department of Agriculture, Washington, D.C., 2004.

24. Ibid.

25. Emilio A. Parrado and William A. Kandel, "Hispanic Population Growth and Rural Income Inequality," *Social Forces* 88 (2010): 1421–1450.

26. Mark A. Grey, "State and Local Immigration Policy in Iowa," in *Immigration's New Frontiers: Experiences from the Emerging Gateway States,* ed. Greg Anrig Jr. and Tova Andrea Wang (New York: Century Foundation Press, 2006), 33–66.

27. Kandel and Cromartie, *New Patterns of Hispanic Settlement,* app. table 2.

28. Roy Beck, *The Case against Immigration* (New York: W. W. Norton, 1996); George J. Borjas, "Do Blacks Gain or Lose from Immigration?" in *Help or Hindrance? The Economic Implications of Immigration for African Americans,* ed. Daniel S. Hamermesh and Frank D. Bean (New York: Russell Sage Foundation, 1998), 51–74; William H. Frey

and Kao-Lee Liaw, "Internal Migration of Foreign-born Latinos and Asians: Are They Assimilating Geographically?" in *Geographic Perspectives on U.S. Migration: The Role of Population Movements in the Economic and Demographic Restructuring of Society,* ed. Kavita Pandit and Suzanne Davies Winters (Lanham, Md.: Rowman and Littlefield, 1999), 212–230; Donald Huddle, *The Net National Cost of Immigration in 1993* (Washington, D.C.: Carrying Capacity Network, 1994); Manuel Pastor Jr. and Enrico Marcelli, "Somewhere over the Rainbow? African Americans, Unauthorized Mexican Immigration and Coalition Building," *Review of Black Political Economy* 31 (2003): 125–155; Michael Rosenfeld and Marta Tienda, "Mexican Immigration, Occupational Niches and Labor Market Competition: Evidence from Los Angeles, Chicago and Atlanta, 1970–1990," in *Immigration and Opportunity: Race, Ethnicity and Employment in the United States,* ed. Frank D. Bean and Stephanie Bell-Rose (New York: Russell Sage Foundation, 1999); Michael A. Stoll, Edwin Melendez, and Abel Valenzuela, "Spatial Job Search and Job Competition among Immigrant and Native Groups in Los Angeles," *Regional Studies* 35 (2002): 97–112.

29. George J. Borjas, "The Economics of Immigration," *Journal of Economic Literature* 32 (1994): 1698. See also Frank D. Bean, B. Lindsay Lowell, and Lowell J. Taylor, "Undocumented Mexican Immigrants and the Earnings of Other Workers in the United States," *Demography* 25 (1988): 35–52; George J. Borjas and Stephen J. Trejo, "Immigrant Participation in the Welfare System," *Industrial and Labor Relations Review* 44 (1991): 195–211; David Card, "The Impact of the Mariel Boatlift on the Miami Labor Market," *Industrial and Labor Relations Review* 43 (1990): 245–257; Louise Lamphere, Alex Stepick, and Guillermo Grenier, eds., *Newcomers in the Workplace: Immigrants and the Restructuring of the U.S. Economy* (Philadelphia: Temple University Press, 1994); Helga Leitner, "The Political Economy of International Labor Migration," in *Companion Guide to Economic Geography,* ed. Eric Sheppard and Trevor J. Barnes (Oxford: Blackwell, 2000), 450–467; Jeffery S. Passel and Rebecca L. Clark, "How Much Do Immigrants Really Cost? A Reappraisal of Huddle's 'The Costs of Immigrants,'" Urban Institute, Washington, D.C., 1994.

30. Theo J. Majka and Linda C. Majka, "Institutional Obstacles to Incorporation: Latino Immigrant Experiences in a Midsized Rust-Belt City," in *Latinos in the Midwest,* ed. Rubén O. Martinez (East Lansing: Michigan State University Press, 2011), 87–118.

31. Thomas Tancredo, *In Mortal Danger: The Battle for America's Border and Security* (Nashville: Cumberland House, 2006).

32. David Goodhart, "Too Diverse?" *Prospect* 95 (February 2004): 30–37, available online at http://www.cceia.org/media/goodhart.pdf (accessed January 9, 2012); Samuel P. Huntington, *Who Are We? The Challenges to America's National Identity* (New York: Simon and Schuster, 2004).

33. Stephen Castles and Mark J. Miller, *The Age of Migration* (Basingstoke: Palgrave Macmillan, 2003); Kathleen N. Conzen, David A. Gerber, Ewa Morawska, George E. Pozzetta, and Rudolph J. Vecoli, "The Invention of Ethnicity: A Perspective from the USA," *Journal of American Ethnic History* 12 (1992): 4–51; Joseph Nevins, *Operation Gatekeeper: The Rise of the "Illegal Alien" and the Making of the U.S.–Mexico Boundary* (New York: Routledge, 2003).

34. Katherine Fennelly, "Prejudice toward Immigrants in the Midwest," in *New Faces in New Places: The Changing Geography of American Immigration,* ed. Douglas Massey (New York: Russell Sage Foundation, 2008), 163.

35. Ibid., 151.

36. Portes and Rumbaut, *Immigrant America.*

37. Richard Alba and Victor Nee, *Remaking the American Mainstream: Assimilation and Contemporary Immigration* (Cambridge, Mass.: Harvard University Press, 2003).

38. Philip Kasinitz, Mary Waters, John Mollenkopf, and Jennifer Holdaway, *Inheriting the City: The Children of Immigrants Come of Age* (New York: Russell Sage Foundation, 2009); Portes and Rumbaut, *Legacies*.

39. Roger Waldinger, ed., *Strangers at the Gates: New Immigrants in Urban America* (Berkeley: University of California Press, 2001).

40. Karen M. Kaufmann, "Immigration and the Future of Black Power in U.S. Cities," *Du Bois Review* 4 (2007): 80. See also Karen M. Kaufmann, "Cracks in the Rainbow: Group Commonality as a Basis for Latino and African-American Coalitions," *Political Research Quarterly* 56 (2003): 199–210.

41. Claudine Gay, "Seeing Difference: The Effect of Economic Disparity on Black Attitudes toward Latinos," *American Journal of Political Science* 50 (2006): 982–997; Karen M. Kaufmann, "Divided We Stand: Mass Attitudes and the Prospects for Black/Latino Urban Political Coalitions," in *Black and Latino/a Politics: Issues in Political Development in the United States*, ed. William E. Nelson Jr. and Jessica Lavareiga Monforti (Miami: Barnhardt and Ashe, 2006), 158–168; Karen M. Kaufmann, *The Urban Voter: Group Conflict and Mayoral Voting Behavior in American Cities* (Ann Arbor: University of Michigan Press, 2004); Paula D. McClain, Niambi M. Carter, Victoria M. DeFrancesco Soto, Monique L. Lyle, Jeffrey D. Grynaviski, Shayla C. Nunnally, Thomas J. Scotto, J. Alan Kendrick, Gerald F. Lackey, and Kendra Davenport Cotton, "Racial Distancing in a Southern City: Latino Immigrants' View of Black Americans," *Journal of Politics* 68 (2006): 571–584; Nicolas Corona Vaca, *The Presumed Alliance: The Unspoken Conflict between Latinos and Blacks and What It Means for America* (New York: Rayo, 2004).

42. Atiya Kai Stokes, "Latino Group Consciousness and Political Participation," *American Politics Research* 31 (2003): 361–378.

43. Rodney Hero, F. Chris Garcia, John Garcia, and Harry Pachon, "Latino Participation, Partisanship and Office Holding," *PS: Political Science and Politics* 33 (2000): 529–534.

44. Angelo Falcon, "Black and Latino Politics in New York City: Race and Ethnicity in a Changing Urban Context," *New Community* 14 (1988): 370–384; F. Chris Garcia, "Hispanic Political Participation and Demographic Correlates," in *Pursing Power: Latinos and the Political System*, 2nd ed. (South Bend, Ind.: University of Notre Dame Press, 1997).

45. Arturo Vega, Rubén O. Martinez, and Tia Stevens, "*Cosas Políticas*: Politics, Attitudes and Perceptions by Region," in *Latinos in the Midwest*, ed. Rubén O. Martinez (East Lansing: Michigan State University Press, 2011), 57–86.

46. John R. Arvizu and F. Chris Garcia, "Latino Voting Participation: Explaining and Differentiating Latino Voting Turnout," *Hispanic Journal of Behavioral Sciences* 18 (1996): 104–123; S. Karthick Ramakrishnan and Mark Baldassare, *The Ties That Bind: Changing Demographics and Civic Engagement in California* (San Francisco: Public Policy Institute of California, 2004); Carole J. Uhlaner, Bruce E. Cain, and D. Roderick Kiewiet, "Political Participation of Ethnic Minorities in the 1980s," *Political Behavior* 11 (1989): 195–231; Stephen White, Neil Nevitte, Andre Blais, Elisabeth Gidengil, and Patrick Fournier, "The Political Resocialization of Immigrants: Resistance of Lifelong Learning," *Political Research Quarterly* 61 (2008): 268–281; Janelle Wong, "The Effects of Age and Political Exposure on the Development of Party Identification among Asian American and Latino Immigrants in the United States," *Political Behavior* 22 (2000): 341–371.

47. Michael Jones-Correa, *Between Two Nations: The Political Predicament of Latinos in New York City* (Ithaca, N.Y.: Cornell University Press, 1998); Sidney Verba, Kay Schlozman, and Henry Brady, *Voice and Equality: Civic Voluntarism in American Politics* (Cambridge, Mass.: Harvard University Press, 1995).

48. Turnout studies include Rodolfo O. de la Garza and Fujia Lu, "Explorations into Latino Voluntarism," in *Nuevos Senderos: Reflections on Hispanics and Philanthropy*, ed. Diana Comoamor, William A. Diaz, and Henry A. J. Ramos (Houston: Arte Publico Press,

1999), 55–78; Louis DeSipio, Rodolfo O. de la Garza, and Mark Setzler, "Awash in the Mainstream: Latinos and the 1996 Elections," in *Awash in the Mainstream: Latinos and the 1996 Elections,* ed. Rodolfo de la Garza and Louis DeSipio (Boulder, Colo.: Westview Press, 1999), 3–46; Daron Shaw, Rodolfo O. de la Garza, and Jongho Lee, "Examining Latino Turnout in 1996: A Three-State, Validated Survey Approach," *American Journal of Political Science* 44 (2000): 338–346. For a nonelectoral participation study, see Robert D. Wrinkle, Joseph Stewart Jr., Kenneth J. Meier, and John R. Arvizu, "Ethnicity and Nonelectoral Participation," *Hispanic Journal of Behavioral Sciences* 18 (1996): 142–151.

49. Karen M. Kaufmann and Antonio Rodriguez, "The Future of Latino Involvement in U.S. Politics: Why Immigrant Destinations Matter," Unpublished ms.

50. Kristi Andersen, "In Whose Interest? Political Parties, Context and Incorporation of Immigrants," in *New Race Politics in America: Understanding Minority and Immigrant Politics,* ed. Jane Junn and Kerry L. Haynie (New York: Cambridge University Press, 2008); Natacha Hritzuk and David Park, "The Question of Latino Participation: From an SES to a Social Structural Explanation," *Social Science Quarterly* 81 (2000): 151–166; Jan E. Leighley, *Strength in Numbers?* (Princeton, N.J.: Princeton University Press, 2001); Janelle S. Wong, *Democracy's Promise: Immigrants and American Civic Institutions* (Ann Arbor: University of Michigan Press, 2006).

51. Louis DeSipio, "Building America, One Person at a Time: Naturalization and Political Behavior of the Naturalized in Contemporary U.S. Politics," in *E Pluribus Unum? Immigrant, Civic Life and Political Incorporation,* ed. John Mollenkopf and Gary Gerstle (New York: Russell Sage Foundation, 2001), 67–106.

52. Jonathan Benjamin-Alvarado, Louis DeSipio, and Celeste Montoya, "Latino Mobilization in New Immigrant Destinations: The Anti–H.R. 4437 Protest in Nebraska's Cities," *Urban Affairs Review* 44 (2009): 718–735.

53. Melissa R. Michelson, "Getting Out the Latino Vote: How Door-to-Door Canvassing Influences Voter Turnout in Rural Central California," *Political Behavior* 25 (2003): 247–263.

54. Korean American Coalition, "Population Change by Race and Ethnicity, 1990–2000: USA, California, Southern California, LA County, Orange County, Koreatown," July 2, 2003, available online at http://www.calstatela.edu/centers/ckaks/census/7203_tables .pdf (accessed August 15, 2011).

55. The report by the Korean American Coalition shows that the rates of change in the five-county area around Los Angeles (including Los Angeles, Orange, Riverside, San Bernardino, and Ventura counties) were 38 percent for Latinos and 32 percent for Asians: ibid.

56. Jody Swilky and Kent Newman, dirs. *A Little Salsa on the Prairie: The Changing Character of Perry, Iowa,* documentary, Full Spectrum Productions, Des Moines, Iowa, 2006.

57. Deborah Fink, *Cutting into the Meatpacking Line: Workers and Change in the Rural Midwest* (Chapel Hill: University of North Carolina Press, 1998), 52–53.

58. Swilky and Newman, *A Little Salsa on the Prairie.*

59. Ibid.

60. Warren, *Tied to the Great Packing Machine.*

61. Fink, *Cutting into the Meatpacking Line,* 58–62.

62. "Perry, Iowa," City-Data.com, available online at http://www.city-data.com/city/ Perry-Iowa.html (accessed May 12, 2010).

63. Warren, *Tied to the Great Packing Machine,* 70.

64. Mark A. Grey, "Meatpacking and the Migration of Refugee and Immigrant Labor in Storm Lake, Iowa," *Changing Face* 2, no. 3 (1996), available online at http://migration .ucdavis.edu/cf/comments.php?id=154_0_2_0 (accessed February 2, 2012).

65. Ibid.; Stephen J. Hedges, Dana Hawkins, and Penny Loeb, "The New Jungle," *U.S. News and World Report,* September 23, 1996, 34–46. For example, employees do not have access to health care until they have worked at IBP for six months. Because of the difficulty of the job and the low wages, turnover at the plant is higher than 100 percent per year, making it difficult for many employees ever to become eligible.

66. Warren, *Tied to the Great Packing Machine,* 70.

67. Grey, "Meatpacking ."

68. Chuck Offenburger, "Storm Lake's Big Statement: $40 Million Project Lets Town Reinvent Itself as a Destination." *Iowa Farm Bureau's Family Living Magazine,* March 2009, available online at http://www.offenburger.com/lspaper.asp?link=20090309 (accessed June 12, 2009).

69. City-Data.com, available online at http://www.city-data.com/city (accessed December 13, 2008).

70. Grey, "Pork, Poultry, and Newcomers," 109–127.

71. Dennis Chong, "Tolerance and Social Adjustment to New Norms and Practices," *Political Behavior* 16 (1994): 21–53 (23).

72. Ibid., 28.

73. Patricia G. Devine, Margo J. Monteith, Julia R. Zuwerink, and Andrew J. Elliot, "Prejudice with and without Compunction," *Journal of Personality and Social Psychology* 60 (1991): 829.

74. Hugh Matthews, Mark Taylor, Kenneth Sherwood, Faith Tucker, and Melanie Lamb, "Growing Up in the Countryside: Children and the Rural Idyll," *Journal of Rural Studies* 16 (2000): 141–153; Cynthia B. Struthers and Janet L. Bokemeier, "Myths and Realities of Raising Children and Creating Family Life in a Rural County," *Journal of Family Issues* 21 (2000): 17–46.

75. Caroline Tauxe, "Heartland Community: Economic Restructuring and the Management of Small Town Identity in the Central U.S.," *Identities* 5 (1998): 335–377.

76. Grey and Woodrick, "Latinos Have Revitalized Our Community." See also Lisa Nelson and Nancy Hiemstra, "Latino Immigrants and the Renegotiation of Place and Belonging in Small Town America," *Social and Cultural Geography* 9 (2008): 319–342.

77. Personal interview with Viivi Shirley, Perry, Iowa, May 25, 2010.

78. Frank M. Bryan, *Politics in the Rural States: People, Parties, and Processes* (Boulder, Colo.: Westview Press, 1981), 7.

79. With the exception of a few policy pieces, a search for "rural America" in political science journals yielded only the following research articles within the past ten years: Peter L. Francia and Jody Baumgartner, "Victim or Victor of the 'Culture War'? How Cultural Issues Affect Support for George W. Bush in Rural America," *American Review of Politics* 26 (2005–2006): 349–367; Garcia, "The Role of Quality of Life"; James G. Gimpel and Kimberly A. Karnes, "The Rural Side of the Urban–Rural Gap," *PS: Political Science and Politics* 39 (2006): 467–472; Helen B. Marrow, "New Destinations and Immigrant Incorporation," *Perspectives on Politics* 3 (2005): 781–799 (note that Marrow is a sociologist, not a political scientist); Seth C. McKee, "Rural Voters in Presidential Elections, 1992–2004," *Forum* 5 (2007): art. 2.

80. H. L. Mencken, "The Calamity of Appomattox," *American Mercury,* September 1930, 29–31.

81. In his bestselling book, Thomas Frank argues that Kansans (and others in predominantly rural states) regularly vote against their economic interests because they have been duped by conservative elites who use "moral" issues as a means to divert attention away from their real passion, fiscal conservatism: Thomas Frank, *What's the Matter with Kansas? How Conservatives Won the Heart of America* (New York: Henry Holt, 2004).

82. Robert A. Dahl, "The City in the Future of Democracy," *American Political Science Review* 61 (1967): 960–961.

83. Bryan, *Politics in the Rural States,* 15.

CHAPTER 2

Epigraph: As quoted in *Improving the Quality of Life for the Black Elderly: Challenges and Opportunities,* hearing before the Select Committee on Aging, U.S. House of Representatives, 100th Cong. (1st sess.), September 25, 1987, 28.

1. David B. Danbom, *Born in the Country: A History of Rural America* (Baltimore: Johns Hopkins University Press, 1995).

2. For a good discussion of how rural areas and small towns have adapted since the 1950s in the Midwest, see Robert Wuthnow, *Remaking the Heartland: Middle America since the 1950s* (Princeton, N.J.: Princeton University Press, 2011).

3. Jared Diamond and James A. Robinson, *Natural Experiments of History* (Boston: Harvard University Press, 2010), 2.

4. For other advantages, see Thad Dunning, "Improving Causal Inference: Strengths and Limitations of Natural Experiments," *Political Research Quarterly* 61 (2008): 282–293.

5. Diamond and Robinson, *Natural Experiments of History,* 267.

6. Rochelle L. Dalla, Amy Ellis, and Sheran C. Cramer, "Immigration and Rural America: Latinos' Perceptions of Work and Residence in Three Meatpacking Communities," *Community, Work, and Family* 8 (2005): 163–185.

7. William Kandel and John Cromartie, *New Patterns of Hispanic Settlement in Rural America,* Rural Development Research Report, no. 99, Economic Research Service, U.S. Department of Agriculture, Washington, D.C., 2004, app. 2.

8. Michael Lewis-Beck and Peverill Squire, "Iowa: The Most Representative State?" *PS: Political Science and Politics* 42 (2009): 39–44.

9. Ibid.

10. Given the title of the book and references to rural America throughout, some may wish to define where the five towns in the study fit into "rural" and "urban" classifications. The short answer is that it depends on the definition of these terms. "Rural" is a highly contested term. The U.S. Department of Agriculture (USDA) has identified several different methods for measuring this term. According to the official U.S. Census Bureau definitions, rural areas consist of open country and settlements with fewer than 2,500 residents. According to this definition, none of these towns would be considered "rural." The USDA's Economic Research Service has measured rural areas by looking at the counties in which they are located. In 1990, U.S. counties were considered metropolitan or non-metropolitan. Metropolitan areas have at least one urbanized area with population of 50,000 or more and include adjacent counties in which at least 25 percent of workers commute to the central counties of the metro/micro area. By these definitions, only one of the towns was located within a county that is included in a metropolitan statistical area: Dallas County (home of Perry), which lies within the Des Moines–West Des Moines metropolitan area. Many researchers contend that counties are too big to serve as building blocks for statistical areas, and sub-units should be used. Some sub-units commonly used are Zip Code areas, block groups, and census tracts: John B. Cromartie and Linda L. Swanson, "Census Tracts More Precisely Define Rural Populations and Areas," *Rural Development Perspectives* 11 (2001): 31–39. In 2000, the U.S. Census Bureau categorized census tracts as either "urban" (adjacent densely settled census blocks that encompass a population of 2,500–49,999) or "rural" (any cluster with fewer than 2,500 people). Within each community, the proportion of individuals living in rural clusters is Boone, 19 percent; Carroll, 42 percent;

Harlan, 62 percent; Perry, 22 percent; Storm Lake, 26 percent. This gives some idea of the difficulty in defining "rural," as well as how a designation of metropolitan or non-metropolitan can be misleading at the town level. Although Perry is inside a "metro area," a greater proportion of its population lives in census tracts defined as rural clusters than in Boone, which is not located in a "metro area." Finally, some rural sociologists have defined a "small town" as an incorporated place that ranges in population from 2,500 to 20,000, a designation that would certainly fit all of these communities: see Charles M. Tolbert, Michael D. Irwin, Thomas A. Lyson, and Alfred R. Nucci, "Civic Community in Small-Town America: How Civic Welfare Is Influenced by Local Capitalism and Civic Engagement," *Rural Sociology* 67 (2002): 90–113.

11. Dorothy Schweider, "Early History of Iowa," *Iowa Official Register,* available online at http://www.legis.state.ia.us/Register/Chapter_7_History_and_Constitution.pdf (accessed May 14, 2010).

12. Nathan E. Goldthwait, ed., *History of Boone County, Iowa,* vols. 1–2 (Chicago: Pioneer Publishing, 1914).

13. James F. Kerwin, *My Hometown, Carroll, Iowa* (Glidden, Iowa: Ferguson, 1992).

14. *Biographical History of Shelby and Audubon Counties, Iowa* (Chicago: W. S. Dunbar, 1889), 260.

15. Phyllis Heller, "Early Shelby County Towns, Post Offices, and Post Masters," available online at http://iagenweb.org/shelby/post-tpom.htm (accessed May 14, 2010).

16. Matt Willett, "History of Rock Island Railroad," available online at http://home .covad.net/~scicoatnsew/rihist3.htm (accessed May 14, 2010).

17. Marjorie Patterson, *A Town Called Perry: Midwest Life in Small-Town Iowa.* (Perry, Iowa: Fullhart-Carnegie Museum Trust, 1997), 6.

18. C. H. Wegerslev and Thomas Walpole, *Past and Present of Buena Vista County, Iowa* (Chicago: S. J. Clarke, 1909), available online at http://iagenweb.org/buenavista/ stormlake.html (accessed May 12, 2010).

19. Robert D. Putnam, *Bowling Alone: The Collapse and Revival of American Community* (New York: Simon and Schuster, 2000), 291. These indicators include (1) measures of community organizational life (e.g., number of civic/social organizations per 1,000 population, number of club meetings annually, mean number of group memberships); (2) measures of engagement in public affairs (e.g., turnout in presidential elections, attendance at public meetings); (3) measures of community volunteerism (e.g., number of nonprofit organizations per 1,000 population, mean number of times worked on a committee project in the previous year, mean number of times did volunteer work in previous year); (4) measures of informal sociability (e.g., agrees with "I spend a lot of time visiting friends," mean number of times entertained in home in previous year); (5) measures of social trust (e.g., agrees with "Most people can be trusted," agrees with "Most people are honest").

20. Frequently Asked Questions Archive, "Tax Exempt Organizations in Iowa," available online at http://www.faqs.org/tax-exempt/index-Iowa.html (accessed April 20, 2011).

21. Michael Irwin, Charles M. Tolbert, and Thomas A. Lyson, "There's No Place Like Home: Nonmigration and Civic Engagement," *Environment and Planning* 31 (1999): 2223–2238.

22. Andrew Greeley, "Coleman Revisited: Religious Structures as a Source of Social Capital," *American Behavioral Scientist* 40 (1997): 587–594.

23. Dave Olson, "A Sample of the Church in Iowa and the Des Moines Metro Areas, 1990–2000," American Church Research Project, 2004, available online at http://the americanchurch.org/sample/IowaStateandMetroSample.ppt (accessed May 15, 2010). These figures are based on a nationwide study of American church attendance, as reported by churches and denominations.

24. Martin B. Bradley, Norman M. Green Jr., Dale E. Jones, Mac Lynn, and Lou McNeil, *Churches and Church Membership in the United States, 1990* (Atlanta: Glenmary Research Center, 1992).

25. "News Audiences Increasingly Polarized," survey report, Pew Research Center for the People and the Press, Washington, D.C., June 8, 2004, available online at http://people -press.org/report/?pageid=834 (accessed September 13, 2010).

26. Charlotte Eby, "Democrat House Leaders Look for Moderation, with High Expectations," *Quad City Times,* January 6, 2007, available online at http://www.qctimes.com/ news/state-and-regional/article_927e8c67-9c78-56c7-9985-ad07a80b6666.html (accessed October 15, 2009).

27. In 2000, Gore won by fewer than 5,000 votes; in 2004, Bush won with just over 10,000 votes of more than 1.5 million cast.

28. Michael O'Brien, "Rep[resentative] Steve King Slams Hate Crimes Bill as Protecting 'Sexual Idiosyncrasies,'" *The Hill* , October 9, 2009, available online at http://thehill .com/blogs/blog-briefing-room/news/62451-rep-steve-king-slams-hate-crimes-bill-as -protecting-sexual-idiosyncrasies?page=2#comments (accessed October 13, 2009).

29. "Senate, White House Agree on Worker Program," *WorldNetDaily,* May 17, 2007, available online at http://www.wnd.com/index.php?fa=PAGE.printable&pageId=41655 (accessed April 22, 2011).

30. Jason Hancock, "In Swing State Iowa, Dallas County Is Key," *Iowa Independent,* August 22, 2008, available online at http://iowaindependent.com/4398/in-swing-state -iowa-dallas-county-is-key (accessed October 13, 2009).

31. Kenneth P. Langton and M. Kent Jennings, "Political Socialization and the High School Civics Curriculum in the United States," *American Political Science Review* 62 (1968): 852–867; Richard G. Niemi and Jane Junn, *Civic Education: What Makes Students Learn* (New Haven, Conn.: Yale University Press, 1998).

32. In Iowa, a "unit" consists of a course or equivalent related components or partial units taught throughout the academic year: Iowa Code, 2009, Title VII Education and Cultural Affairs, Subtitle 1 Elementary and Secondary Education, Chapter 256.11, available online at http://search.legis.state.ia.us (accessed February 24, 2011).

33. CTI College Search, available online at http://www.citytowninfo.com/school -profiles/buena-vista-university (accessed May 13, 2010).

34. U.S. Bureau of the Census, Decennial Censuses, 1990 Census: Summary Tape File 3, American Factfinder, Table P070, prepared by the State Library of Iowa, State Data Center Program, 800-248-4483, available online at http://www.silo.lib.ia.us/datacenter (accessed March 2, 2011).

CHAPTER 3

Epigraph: Stephen Colbert, *The Colbert Report,* Comedy Central, episode no. 2138, November 2, 2006. Other punchlines to this repeating joke have included ". . . because I have my own late-night talk show" (episode no. 3034, March 13, 2007), ". . . because I can't say the 'N' word, I have to say 'the "N" word' instead" (episode no. 3053, April 23, 2007), and ". . . because I shop at Eddie Bauer" (episode no. 2150, November 30, 2006).

1. David Evans, "Diversity in Iowa," *Chronicle of Higher Education,* November 25, 2009, available online at http://chronicle.com/blogPost/Diversity-in-Iowa/8995 (accessed November 26, 2009).

2. Intolerant attitudes have also been found among White populations in sparsely populated rural areas where Blacks, immigrants, and ethnic rivals do not constitute a credible threat: see J. Eric Oliver and Tali Mendelberg, "Reconsidering the Environmental

Determinants of White Racial Attitudes," *American Journal of Political Science* 44 (2000): 574–589; D. Stephen Voss, "Beyond Racial Threat: Failure of an Old Hypothesis in the New South," *Journal of Politics* 58 (1996): 1156–1170.

3. In this study, the terms "White" and "Anglo" are used interchangeably to refer to the predominantly non-Hispanic White communities in Iowa's small towns. I realize that "White" is a racial term that encompasses some of the ethnic minorities studied here. The community's residents, both Anglo and Latino, used "White" synonymously with Anglo in their conversations.

4. James G. Gimpel and J. Celeste Lay, "Political Socialization and Reactions to Immigration-Related Diversity in Rural America," *Rural Sociology* 73 (2008): 180–204.

5. Diane Hughes, James Rodriguez, Emilie P. Smith, Deborah J. Johnson, Howard C. Stevenson, and Paul Spicer, "Parents' Ethnic-Racial Socialization Practices: A Review of Research and Directions for Future Study," *Developmental Psychology* 42 (2006): 761.

6. Amanda E. Lewis, "There Is No 'Race' in the Schoolyard: Color-Blind Ideology in an (Almost) All-White School," *American Educational Research Journal* 38 (2001): 781–811.

7. On hostility to racial integration, see ; Mark A. Fossett and K. Jill Kiecolt, "The Relative Size of Minority Populations and White Racial Attitudes," *Social Science Quarterly* 70 (1989): 820–835; Jerry Wilcox and W. Clark Roof, "Percent Black and Black-White Status Inequality: Southern versus Non-Southern Patterns," *Social Science Quarterly* 59 (1978): 421–434. On higher turnout to protect self-interest, see V. O. Key, *Southern Politics in State and Nation* (New York: Alfred A. Knopf, 1949). On increased racial violence, see Jay Corzine, James Creech, and Lin Corzine, "Black Concentration and Lynchings in the South: Testing Blalock's Power-Threat Hypothesis," *Social Forces* 61 (1983): 774–795; Donald P. Green, Dara Strolovich, and Janelle Wong, "Defended Neighborhoods, Integration and Racially Motivated Crime," *American Journal of Sociology* 104 (1998): 372–403. On ideological conservatism, see Michael Giles and Kaenan Hertz, "Racial Threat and Partisan Identification," *The American Political Science Review* 88 (1994): 317–326.

8. Kim Quaile Hill and Jan E. Leighley, "Racial Diversity, Voter Turnout and Mobilizing Institutions in the United States," *American Political Quarterly* 27 (1999): 275–295.

9. Stephen D. Voss, "Huddled Masses or Immigrant Menace? The Black Belt Hypothesis Did Not Emigrate," *American Review of Politics* 22 (2001): 217–232.

10. Michael A. Zarate and Moira P. Shaw, "The Role of Cultural Inertia in Reactions to Immigration on the U.S./Mexico Border," *Journal of Social Issues* 66 (2010): 45–57.

11. Joseph A. Amato, *To Call It Home: The New Immigrants of Southwestern Minnesota* (Marshall, Minn.: Crossings Press, 1996); Jorge Chapa, Rogelio Saenz, Refugio I. Rochin, and Eileen Diaz McConnell, "Latinos and the Changing Demographic Fabric of the Rural Midwest," in *Apple Pie and Enchiladas: Latino Newcomers to the Midwest*, ed. Ann V. Millard and Jorge Chapa (Austin: University of Texas Press, 2001), 47–73.

12. Gimpel and Lay, "Political Socialization and Reactions to Immigration-Related Diversity in Rural America."

13. Hubert Blalock, *Toward a Theory of Minority Group Relations* (New York: John Wiley and Sons, 1967). See also Regina P. Branton and Bradford S. Jones, "Re-examining Racial Attitudes: The Conditional Relationship between Diversity and Socioeconomic Environment," *American Journal of Political Science* 49 (2005): 359–372; Susan Olzak, *The Dynamics of Ethnic Competition and Conflict* (Stanford, Calif.: Stanford University Press, 1992).

14. Katherine Fennelly and Christopher Federico, "Rural Residence as a Determinant of Attitudes Toward U.S. Immigration Policy," *International Migration* 46 (2008): 151–190; Jeannie Haubert and Elizabeth Fussell, "Explaining Pro-Immigrant Sentiment in the

U.S.: Social Class, Cosmopolitanism, and Perceptions of Immigrants," *International Migration Review* 40 (2006): 489–507; Marilyn Hoskin and William Mishler, "Public Opinion toward New Migrants: A Comparative Analysis," *International Migration* 21 (1983): 440–462; Yueh-Ting Lee and Victor Ottati, "Attitudes toward U.S. Immigration Policy: The Roles of In-Group–Out-Group Bias, Economic Concern and Obedience to Law," *Journal of Social Psychology* 142 (2002): 617–634; Rita J. Simon, "Immigration and American Attitudes," *Public Opinion* 10 (1987): 47–50.

15. Jack Citrin, Donald P. Green, Christopher Muste, and Cara Wong, "Public Opinion toward Immigration Reform: The Role of Economic Motivations," *Journal of Politics* 59 (1997): 858–881; Ann V. Millard, Jorge Chapa, and Eileen Diaz McConnell, "'Not Racist Like Our Parents': Anti-Latino Prejudice and Institutional Discrimination," in *Apple Pie and Enchiladas: Latino Newcomers to the Midwest,* ed. Ann V. Millard and Jorge Chapa (Austin: University of Texas Press, 2001), 102–124.

16. Gordon W. Allport, *The Nature of Prejudice* (Reading, Mass.: Addison-Wesley, 1954); Rupert Brown and Miles Hewstone, "An Integrative Theory of Intergroup Contact," in *Advances in Experimental Social Psychology,* vol. 37, ed. Mark P. Zanna (San Diego, Calif.: Academic Press, 2005), 255–343; Thomas Carsey, "The Contextual Effects of Race on White Voter Behavior: The 1989 New York City Mayoral Election," *Journal of Politics* 57 (1995): 221–228; M. V. Hood III and Irwin L. Morris, "Amigo o Enemigo? Context, Attitudes, and Anglo Public Opinion toward Immigration," *Social Science Quarterly* 78 (1997): 309–323; Thomas F. Pettigrew, "Intergroup Contact Theory," *Annual Review of Psychology* 49 (1998): 65–85; Thomas F. Pettigrew and Linda Tropp, "A Meta-Analytic Test of Intergroup Contact Theory," *Journal of Personality and Social Psychology* 90 (2006): 751–783; Voss, "Beyond Racial Threat"; Susan Welch, Lee Sigelman, Timothy Bledsoe, and Michael Combs, *Race and Place: Race Relations in an American City* (Cambridge: Cambridge University Press, 2001); Daniel M. Wilner, Rosabelle Price Walkley, and Stuart W. Cook, *Human Relations in Interracial Housing: A Study of the Contact Hypothesis* (Minneapolis: University of Minnesota Press, 1976).

17. Justin Allen Berg, "Core Networks and Whites' Attitudes toward Immigrants and Immigration Policy," *Public Opinion Quarterly* 73 (2009): 7–31.

18. John Dixon, "Contact and Boundaries: 'Locating' the Social Psychology of Intergroup Relations," *Theory and Psychology* 11 (2001): 587–608.

19. Shang E. Ha, "The Consequences of Multiracial Contexts on Public Attitudes toward Immigration," *Political Research Quarterly* 63 (2010): 29–42. See also Mary R. Jackman and M. Crane, "'Some of My Best Friends Are Black . . .' Interracial Friendship and Whites' Racial Attitudes," *Public Opinion Quarterly* 50 (1986): 459–486; J. Eric Oliver and Janelle Wong, "Intergroup Prejudice in Multiethnic Settings," *American Journal of Political Science* 47 (2003): 567–582.

20. Robert M. Stein, Stephanie Shirley Post, and Allison Rinden, "Reconciling Context and Contact Effects on Racial Attitudes," *Political Research Quarterly* 53 (2000): 285–303. See also Michael O. Emerson, Karen J. Chai, and George Yancey, "Does Race Matter in Residential Segregation? Exploring the Preferences of White Americans," *American Sociological Review* 66 (2001): 922–935.

21. J. Eric Oliver, *The Paradoxes of Integration: Race, Neighborhood, and Civic Life in Multiethnic America* (Chicago: University of Chicago Press, 2010).

22. Gunnar Myrdal, *An American Dilemma: The Negro Problem and Modern Democracy* (New York: Harper and Brothers, 1944).

23. Allport, *The Nature of Prejudice.* See also John F. Dovidio, Samuel L. Gaertner, and Ana Validzic, "Intergroup Bias: Status, Differentiation, and a Common In-Group Identity," *Journal of Personality and Social Psychology* 75 (1998): 109–120; Jackman and

Crane, "Some of My Best Friends Are Black"; Muzafer Sherif, O. J. Harvey, B. J. White, W. R. Hood, and Carolyn W. Sherif, *Intergroup Conflict and Cooperation: The Robber's Cave Experiment* (Norman: University of Oklahoma Book Exchange, 1961); Lee Sigelman and Susan Welch, "The Contact Hypothesis Revisited: Black–White Interaction and Positive Racial Attitudes," *Social Forces* 71 (1993): 781–795; Ernest Works, "The Prejudice-Interaction Hypothesis from the Point of View of the Negro Minority Group," *American Journal of Sociology* 67 (1961): 47–52. Some have criticized contact theory precisely for its many conditions, arguing that it is unfalsifiable. This theory is also prone to self-selection bias: see Jeffrey C. Dixon, "The Ties That Bind and Those That Don't: Toward Reconciling Group Threat and Contact Theories of Prejudice." *Social Forces* 84 (2006): 2179–2204.

24. Bernard Meer and Edward Freedman, "The Impact of Negro Neighborhoods on White Home Owners," *Social Forces* 45 (1966): 11–19.

25. Stuart W. Cook, "Experimenting on Social Issues: The Case of School Desegregation," *American Psychologist* 40 (1985): 452–460; Jackman and Crane, "Some of My Best Friends Are Black."

26. Robert E. Slavin, "Cooperative Learning and Intergroup Relations," in *Handbook of Research on Multicultural Education,* ed. James A. Banks and Cherry A. McGee Banks (New York: Simon and Schuster–Macmillan, 1996), 631.

27. Cynthia T. Garcia Coll and Heidie A. Vazquez Garcia, "Developmental Processes and Their Influence on Interethnic and Interracial Relations," in *Toward a Common Destiny: Improving Race and Ethnic Relations in America,* ed. Willis D. Hawley and Anthony W. Jackson (San Francisco: Jossey-Bass, 1995), 103–130.

28. Christopher Ellison and Daniel A. Powers, "The Contact Hypothesis and Racial Attitudes among Black Americans," *Social Science Quarterly* 75 (1994): 385–399.

29. Drew Nesdale, "Developmental Changes in Children's Ethnic Preferences and Social Cognition," *Journal of Applied Developmental Psychology* 20 (1999): 501–519; Drew Nesdale, "Social Identity Processes and Children's Ethnic Prejudice," in *The Development of the Social Self,* ed. Mark Bennett and Fabio Sani (East Sussex: Psychology Press, 2004), 219–246.

30. Beverly D. Tatum argues that when young people hit puberty, attitudes change with regard to race and ethnicity. Children who once had racially diverse birthday parties are unlikely to continue inviting members of other races once parties become girl–guy events and sleepovers: Beverly D. Tatum, *Why Are All the Black Kids Sitting Together in the Cafeteria?* (New York: Basic Books, 1997). Others who argue that racial categorization and stereotypes do not begin until middle or later childhood include Frances E. Aboud, *Children and Prejudice* (London: Blackwell, 1988); Phyllis A. Katz, "Development of Children's Racial Awareness and Intergroup Attitudes," *Current Topics in Early Childhood Education* 4 (1982): 17–54; Patricia G. Ramsey, "Young Children's Thinking about Ethnic Differences," in *Children's Ethnic Socialization,* ed. Jean S. Phinney and Mary Jane Rotheram (Newbury Park, Calif.: Sage, 1987), 56–72. Others argue that even young children understand many aspects of racial stereotypes: Debra Van Ausdale and Joe R. Feagin, *The First R: How Children Learn Race and Racism* (Lanham, Md.: Rowman and Littlefield, 2001).

31. Deborah O. Erwin, "An Ethnographic Description of Latino Immigration in Rural Arkansas: Intergroup Relations and Utilization of Healthcare Services," *Southern Rural Sociology* 19 (2003): 46–72; Helen B. Marrow, *New Destination Dreaming: Immigration, Race, and Legal Status in the Rural American South* (Stanford, Calif.: Stanford University Press, 2011); Eileen Diaz McConnell and Faranak Miraftab, "Sundown Town 'Little Mexico': Old-Timers and Newcomers in an American Small Town," *Rural Sociology* 75 (2009): 605–629.

32. Philip E. Converse and Gregory B. Markus, "Plus ça change . . . The New CPS Election Study Panel," *American Political Science Review* 73 (1979): 32–49; Donald R. Kinder and Lynn M. Sanders, *Divided by Color: Racial Politics and Democratic Ideals* (Chicago: University of Chicago Press, 1996); David O. Sears, "The Persistence of Early Political Predispositions: The Role of Attitude Object and Life Stage," in *Review of Personality and Social Psychology,* vol. 4, ed. Ladd Wheeler and Philip Shaver (Beverly Hills, Calif.: Sage, 1983), 79–116.

33. David O. Sears, Jack Citrin, Sharmaine V. Cheleden, and Colette van Laar, "Cultural Diversity and Multicultural Politics: Is Ethnic Balkanization Psychologically Inevitable?" in *Cultural Divides: Understanding and Overcoming Group Conflict,* ed. Deborah A. Prentice and Dale T. Miller (New York: Russell Sage, 1999), 42.

34. Lawrence Bobo and Ryan A. Smith, "Antipoverty Policy, Affirmative Action, and Racial Attitudes," in *Confronting Poverty: Prescriptions for Change,* ed. Sheldon H. Danziger, Gary D. Sandefur, and Daniel H. Weinberg (Cambridge, Mass.: Harvard University Press, 1994); Martin Gilens, *Why Americans Hate Welfare: Race, Media, and the Politics of Antipoverty Policy* (Chicago: University of Chicago Press, 2000); Martin Gilens, Paul M. Sniderman, and James H. Kuklinski, "Affirmative Action and the Politics of Realignment," *British Journal of Political Science* 28 (1998): 159–183; Donald R. Kinder and David O. Sears, "Prejudice and Politics: Symbolic Racism versus Racial Threats to the Good Life," *Journal of Personality and Social Psychology* 40 (1982): 414–431; David O. Sears, Colette van Laar, M. Carrillo, and R. Kosterman, "Is It Really Racism? The Origins of White Americans' Opposition to Race-Targeted Policies," *Public Opinion Quarterly* 61 (1997): 16–53.

35. John W. Ayers, C. Richard Hofstetter, Keith Schnakenberg, and Bohdan Kolody, "Is Immigration a Racial Issue? Anglo Attitudes on Immigration Policies in a Border County," *Social Science Quarterly* 90 (2009): 593–610.

36. P. J. Henry and David O. Sears, "The Symbolic Racism 2000 Scale," *Political Psychology* 23 (2002): 253–283; Donald R. Kinder and David O. Sears, "Prejudice and Politics: Symbolic Racism versus Racial Threats to the Good Life," *Journal of Personality and Social Psychology* 40 (1981): 414–431; David O. Sears and P. J. Henry, "The Origins of Symbolic Racism," *Journal of Personality and Social Psychology* 85 (2003): 259–275; Sears et al., "Is It Really Racism?"

37. David O. Sears and Victoria Savalei, "The Political Color Line in America: Many 'Peoples of Color' or Black Exceptionalism?" *Political Psychology* 27 (2006): 895–924.

38. Joe R. Feagin, *Racist America: Roots, Current Realities, and Future Reparations* (New York: Routledge, 2000), 267.

39. Jeffrey C. Dixon and Michael S. Rosenbaum, "Nice to Know You? Testing Contact, Cultural and Group Threat Theories of Anti-Black and Anti-Hispanic Stereotypes," *Social Science Quarterly* 85 (2004): 257–280.

40. Peter Burns and James G. Gimpel, "Economic Insecurity, Prejudicial Stereotypes, and Public Opinion on Immigration Policy," *Political Science Quarterly* 115 (2000): 201–225.

41. Dixon, "The Ties That Bind and Those That Don't." See also Marylee C. Taylor, "How White Attitudes Vary with the Racial Composition of Local Populations: Numbers Count," *American Sociological Review* 63 (1998): 512–535.

42. Sears et al., "Cultural Diversity and Multicultural Politics," 37.

43. Benjamin Bailey, "Dominican-American Ethnic/Racial Identities and United States Social Categories," *International Migration Review* 35 (2001): 677–708; Alex Stepick, *Pride against Prejudice: Haitians in the United States* (Boston: Allyn and Bacon 1998); Alex Stepick, Carol Dutton Stepick, Emmanuel Eugene, Deborah Teed, and Yves Labissiere, "Shifting Identities and Inter-generational Conflict: Growing Up Haitian in Miami," in

Ethnicities: Children of Immigrants in America, ed. Ruben Rumbaut and Alejandro Portes (Berkeley: University of California Press, 2001), 229–266.

44. Sears et al., "Cultural Diversity and Multicultural Politics," 42.

45. Won Moo Hurh and Kwang Chung Kim, "The 'Success' Image of Asian Americans: Its Validity, and Its Practical and Theoretical Implications," *Ethnic and Racial Studies* 12 (1989): 514–561; Keith Osajima, "Asian Americans as the Model Minority: An Analysis of the Popular Press Image in the 1960s and 1980s," in *Reflections on Shattered Windows,* ed. Gary Y. Okihiro, John M. Liu, Arthur A. Hansen, and Shirley Hune (Pullman: Washington State University Press, 1988), 165–174; Stanley Sue and Harry H. L. Kitano, "Stereotypes as a Measure of Success," *Journal of Social Issues* 29 (1973): 83–98; Paul Wong, Chienping Faith Lai, Richard Nagasawa, and Tieming Lin, "Asian Americans as a Model Minority: Self-Perceptions and Perceptions by Other Racial Groups," *Sociological Perspectives* 41 (1998): 95–118.

46. Katherine D. Kinzler, Kristin Shutts, Jasmine DeJesus, and Elizabeth S. Spelke, "Accent Trumps Race in Guiding Children's Social Preferences," *Social Cognition* 27 (2009): 623–634; Stephanie Lindemann, "Koreans, Chinese or Indians? Attitudes and Ideologies about Non-native English Speakers in the United States," *Journal of Sociolinguistics* 7 (2003): 348–364; Stephanie Lindemann, "Who Speaks 'Broken English'? U.S. Undergraduates' Perceptions of Non-native English," *International Journal of Applied Linguistics* 15 (2005): 187–212; Rosina Lippi-Green, *English with Accents: Language, Ideology, and Discrimination in the United States* (New York: Routledge, 1997). John F. Dovidio and his colleagues also find that people with non-native accents feel they do not belong, feel they are outsiders, and perceive more discrimination from native-English speakers: John F. Dovidio, Agata Gluszek, Melissa-Sue John, Ruth Ditlmann. and Paul Lagunes, "Understanding Bias toward Latinos: Discrimination, Dimensions of Differences, and Experience of Exclusion," *Journal of Social Issues* 66 (2010): 59–78.

47. T. R. Reid, "Spanish at School Translates to Suspension," *Washington Post,* December 9, 2005; Anne Ryman and Ofelia Madrid, "Hispanics Upset by Teacher's Discipline," *Arizona Republic,* January 17, 2004.

48. "87 Percent Say English Should Be U.S. Official Language," *Rasmussen Reports,* May 11, 2010, available online at http://www.rasmussenreports.com/public_content/ politics/general_politics/may_2010/87_say_english_should_be_u_s_official_language (accessed June 29, 2010).

49. Francine Segovia and Renatta Defever, "The Polls-Trends: American Public Opinion on Immigrants and Immigration Policy," *Public Opinion Quarterly* 74 (2010): 374–394.

50. Fox News/Opinion Dynamics Poll, May 18–19, 2010, available online at http:// www.pollingreport.com/immigration.htm (accessed June 29, 2010).

51. It would be ideal to have attitudinal measures that capture specific perceptions of threat, but these are not available in the survey.

52. Glen H. Elder and Rand D. Conger, *Children of the Land: Adversity and Success in Rural America* (Chicago: University of Chicago Press, 2000); Chrystal C. Ramirez-Barranti, "The Grandparent/Grandchild Relationship: Family Resource in an Era of Voluntary Bonds," *Family Relations* 34 (1985): 343–352.

53. Elder and Conger, *Children of the Land*; Daniel J. McGrath, Raymond R. Swisher, Glen H. Elder Jr., and Rand D. Conger, "Breaking New Ground: Diverse Routes to College in Rural America," *Rural Sociology* 66 (2001): 244–267.

54. Donald R. Kinder and Cindy D. Kam, *Us versus Them: Ethnocentric Foundations of American Opinion* (Chicago: University of Chicago Press, 2009), 47.

55. Citrin et al., "Public Opinion toward Immigration Reform."

56. See, e.g., Martin Gilens, "Racial Attitudes and Opposition to Welfare," *Journal of Politics* 57 (1995): 994–1014; Martin Gilens, *Why Americans Hate Welfare: Race, Media, and the Politics of Antipoverty Policy* (Chicago: University of Chicago Press, 2000); Sears and Savalei, "The Political Color Line in America"; Sears et al., "Is It Really Racism?"

57. Reynolds Farley, Charlotte Steeh, Tara Jackson, Maria Krysan, and Keith Reeves, "Continued Racial Residential Segregation in Detroit: 'Chocolate City, Vanilla Suburbs' Revisited," *Journal of Housing Research* 4 (1993): 1–38. See also Lawrence Bobo and Camille L. Zubrinsky, "Attitudes on Racial Integration: Perceived Status Differences, Mere In-Group Preferences, or Racial Prejudice?" *Social Forces* 74 (1996): 883–909; Camille Z. Charles, "Neighborhood Racial-Composition Preferences: Evidence from a Multiethnic Metropolis," *Social Problems* 47 (2000): 379–407; Nancy A. Denton and Douglas S. Massey, "Residential Segregation of Blacks, Hispanics, and Asians by Socioeconomic Status and Generation," *Social Science Quarterly* 69 (1988): 797–817; Reynolds Farley, "Residential Segregation in Urbanized Areas of the United States in 1970: An Analysis of Social Class and Racial Differences," *Demography* 14 (1977): 497–518; Douglas S. Massey and Nancy A. Denton, *American Apartheid: Segregation and the Making of the Underclass* (Cambridge, Mass.: Harvard University Press, 1993); Craig St. John and Nancy A. Bates, "Racial Composition and Neighborhood Evaluation," *Social Science Research* 1 (1990): 47–61; Karl E. Taeubur, "The Effect of Income Redistribution on Racial Residential Segregation," *Urban Affairs Quarterly* 4 (1965): 5–14.

58. Camille L. Zubrinsky and Lawrence Bobo, "Prismatic Metropolis: Race and Residential Segregation in the City of the Angels," *Social Science Research* 25 (1996): 335–374.

59. Emerson et al., "Does Race Matter in Residential Segregation?"

60. Lawrence Bobo, "Keeping the Linchpin in Place: Testing the Multiple Sources of Opposition to Residential Integration," *Revue Internationale de Psychologie Sociale* 2 (1989): 307.

61. Daniel J. Hopkins, "Politicized Places: Explaining Where and When Immigrants Provoke Local Opposition," *American Political Science Review* 104 (2010): 40–60.

62. Rodolfo de la Garza, "Attitudes toward Immigration Policy," *Migration World Magazine* 21 (1993): 13–17; Rodolfo de la Garza, Jerry L. Polinard, Robert D. Wrinkle, and Tomás Longoria, "Understanding Intra-Ethnic Attitude Variations: Mexican Origin Population Views of Immigration," *Social Science Quarterly* 72 (1991): 379–387.

63. Bruce Cain and Roderick Kiewiet, "California's Coming Minority Majority," *Public Opinion* 9 (1986): 50–52; Lawrence W. Miller, Jerry L. Polinard, and Robert D. Wrinkle, "Attitudes toward Undocumented Workers: The Mexican American Perspective," *Social Science Quarterly* 65 (1984): 482–492; Dale C. Nelson, "Ethnicity and Socioeconomic Status as Sources of Participation: The Case for Ethnic Political Culture," *American Political Science Review* 73 (1979): 1024–1038.

64. Miller et al., "Attitudes toward Undocumented Workers."

65. Thomas J. Espenshade and Charles A. Calhoun, "An Analysis of Public Opinion toward Undocumented Immigration," *Population Research and Policy Review* 12 (1993): 189–224; Marilyn Hoskin and William Mishler, "Public Opinion toward New Migrants: A Comparative Analysis," *International Migration* 21 (1983): 440–462.

66. de la Garza et al., "Understanding Intra-Ethnic Attitude Variations"; M. V. Hood III, Irwin L. Morris, and Kurt A. Shirkey, "'Quedate o Vente!' Uncovering the Determinants of Hispanic Public Opinion toward Immigration," *Political Research Quarterly* 50 (1997) 627–647.

67. Ann V. Millard, Jorge Chapa, and Eileen Diaz McConnell, "Ten Myths about Latinos," in *Apple Pie and Enchiladas: Latino Newcomers to the Midwest,* ed. Ann V. Millard and Jorge Chapa (Austin: University of Texas Press, 2001), 22–25.

68. Alejandro Portes and Rubén G. Rumbaut, *Legacies: The Story of the Immigrant Second Generation* (Berkeley: University of California Press, 2001).

69. Personal interview with Doug Bruce, Perry, Iowa, May 25, 2010.

70. Neil Chakraborti and Jon Garland, *Rural Racism* (Portland, Ore.: Willan Publishing, 2004); James W. Loewen, *Sundown Towns: A Hidden Dimension of American Racism* (New York: The New Press, 2005).

71. Adrienne D. Dixson and Celia K. Rousseau, "And We Are Still Not Saved: Critical Race Theory in Education Ten Years Later," in *Critical Race Theory in Education: All God's Children Got a Song,* ed. Adrienne D. Dixson and Celia K. Rousseau (New York: Routledge, 2006), 33; Jennifer S. Trainor, *Rethinking Racism: Emotion, Persuasion and Literacy Education in an All-White High School* (Carbondale: Southern Illinois University Press, 2008).

72. Oliver and Mendelberg, "Reconsidering the Environmental Determinants of White Racial Attitudes," 576.

73. P. J. Henry and David O. Sears, "The Crystallization of Contemporary Racial Prejudice across the Lifespan," *Political Psychology* 30 (2009): 569–590.

CHAPTER 4

Epigraph: Robert D. Putnam, "*E Pluribus Unum*: Diversity and Community in the Twenty-First Century, the 2006 Johan Skytte Prize Lecture," *Scandinavian Political Studies* 30 (2007): 137–174.

1. Robert D. Putnam, *Bowling Alone: The Collapse and Revival of American Community* (New York: Simon and Schuster, 2000). See also James Coleman, "Social Capital and the Creation of Human Capital," *American Journal of Sociology* 94 (1988): S95–S121.

2. The aim of this study is not to make a normative claim that social capital is always beneficial for individuals or communities. Many studies show a variety of benefits of social capital, but others disagree on the universally beneficial nature of strong social networks and trust. Most famously, perhaps, is Pierre Bourdieu, who argues that social capital is linked to economic and political power structures; it perpetuates inequalities between the powerful and the powerless: Pierre Bourdieu, "The Forms of Capital," in *Handbook of Theory and Research for the Sociology of Education,* ed. J. G. Richardson (Westport, Conn.: Greenwood Press, 1985). Cynthia Duncan also finds that social capital is mediated by inequality and that small towns with less inequality have higher levels of social capital: Cynthia Duncan, *Worlds Apart: Why Poverty Persists in Rural America* (New Haven, Conn.: Yale University Press, 1999). Other research demonstrates that social capital is beneficial for individuals and communities. Higher social capital is associated with higher individual incomes (Ronald S. Burt, "The Contingent Value of Social Capital," *Administrative Science Quarterly* 42 [1997]: 339–365; Mark Granovetter, "The Strength of Weak Ties," *American Journal of Sociology* 78 [1973]: 1360–1380; Nan Lin, "Social Networks and Status Attainment," *Annual Review of Sociology* 25 [1999]: 467–487); with better personal and public health (Lisa F. Berkman, "The Role of Social Relations in Health Promotion," *Psychosomatic Medicine* 57 [1995]: 245–254; James S. House, Karl R. Landis, and Debra Umberson, "Social Relationships and Health," *Science* 241 [1988]: 540–545; Teresa E. Seeman, "Social Ties and Health: The Benefits of Social Integration," *Annals of Epidemiology* 6 [1996]: 442–451); with lower levels of crime (Robert J. Sampson, "Crime and Public Safety: Insights from Community-Level Perspectives on Social Capital," in *Social Capital*

and Poor Communities, ed. Susan Saegert, J. Phillip Thompson, and Mark R. Warren [New York: Russell Sage Foundation, 2001], 89–114; Robert J. Sampson, Steven W. Raudenbush, and Felton Earls, "Neighbourhoods and Violent Crime: A Multilevel Study of Collective Efficacy," *Science* 277 [1997]: 918–924); and with economic growth (Stephen Knack and Philip Keefer, "Does Social Capital Have an Economic Payoff? A Cross-Country Investigation," *Quarterly Journal of Economics* 112 [1997]: 251–288).

3. Putnam, "*E Pluribus Unum,*" 138.

4. Putnam, *Bowling Alone,* 358–363.

5. Rodney Hero, *Social Capital and Racial Diversity: Equality and Community in America* (Cambridge: Cambridge University Press, 2007); Rodney Hero, "Social Capital and Racial Inequality in America," *Perspectives on Politics* 1 (2003): 113–122. Looking at aggregate data on the effects of social capital, Hero shows that states with high rates of social capital are also racially homogeneous, and in these states racial and ethnic minorities are actually worse off. The gap in high school graduation rates between minorities and Whites is greater in these states, as are the gaps in school suspension rates, Black incarceration rates, voter turnout, and poverty.

6. Putnam, "*E Pluribus Unum,*" 149.

7. Ibid., 144.

8. On reduced support for public good expenditures, see Alberto Alesina, Reza Baquir, and William Easterly, "Public Goods and Ethnic Divisions," *Quarterly Journal of Economics* 114 (1999): 243–285; Erzo F. P. Luttmer, "Group Loyalty and the Taste for Redistribution," *Journal of Political Economy* 109 (2001): 500–528; James M. Poterba, "Demographic Structure and the Political Economy of Public Education," *Journal of Policy Analysis and Management* 16 (1997): 48–66. However, Daniel J. Hopkins argues that sudden demographic change corresponds with less support for tax increases, not simply levels of diversity per se. "To understand how diversity influence public good provisions, we should look to those towns that are diversifying, not those towns that are diverse": Daniel J. Hopkins, "The Diversity Discount: When Increasing Ethnic and Racial Diversity Prevents Tax Increases," *Journal of Politics* 71 (2009): 160. On less participation in social activities, see Alberto Alesina and Eliana La Ferrara, "Participation in Heterogeneous Communities," *Quarterly Journal of Economics* 115 (2000): 847–904. On lower levels of trust, see Alberto Alesina and Eliana La Ferrara, "Who Trusts Others?" *Journal of Public Economics* 85 (2002): 207–234.

9. Dora L. Costa and Matthew E. Kahn, "Civic Engagement and Community Heterogeneity: An Economist's Perspective," *Perspectives on Politics* 1 (2003): 103–111. Others have also found that ethnic heterogeneity decreases trust, civic engagement, and political participation: Hilde Coffé and Benny Geys, "Community Heterogeneity: A Burden for the Creation of Social Capital?" *Social Science Quarterly* 87 (2006): 1053–1072; Jan Delhey and Kenneth Newton, "Predicting Cross-National Levels of Social Trust: Global Pattern or Nordic Exceptionalism?" *European Sociological Review* 21 (2005): 311–327; Edward Fieldhouse and David Cutts, "Does Diversity Damage Social Capital? A Comparative Study of Neighbourhood Diversity and Social Capital in the U.S. and Britain," *Canadian Journal of Political Science* 43 (2010): 289–318; Christel Kesler and Irene Bloemraad, "Does Immigration Erode Social Capital? The Conditional Effects of Immigration-Generated Diversity on Trust, Membership, and Participation across 19 Countries, 1981–2000," *Canadian Journal of Political Science* 43 (2010): 319–347.

10. Robert J. Sampson, "Disparity and Diversity in the Contemporary City: Social (Dis)Order Revisited," *British Journal of Sociology* 60 (2009): 1–31; Robert J. Sampson and Stephen W. Raudenbush, "Seeing Disorder: Neighborhood Stigma and the Social Construction of Broken Windows," *Social Psychology Quarterly* 67 (2004): 319–342.

11. Tom W. Rice and Brent Steele, "White Ethnic Diversity and Community Attachment in Small Iowa Towns," *Social Science Quarterly* 82 (2001): 397–407.

12. Christopher J. Anderson and Aida Paskeviciute, "How Ethnic and Linguistic Heterogeneity Influence the Prospects for Civil Society: A Comparative Study of Citizenship Behavior," *Journal of Politics* 68 (2006): 783–802. See also J. Eric Oliver and Janelle Wong, "Intergroup Prejudice in Multiethnic Settings," *American Journal of Political Science* 47 (2003): 567–582.

13. Anderson and Paskeviciute, "How Ethnic and Linguistic Heterogeneity Influence the Prospects for Civil Society." See also Melissa J. Marschall and Dietlind Stolle, "Race and the City: Neighborhood Context and the Development of Generalized Trust," *Political Behavior* 26 (2004): 125–153; Diana C. Mutz, "Cross-Cutting Social Networks: Testing Democratic Theory in Practice," *American Political Science Review* 96 (2002): 111–126.

14. Anderson and Paskeviciute, "How Ethnic and Linguistic Heterogeneity Influence the Prospects for Civil Society," 792. See also Jan Leighley, *Strength in Numbers? The Political Mobilization of Racial and Ethnic Minorities* (Princeton, N.J.: Princeton University Press, 2001); J. Eric Oliver, *Democracy in Suburbia* (Princeton, N.J.: Princeton University Press, 2001).

15. Putnam, "*E Pluribus Unum.*" See also David E. Campbell, *Why We Vote: How Schools and Communities Shape Our Civic Life* (Princeton, N.J.: Princeton University Press, 2006).

16. Michael X. Delli Carpini and Scott Keeter, *What Americans Know about Politics and Why It Matters* (New Haven, Conn.: Yale University Press, 1995); Sidney Verba, Kay Schlozman, and Henry Brady, *Voice and Equality: Civic Voluntarism in American Politics* (Cambridge, Mass.: Harvard University Press, 1995).

17. Richard G. Niemi and Jane Junn, *Civic Education: What Makes Students Learn* (New Haven, Conn.: Yale University Press, 1998); Judith Torney-Purta, Rainer Lehmann, Hans Oswald, and Wolfram Schulz, *Citizenship and Education in Twenty-Eight Countries: Civic Knowledge and Engagement at Age Fourteen* (Amsterdam: International Association for the Evaluation of Educational Achievement, 2001).

18. Gina M. Garramone and Charles K. Atkin, "Mass Communication and Political Socialization: Specifying the Effects," *Public Opinion Quarterly* 50 (1986): 76–86.

19. In 2007, for example, only 69 percent of Americans could correctly name the current vice president. About the same proportion (64 percent) could identify Beyoncé Knowles as could identify Condoleezza Rice: Andrew Kohut, Richard Morin, and Scott Keeter, *What Americans Know: 1989–2007—Public Knowledge of Current Affairs Little Changed by News and Information Revolutions,* Pew Research Center for the People and the Press, 2007, available online at http://people-press.org/reports/pdf/319.pdf (accessed October 1, 2009).

20. Anthony D. Lutkus and Andrew R. Weiss, *The Nation's Report Card: Civics 2006,* U.S. Department of Education, National Center for Education Statistics, NCES 2007-476. Washington, D.C.: U.S. Government Printing Office, 2007.

21. William Galston, "Political Knowledge, Political Engagement, and Civic Education." *Annual Review of Political Science* 4 (2001): 219.

22. Delli Carpini and Keeter, *What Americans Know about Politics and Why It Matters,* 230–267; Norman Nie, Jane Junn, and Kathleen Stehlik-Barry, *Education and Democratic Citizenship in America* (Chicago: University of Chicago Press, 1996); Samuel L. Popkin and Michael Dimock, "Knowledge, Trust and International Reasoning," in *Elements of Reason: Cognition, Choice, and the Bounds of Rationality,* ed. Arthur Lupia, Michael McCubbins, and Samuel L. Popkin (New York: Cambridge University Press, 2000), 214–238; Verba et al., *Voice and Equality.*

23. Ilya Somin, "When Ignorance Isn't Bliss: How Political Ignorance Threatens Democracy," Policy Analysis no. 525, Cato Institute, September 22, 2004, available online at http://www.cato.org/pub_display.php?pub_id=2372 (accessed October 2, 2009).

24. Galston, "Political Knowledge, Political Engagement, and Civic Education," 224.

25. Benjamin Barber, *Strong Democracy: Participatory Politics for a New Age* (Berkeley: University of California Press, 1984), 133, 126.

26. Delli Carpini and Keeter, *What Americans Know about Politics and Why It Matters,* 6–7.

27. Albert Bandura, "Perceived Self-Efficacy in Cognitive Development and Functioning," *Educational Psychologist* 28 (1993): 118.

28. Paul R. Abramson and John H. Aldrich, "The Decline of Electoral Participation in America," *American Political Science Review* 76 (1982): 502–521; Angus Campbell, Gerald Gurin, and Warren E. Miller, *The Voter Decides* (Evanston, Ill.: Row, Peterson, 1954).

29. "Short-Term Impacts, Long-Term Opportunities: The Political and Civic Engagement of Young Adults in America," report, Center for Information and Research in Civic Learning and Engagement and Center for Democracy and Citizenship, March 2002, available online at http://www.civicyouth.org/research/products/National_Youth_Survey_out side2.htm (accessed October 2, 2009).

30. Albert Bandura, *Self-Efficacy: The Exercise of Control* (New York: W. H. Freeman, 1997), 2.

31. Campbell et al., *The Voter Decides.*

32. George I. Balch, "Multiple Indicators in Survey Research: The Concept of 'Sense of Political Efficacy,'" *Political Methodology,* 1 (1974): 1–43; Stephen C. Craig, Richard G. Niemi, and Glenn E. Silver, "Political Efficacy and Trust: A Report on the NES Pilot Study Items," *Political Behavior* 12 (1990): 289–313.

33. Michael E. Morrell argues that both dimensions are parts of the broader psychological concept of self-efficacy. He states, "Believing that I can influence the political system in a representative democracy requires that I feel capable of participation in the system (internal efficacy) and that the system is responsive to my input (external efficacy)": Michael E. Morrell, "Deliberation, Democratic Decision-making, and Internal Political Efficacy," *Political Behavior* 27 (2005): 56.

34. Nicholas A. Valentino, Krysha Gregorowicz, and Eric W. Groenendyk, "Efficacy, Emotions, and the Habit of Participation," *Political Behavior* 31 (2009): 307–330.

35. Gabriel Almond and Sidney Verba, *The Civic Culture* (Princeton, N.J.: Princeton University Press, 1963).

36. David Easton and Jack Dennis, "The Child's Acquisition of Regime Norms: Political Efficacy," *American Political Science Review* 61 (1967): 26–38; Robert D. Hess and Judith V. Torney, *The Development of Political Attitudes in Children* (Chicago: Aldine, 1967); M. Kent Jennings and Richard Niemi, *Generations and Politics* (Princeton, N.J.: Princeton University Press, 1981).

37. Erica Austin and C. Leigh Nelson, "Influences of Ethnicity, Family Communication and Media on Adolescents' Socialization to U.S. Politics," *Journal of Broadcasting and Electronic Media,* 37 (1993): 419–435; Bruce E. Pinkelton and Erica Austin, "Individual Motivations, Perceived Media Importance, and Political Disaffection," *Political Communication,* 18 (2001): 321–334; Bruce E Pinkelton and Erica Austin, "Media Perceptions and Public Affairs Apathy in the Politically Inexperienced," *Mass Communication and Society* 7 (2004): 319–337.

38. Joseph Kahne and Joel Westheimer, "The Limits of Political Efficacy: Educating Citizens for a Democratic Society," *PS: Political Science and Politics* 39 (2006): 289–296; John Pasek, Lauren Feldman, Daniel Romer, and Kathleen Hall Jamieson, "Schools as

Incubators of Democratic Participation: Building Long-Term Political Efficacy with Civic Education," *Applied Developmental Science* 12 (2008): 28.

39. Valentino et al., "Efficacy, Emotions, and the Habit of Participation," 308.

40. Shanto Iyengar, "Subjective Political Efficacy as a Measure of Diffuse Support," *Public Opinion Quarterly* 44 (1980): 249–256.

41. Craig et al., "Political Efficacy and Trust."

42. More information about these measures can be found in Table A.2.

43. Francisco Herreros, *The Problems of Forming Social Capital: Why Trust?* (New York: Palgrave, 2004); Putnam, *Making Democracy Work*. But see Michele P. Claibourn and Paul S. Martin, "Trusting and Joining? An Empirical Test of the Reciprocal Nature of Social Capital," *Political Behavior* 22 (2000): 267–291; Eric M. Uslaner, *The Moral Foundations of Trust* (Cambridge: Cambridge University Press, 2002); Eric M. Uslaner and Mitchell Brown, "Inequality, Trust, and Civic Engagement," *American Politics Research* 31 (2003): 1–28.

44. Some argue that generalized trust improves economic growth (Robert D. Putnam, *Making Democracy Work: Civic Traditions in Modern Italy* [Princeton, N.J.: Princeton University Press, 1993]; Paul F. Whiteley, "Economic Growth and Social Capital," *Political Studies* 48 [2000]: 443–466; Paul J. Zak and Stephen Knack, "Trust and Growth," *Economics Journal* 111 [2001]: 295–321), but others disagree (Uslaner, *The Moral Foundations of Trust*). Stephen Knack finds positive associations between generalized trust and indicators of government performance: Stephen Knack, "Social Capital and the Quality of Government: Evidence from the United States," *American Journal of Political Science* 46 (2002): 772–785. In *The Moral Foundations of Trust,* Uslaner finds that trust is highly related to corruption—countries low in trust have more corruption.

45. John Brehm and Wendy Rahn, "Individual-Level Evidence for the Causes and Consequences of Social Capital," *American Journal of Political Science* 41 (1997): 999–1023; Allan Cigler and Mark R. Joslyn, "The Extensiveness of Group Membership and Social Capital: The Impact on Political Tolerance Attitudes," *Political Research Quarterly* 55 (2002): 7–25.

46. The most common question is, "Generally speaking, would you say that most people can be trusted or that you can't be too careful in dealing with people?" It is used in the World Values Survey, the General Social Survey, the American National Election Studies, the Afrobarometer, the Asian Barometer, the Latinobarometer, and many other surveys. This question is a bit more specific, asking respondents whether people can be trusted *to do the right thing,* but like the more common question, it leaves a great deal up to the respondent. Peter Nannestad's review of the literature on generalized trust points out that the question has a "remarkably high level of test-retest stability at the aggregate level," and individual respondents "do not in general seem to find the generalized trust question difficult": Peter Nannestad, "What Have We Learned about Generalized Trust, If Anything?" *Annual Review of Political Science,* 11 (2008): 418–419.

47. Uslaner, *The Moral Foundations of Trust.*

48. Eric M. Uslaner, "The Foundations of Trust: Macro and Micro," *Cambridge Journal of Economics* 32 (2008): 290. Uslaner's interpretation is not without its critics: see Sjoerd Beugelsdijk, "A Note on the Theory and Measurement of Trust in Explaining Differences in Economic Growth," *Cambridge Journal of Economics* 30 (2006): 371–387; Edward L. Glaeser, David Laibson, Jose A. Scheinkman, and Christine L. Soutter, "Measuring Trust," *Quarterly Journal of Economics* 115 (2000): 811–846; Russell Hardin, *Trust* (Cambridge: Polity, 2006).

49. Steven J. Rosenstone and John Mark Hansen, *Mobilization, Participation, and Democracy in America* (New York: Macmillan, 1993); Uslaner, *The Moral Foundations of Trust.*

50. Alexander W. Astin, Linda J. Sax and Juan Avalos, "Long-Term Effects of Volunteerism during the Undergraduate Years," *Review of Higher Education* 22 (1999): 187–202; James Beane, Joan Turner, David Jones, and Richard Lipka, "Long-Term Effects of Community Service Programs," *Curriculum Inquiry* 11 (1981): 143–155; Constance Flanagan and Lonnie Sherrod, "Youth Political Development: An Introduction," *Journal of Social Issues* 54 (1998): 447–456; Michael Hanks and Bruce K. Eckland, "Adult Voluntary Association and Adolescent Socialization," *Sociological Quarterly* 19 (1978): 481–490; James Youniss, Jeffrey A. McLellan, and Miranda Yates, "What We Know about Engendering a Civic Identity," *American Behavioralist Scientist* 40 (1997): 620–631.

51. Youniss et al., "What We Know about Engendering a Civic Identity," 624.

52. Some might argue that a good measure of adolescent participation should also include volunteerism. I excluded this for both empirical and theoretical reasons. First, there were no data on the amount of volunteerism in the surveys; we did not ask the questions. Second, although many studies show a positive association between community service and democratic attitudes, other research points out some problems with this link. The causal arrow is often obfuscated because we do not know whether young people gained knowledge through service or whether knowledgeable young people are those most inclined to engage in service anyway. Further, most community service activities have no explicit link to politics. Helping others, though obviously a value worth instilling in young people, is not the same thing as engagement in political activities or service that is explicitly linked, through discussions or external readings, with political problems and solutions.

53. Theodore Coladarci and Casey D. Cobb, "Extracurricular Participation, School Size, and Achievement and Self-Esteem among High School Students: A National Look," *Journal of Research in Rural Education* 12 (1996): 92–103; Joseph L. Mahoney and Robert B. Cairns, "Do Extracurricular Activities Protect against Early School Leaving?" *Developmental Psychology* 33 (1997): 241–253; Herbert W. Marsh, "Extracurricular Activities: Beneficial Extension of the Traditional Curriculum or Subversion of Academic Goals?" *Journal of Educational Psychology* 84 (1992): 553–562; Ralph B. McNeal, "Extracurricular Activities and High School Dropouts," *Sociology of Education* 68 (1995): 62–81.

54. Niemi and Junn, *Civic Education*.

55. Jacquelynne S. Eccles and Bonnie Barber, "Student Council, Volunteering, Basketball, or Marching Band: What Kind of Extracurricular Involvement Matters?" *Journal of Adolescent Research* 14 (1999): 10–34.

56. Patrick C. Meirick and Daniel B. Wackman, "Kids Voting and Political Knowledge: Narrowing Gaps, Informing Voters," *Social Science Quarterly* 85 (2004): 1161–1177.

57. Alfonso J. Damico, Sandra Bowman Damico, and M. Margaret Conway, "The Democratic Education of Women: High School and Beyond," *Women and Politics* 19 (1998): 4.

58. Jennifer L. Glanville, "Political Socialization or Selection? Adolescents' Extracurricular Participation and Political Activity in Early Adulthood," *Social Science Quarterly* 80 (1999): 285.

59. Beane et al., "Long-Term Effects of Community Service Programs"; Hanks and Eckland, "Adult Voluntary Associations and Adolescent Socialization."

60. Anderson and Paskeviciute, "How Ethnic and Linguistic Heterogeneity Influence the Prospects for Civil Society," 784. See also Pamela J. Conover, Donald D. Searing, and Ivor M. Crewe, "The Deliberative Potential of Political Discussion," *British Journal of Political Science* 32 (2002): 21–62; Jack Knight and James Johnson, "Aggregation and Deliberation: On the Possibility of Democratic Legitimacy," *Political Theory* 22 (1994): 277–296.

61. Nina Eliasoph, *Avoiding Politics: How Americans Produce Apathy in Everyday Life* (New York: Cambridge University Press, 1998).

62. John Gastil, "Adult Civic Education through the National Issues Forums: Developing Democratic Habits and Dispositions through Public Deliberation," *Adult Education Quarterly* 54 (2004): 308–328; John Gastil and James P. Dillard, "The Aims, Methods, and Effects of Deliberative Civic Education through the National Issues Forums," *Communication Education* 48 (1999): 179–192; Edward S. Greenberg, Leon Grunberg and Kelley Daniel, "Industrial Work and Political Participation: Beyond 'Simple Spillover,'" *Political Research Quarterly* 49 (1996): 305–330.

63. Barber, *Strong Democracy*; Matthew C. Nisbet and Dietram A. Scheufele, "Political Talk as a Catalyst for Online Citizenship," *Journalism and Mass Communication Quarterly* 81 (2004): 877–896; Carole Pateman, *Participation and Democratic Theory* (New York: Cambridge University Press, 1970).

64. Philip E. Converse, "Attitudes and Nonattitudes: Continuation of a Dialogue," in *The Quantitative Analysis of Social Problems,* ed. Edward R. Tufte (Reading, Mass.: Addison-Wesley, 1970), 168–189; M. Kent Jennings, Jan W. van Deth, Samuel Barnes, Dieter Fuchs, Felix Heunks, Ronald Inglehart, Max Kaase, Hans-Dieter Klingemann, and Jacques Thomassen, *Continuities in Political Action: A Longitudinal Study of Political Orientations in Three Western Democracies* (New York: de Gruyter, 1989); Jan W. van Deth, "Politicization and Political Interest," in *Eurobarometer: The Dynamics of European Public Opinion,* ed. Karlheinz Reif and Ronald Inglehart (New York: St. Martin's Press, 1991), 201–213.

65. "Short-Term Impacts, Long-Term Opportunities," 8.

66. Diana C. Mutz, *Hearing the Other Side: Deliberative versus Participatory Democracy* (Cambridge: Cambridge University Press, 2006).

67. Leon Festinger, *A Theory of Cognitive Dissonance* (Evanston, Ill.: Row, Peterson, 1957); Melanie C. Green, Penny S. Visser, and Philip E. Tetlock, "Coping with Accountability Cross-Pressures: Low-Effort Evasive Tactics and High-Effort Quests for Complex Compromises," *Personality and Social Psychology Bulletin* 26 (2000): 1380–1391; Joseph T. Klapper, *The Effects of Mass Communication* (New York: Free Press, 1960).

68. Elizabeth Noelle-Neumann, "The Spiral of Silence: A Theory of Public Opinion," *Journal of Communication* 24 (1974): 43–51; Elizabeth Noelle-Neumann, *The Spiral of Silence: Public Opinion—Our Social Skin,* 2d ed. (Chicago: University of Chicago Press, 1993).

69. Mutz, "Cross-Cutting Social Networks."

70. Carroll J. Glynn, Andrew F. Hayes, and James Shanahan, "Perceived Support for One's Opinions and Willingness to Speak Out: A Meta-analysis of Survey Studies on the Spiral of Silence," *Public Opinion Quarterly* 61 (1997): 452–461; Morris Rosenberg, "Some Determinants of Political Apathy," *Public Opinion Quarterly* 18 (1954–1955): 349–366. Individuals who perceive they are at odds with their neighbors are less likely to support their preferred party's candidate and are more likely to avoid interpersonal conflict by withdrawing from politics: James G. Gimpel, Joshua J. Dyck and Daron R. Shaw, "Registrants, Voters and Turnout Variability Across Neighborhoods," *Political Behavior* 26 (2004): 343–375. Lauren Feldman and Vincent Price show that individuals with heterogeneous networks do not benefit from frequent political discussions, while political knowledge increases among those who regularly discuss politics within the safety of homogeneous networks: Lauren Feldman and Vincent Price, "Confusion or Enlightenment? How Exposure to Disagreement Moderates the Effects of Political Discussion and Media Use on Candidate Knowledge," *Communication Research* 35 (2008): 61–87.

71. Katherine Cramer Walsh, *Talking about Politics: Informal Groups and Social Identity in American Life* (Chicago: University of Chicago Press, 2004).

72. Meira Levinson, "The Civic Achievement Gap," CIRCLE Working Paper 51, January 2007, available online at http://civicyouth.org/PopUps/WorkingPapers/WP51

Levinson.pdf (accessed October 12, 2009); Martin Sanchez-Jankowski, "Minority Youth and Civic Engagement: The Impact of Group Relations," *Applied Developmental Science* 6 (2002): 237–245; Nie, Junn, and Stehlik-Barry, *Education and Democratic Citizenship in America*; Robert C. Smith and Richard Seltzer, *Contemporary Controversies and the American Racial Divide* (Lanham, Md.: Rowman and Littlefield, 2000); Verba et al., *Voice and Equality*; Putnam, *Bowling Alone*.

73. Judith Torney-Purta, Carolyn H. Barber, and Britt Wilkenfeld, "Latino Adolescents' Civic Development in the United States: Research Results from the IEA Civic Education Study," *Journal of Youth and Adolescence* 36 (2007): 111–125.

74. Verba et al., *Voice and Equality*. See also Jeffrey E. Cohen, Patrick R. Cotter and Philip B. Coulter, "The Changing Structure of Southern Political Participation: Matthews and Prothro 20 Years Later," *Social Science Quarterly* 64 (1983): 536–549; Donald R. Matthews and James W. Prothro, *Negroes and the New Southern Politics* (New York: Harcourt Brace, 1966); Lester W. Milbrath and M. Lal Goel, *Political Participation: How and Why Do People Get Involved in Politics?* 2d ed. (Chicago: Rand McNally, 1977); Marvin E. Olsen, "Social and Political Participation of Blacks," *American Sociological Review* 35 (1970): 682–687; Sidney Verba and Norman H. Nie, *Participation in America: Political Democracy and Social Equality* (New York: Harper and Row, 1972); Raymond E. Wolfinger and Steven J. Rosenstone, *Who Votes?* (New Haven, Conn.: Yale University Press, 1980).

75. Donald Hossler, John Braxton, and G. Coopersmith, "Understanding Student College Choice," in *Higher Education: Handbook of Theory and Research*, vol. 5, ed. John C. Smart (New York: Agathon, 1985), 231–288; Donald Hossler and Karen S. Gallagher, "Studying Student College Choice," *College and University* 62 (1987): 207–221; William H. Sewell and Robert M. Hauser, *Education, Occupation, and Earnings: Achievement in the Early Career* (New York: Academic Press, 1975).

76. Pierre Bourdieu, "Cultural and Social Reproduction," in *Power and Ideology in Education*, ed. Jerome Karabel and A. H. Halsey (New York: Oxford University Press, 1977), 487–511; Aaron V. Cicourel and John I. Kitsuse, "The School as a Mechanism of Social Differentiation," in *Power and Ideology in Education*, ed. Jerome Karabel and A. H. Halsey (New York: Oxford University Press, 1977), 282–292; Elavie Ndura, Michael Robinson, and George Ochs, "Minority Students in High School Advanced Placement Courses: Opportunity and Equity Denied," *American Secondary Education* 32 (2003): 21–38.

77. Glen H. Elder Jr. "Achievement Orientations and Career Patterns of Rural Youth," *Sociology of Education* 37 (1963): 30–58; Daniel J. McGrath, Raymond R. Swisher, Glen H. Elder Jr., and Rand D. Conger, "Breaking New Ground: Diverse Routes to College in Rural America," *Rural Sociology* 66 (2001): 244–267.

78. Judith V. Torney-Purta, "The School's Role in Developing Civic Engagement: A Study of Adolescents in Twenty-Eight Countries," *Applied Developmental Science* 6 (2002): 203–212.

79. Jonathan F. Zaff, James Youniss and Cynthia M. Gibson, "An Inequitable Invitation to Citizenship: Non-College-Bound Youth and Civic Engagement," prepared for Philanthropy for Active Civic Engagement, 2009.

80. But see Michael McDevitt, "The Partisan Child: Developmental Provocation as a Model of Political Socialization," *International Journal of Public Opinion Research* 18 (2006): 67–70.

81. Janelle Wong and Vivian Tseng, "Political Socialisation in Immigrant Families: Challenging Top-Down Parental Socialisation Models," *Journal of Ethnic and Migration Studies* 34 (2008): 151–168.

82. Alejandro Portes and Rubén G. Rumbaut, *Immigrant America: A Portrait* (Berkeley: University of California Press, 1996).

83. Jerome H. Black, "The Practice of Politics in Two Settings: Political Transferability among Recent Immigrants to Canada," *Canadian Journal of Political Science* 20 (1987): 731–754; Janelle S. Wong, *Democracy's Promise: Immigrants and American Civic Institutions.* Ann Arbor, MI: University of Michigan Press, 2006.

84. Tom W. Rice and Jan L. Feldman, "Civic Culture and Democracy from Europe to America," *Journal of Politics* 59 (1997): 1159.

85. Mark Hugo Lopez and Karlo Barrios Marcelo, "The Civic Engagement of Immigrant Youth: New Evidence from the 2006 Civic and Political Health of the Nation Survey," *Applied Developmental Science* 12 (2008): 66–73.

86. Alex Stepick and Carol Dutton Stepick, "Becoming American, Constructing Ethnicity: Immigrant Youth and Civic Engagement," *Applied Developmental Science* 6 (2002): 246–257.

87. Lyman Kellstedt, "Ethnicity and Political Behavior: Inter-group and Inter-generational Differences," *Ethnicity* 1 (1974): 393–415; James W. Lamare, "The Political Integration of Mexican-American Children: A Generational Analysis," *International Migration Review* 16 (1982): 169–188; Dario Moreno, "Cuban-American Political Empowerment," in *Pursuing Power: Latinos and the Political System,* ed. F. Chris Garcia (Notre Dame, Ind.: University of Notre Dame Press, 1997), 208–226.

88. Melissa Michelson's results in a study of Latinos in Chicago demonstrate that, depending on the survey item, Latinos are more efficacious than Anglos and Blacks: Melissa Michelson "Political Efficacy and Electoral Participation of Chicago Latinos," *Social Science Quarterly* 81 (2000): 136–150. See also Robert A. Jackson, "Latino Political Connectedness and Electoral Participation," *Journal of Political Marketing,* 8 (2009): 233–262.

89. Shaun Bowler, Francisco Pedraza, and Gary Segura, "The Efficacy and Trust of Juan Q. Public: How the Immigration Marches Reflect Surprising Support for American Institutions of Governance," paper presented at the Western Political Science Conference, Las Vegas, March 8–11, 2007.

90. Arturo Vega, Rubén O. Martinez, and Tia Stevens, "*Cosas Políticas*: Politics, Attitudes, and Perceptions by Region," in *Latinos in the Midwest,* ed. Rubén O. Martinez (East Lansing: Michigan State University Press, 2011), 57–86.

91. The results are the same when looking instead at those whose parents were born outside the United States, so I chose to include only one table. Because of the co-linearity between these two variables, it is unadvisable to include them both in a single regression model.

92. There were no significant differences between the immigrants in Storm Lake and Perry. I included an interaction term for immigrants in Storm Lake in the models, but it was not significant, so I eliminated it.

93. Putnam finds that diversity is associated with *more* civic knowledge, but he uses only a single item—naming U.S. senators from one's state: Putnam, *"E Pluribus Unum,"* 149. Feldman and Price show that political heterogeneity in one's networks is associated with lower levels of political knowledge; however, they look at political diversity, not racial or ethnic diversity: Feldman and Price, "Confusion or Enlightenment?"

94. Hopkins, "The Diversity Discount," 175.

95. Anderson and Paskeviciute, "How Ethnic and Linguistic Heterogeneity Influence the Prospects for Civil Society"; Oliver and Wong, "Intergroup Prejudice in Multiethnic Settings."

96. Muzafer Sherif, O. J. Harvey, B. J. White, W. R. Hood, and Carolyn W. Sherif, *Intergroup Conflict and Cooperation: The Robber's Cave Experiment* (Norman: University of Oklahoma Book Exchange, 1961).

97. Norman Miller and Hugh J. Harrington, "Social Categorization and Intergroup Acceptance: Principles for the Design and Development of Cooperative Learning Teams," in *Interaction in Cooperative Groups,* ed. Rachel Hertz-Lazarowitz and Norman Miller (New York: Cambridge University Press, 1992), 203–227; Janet Ward Schofield, "The Impact of Positively Structured Contact on Intergroup Behavior: Does It Last Under Adverse Conditions?" *Social Psychology Quarterly* 42 (1979): 280–284; Robert E. Slavin, "Enhancing Intergroup Relations in Schools: Cooperative Learning and Other Strategies," in *Toward a Common Destiny: Improving Race and Ethnic Relations in America,* ed. Willis D. Hawley and Anthony W. Jackson (San Francisco: Jossey-Bass, 1995), 291–314.

98. Personal interview with Teresa Coenen, principal (2007–2010), Storm Lake High School, May 26, 2010.

99. Putnam, *"E Pluribus Unum,"* 161.

CHAPTER 5

Epigraph: "Interview with Mark Prosser," *The Iowa Journal,* Iowa Public Television, April 19, 2007.

1. In fact, we made our original trip on September 11, 2001, and on our way to the airport, we drove past the Pentagon just moments after a plane had crashed into it.

2. "Interview with Mark Prosser."

3. "Storm Lake Community Schools Comprehensive School Improvement Plan Report," June 21, 2007, available online at http://www.storm-lake.k12.ia.us/SLCSD/Central_Office/documents/CSIP_06.pdf (accessed April 12, 2011).

4. "Minority Students in Majority in Storm Lake Schools," Associated Press State and Local Wire, February 4, 2003.

5. Mark A. Grey, "Pork, Poultry, and Newcomers in Storm Lake, Iowa," in *Any Way You Cut It: Meat Processing and Small-Town America,* ed. Donald D. Stull, Michael J. Broadway, and David Griffith (Lawrence: University of Kansas Press, 1995), 120.

6. "Immigration in Storm Lake," *The Iowa Journal,* Iowa Public Television, April 19, 2007, available online at http://www.iptv.org/iowajournal/story.cfm/29 (accessed April 9, 2011).

7. Steven A. Holmes, "In Iowa Town, Strains of Diversity," *New York Times,* February 17, 1996.

8. According to Roy Beck, residents in Clay County, Iowa, blocked the opening of a plant in Spencer because the experience in Storm Lake "showed an unacceptable change in a previously egalitarian way of life": Roy Beck, *The Case against Immigration* (New York: W. W. Norton, 1996), 22.

9. Personal interview with Dale Carver, Storm Lake, Iowa, May 26, 2010.

10. Art Cullen, "Immigrants, Meatpacking and My Town: I Confess My Confusion," *Progressive Populist,* 1995–1997, available online at http://www.populist.com/4.97.mytown.html (accessed March 27, 2011).

11. Marc Cooper and Mark Grey, "The Heartland's Raw Deal," *Nation,* vol. 264, 1997, 11–17.

12. Cullen, "Immigrants, Meatpacking and My Town."

13. "Immigration in Storm Lake."

14. "Storm Lake Elects Hispanic to Council," AP State and Local Wire, December 7, 2000.

15. Dana Larsen, "Day of Peace," *Storm Lake Pilot Tribune,* November 20, 2007.

16. Quoted in "Immigration in Storm Lake."

17. Bret Hayworth, "Storm Lake Program Provides National Model," *Sioux City Journal,* May 8, 2010.

18. Dana Larsen, "Letter from the Editor," *Storm Lake Pilot Tribune,* December 19, 2007.

19. Dominic Pulera, *Visible Differences: Why Race Will Matter to Americans in the Twenty-First Century* (New York: Continuum International, 2002), 174.

20. Personal interview with Dale Carver.

21. "Acceptance Is Key," editorial, *Perry Chief,* August 16, 1990.

22. Allie Schwarzen, "Letter to the Editor," *Perry Chief,* August 23, 1990.

23. Ellen Hobbs Burton, "Letter to the Editor," *Perry Chief,* August 30, 1990.

24. Personal interview with Viivi Shirley, Perry, Iowa, May 25, 2010.

25. Juli Probasco, "Test Results Indicate Bias," *Perry Chief,* September 19, 1991.

26. Juli Probasco, "Cultural Diversity: Perry's Hispanic Community Grows," *Perry Chief,* April 30, 1992.

27. Juli Probasco, "Language Barriers: Many Attempt to Tackle Obstacle," *The Perry Chief,* May 14, 1992.

28. Jody Swilky and Kent Newman, dirs., *Little Salsa on the Prairie: The Changing Character of Perry, Iowa,* documentary, Full Spectrum Productions, 2006.

29. Ibid.

30. Perry LINK stands for "Perry—Linking parents with schools; Involving all generations in community dialogue; Nourishing families, parents and youth through education; Keeping and supporting diverse ethnic heritages."

31. Micah Chaplin, "Walstrom Bids Adios to PHS," *Perry Chief,* May 28, 2010.

32. Juli Probasco-Sowers, "Perry Answers Diversity Challenge," *Des Moines Register,* November 20, 2005.

33. Quoted in Laura Sternweis, "Perry Residents Connect with Latino Neighbors—via Mexico," *Extension Connection,* Spring 2007 available online at http://www.extension.iastate.edu/news/2007/apr/121904.htm (accessed November 18, 2010).

34. Teresa Puente, "Wave of Hispanic Immigrants Alters Demographics in the Heartland," *Chicago Tribune,* January 16, 2000.

35. We were unable to conduct focus groups in Storm Lake.

36. Personal interview with Angelica Diaz-Cardenas, Perry, Iowa, May 25, 2010.

37. Personal interview with Guadalupe Duarte, Perry, Iowa, May 25, 2010.

38. Personal interview with Jay Pattee, Perry, Iowa, May 24, 2010.

39. Personal interview with Doug Bruce, Perry, Iowa, May 25, 2010.

40. "Perry Buys Software to Translate Documents into Spanish," AP State and Local Wire, March 27, 2002.

41. Swilky and Newman, *Little Salsa on the Prairie.*

CHAPTER 6

Epigraph: Charles Hirschman, "The Impact of Immigration on American Society: Looking Backward to the Future," in *Border Battles: U.S. Immigration Debates,* report, Social Science Research Council, July 28, 2006, available online at http://borderbattles.ssrc.org/Hirschman (accessed February 28, 2010).

1. Jim Tankersley and Christi Parsons, "Immigration Polarizes Small-Town America," *Chicago Tribune,* September 25, 2008.

2. Paul Waldman, Elbert Ventura, Robert Savillo, Susan Lin, and Greg Lewis, "Fear and Loathing in Prime Time: Immigration Myths and Cable News," report, Media Matters Action Network, May 21, 2008, available online at http://mediamattersaction.org/static/pdfs/fear-and-loathing.pdf (accessed January 30, 2011).

3. The Support Our Law Enforcement and Safe Neighborhoods Act (Arizona Senate Bill 1070) was signed into law by Governor Jan Brewer on April 23, 2010.

4. National Conference of State Legislatures, "2011 Immigration-Related Laws, Bills, and Resolutions in the States (January 1– March 31, 2011), available online at http://www.ncsl.org/issues-research/immigration34/2011-immigration-related-laws-bills-and-reso lutio.aspx (accessed January 16, 2012).

5. Dianne Solis, "Farmers Branch Files Federal Appeal on Immigration Ordinance," *Dallas Morning News,* January 6, 2011.

6. Mauricia Ann Proper, "Letter to the Editor," *Storm Lake Pilot Tribune,* January 13, 2004.

7. At this writing, the entirety of the 2010 U.S. Census file had not been released. Those data that were unavailable are based on the American Community Survey five-year estimates, which represent the average characteristics of the population between January 2005 and December 2009. These data are collected from a sample of housing units, not a full count of the population.

8. Emily Gersema and Paul Goodsell, "Trend in Meatpacking Towns Raises Question of 'White Flight,'" *Omaha World Herald,* August 22, 2004.

9. American Youth Policy Forum, "Diverse Schools: Building Strong Communities, in School and Beyond," June 6, 2003, available online at http://www.aypf.org/forum briefs/2003/fb060603.htm (accessed June 4, 2009).

10. Steven Gravelle, "Safe Place: Doesn't Fit State Department Rules," *Cedar Rapids Gazette,* May 11, 2010.

11. Douglas Burns, "Taking Note: King Unplugged: Paper Car Windows and Tax Hookers," *Daily Times Herald,* April 24, 2006; Jane Norman, "King Says Immigration Views Based on 'Rule of Law,'" *Des Moines Register,* April 1, 2008.

12. John Mueller, *Quiet Cataclysm: Reflections on the Recent Transformation of World Politics* (New York: HarperCollins, 1995), 14.

13. Diane Crispell, "Which Good Old Days?" *American Demographics* 18 (1996): 35.

14. Ann V. Millard and Jorge Chapa, "*Aqui* in the Midwest," in *Apple Pie and Enchiladas: Latino Newcomers to the Midwest,* ed. Ann V. Millard and Jorge Chapa (Austin: University of Texas Press, 2001), 3.

15. Cynthia M. Duncan, *Worlds Apart: Why Poverty Persists in Rural America* (New Haven, Conn.: Yale University Press, 1999).

16. Zaragosa Vargas, *Proletarians of the North: A History of Mexican Industrial Workers in Detroit and the Midwest, 1917–1933* (Berkeley: University of California Press, 1993).

17. "Iowa: Immigration," poll results compiled by the Center for the Study of Politics and Governance, Humphrey Institute of Public Affairs, University of Minnesota, available online at http://www.politicsandgovernance.org/public_opinion/um_polls/ia/issues_immi gration.html (accessed January 16, 2012).

18. Mark A. Grey, Michele Devlin, and Aaron Goldsmith, *Postville, U.S.A.: Surviving Diversity in Small-Town America* (Boston: GemmaMedia, 2009).

19. Patrick J. Carr and Maria J. Kefalas, *Hollowing Out the Middle: The Rural Brain Drain and What It Means for America* (Boston: Beacon Press, 2009), 5.

20. Rick Stouffer, "The Soul of Ravenswood, W[est] V[irginia], Is in Aluminum," *Pittsburgh Tribune-Review,* August 1, 2010. In 2010, the steel mill in Georgetown, South Carolina, reopened: see "Workers Return to ArcelorMittal Mill in South Carolina," Associated Press, October 14, 2010.

21. Scott Pelley, "Newton, Iowa: Anger in the Heartland," *60 Minutes,* CBS Television, October 31, 2010.

22. Rick Hampson, "New Ghost Towns: Industrial Communities Teeter on the Edge," *USA Today,* March 2, 2010.

23. Richard C. Longworth, "Can the Midwest Regain Its Economic Clout?" *Chicago Tribune Magazine,* January 6, 2008, available online at http://articles.chicagotribune.com/2008-01-06/features/0712310090_1_globalization-midwest-regions (accessed June 12, 2009). See also Richard C. Longworth, *Caught in the Middle: America's Heartland in the Age of Globalism* (New York: Bloomsbury, 2008).

24. Hampson, "New Ghost Towns."

25. Michael J. Broadway and Donald D. Stull, "Meat Processing and Garden City, KS: Boom and Bust," *Journal of Rural Studies* 22 (2006): 55–66.

26. Michele Linck, "Sioux City Buys Defunct John Morrell Plant," *Sioux City Journal,* March 7, 2011.

27. Patrik Johnson, "Crackdown on Immigrants Empties a Town and Hardens Views," *Christian Science Monitor,* October 3, 2006.

28. Evan Perez and Corey Dade, "An Immigration Raid Aids Blacks for a Time," *Wall Street Journal,* January 17, 2007.

29. "ICE Raid of Swift Plant Creates a Ghost Town," *Greeley Tribune* (wire reports), February 10, 2007.

30. Debbie Elliott, "Labor Worries Rise as Planting Season Nears in Alabama," *Morning Edition,* National Public Radio, October 24, 2011; Jay Reeves and Alicia A. Caldwell, "After Alabama Immigration Law, Few Americans Taking Immigrants' Work," Associated Press, October 21, 2001, available online at http://www.huffingtonpost.com/2011/10/21/after-alabama-immigration-law-few-americans-taking-immigrants-work_n_1023635.html (accessed January 16, 2012).

31. Campbell Robertson, "After Ruling, Hispanics Flee an Alabama Town," *New York Times,* October 3, 2011. Available at http://www.nytimes.com/2011/10/04/us/after-ruling-hispanics-flee-an-alabama-town.html?pagewanted=all (accessed October 4, 2011).

32. Stephen G. Bloom, *Postville: A Clash of Cultures in Heartland America* (Orlando, Fla.: Harcourt, 2000).

33. Jackie Northam, National Public Radio story, 1998, quoted in Grey et al., *Postville, U.S.A.*

34. Jean Caspers-Simmet, "Agri Star Promises Big Economic Effect in Postville," *Agrinews,* April 29, 2010.

35. Grey et al., *Postville, U.S.A.*

36. Henry C. Jackson, "Town Wonder If It's Next to Face Immigration Raid," Associated Press, August 27, 1998.

37. Katherine Fennelly and Christopher Federico, "Rural Residence as a Determinant of Attitudes toward U.S. Immigration Policy," *International Migration* 46 (2008): 151–190.

38. U.S. Congressional Budget Office, "The Impact of Unauthorized Immigrants on the Budgets of State and Local Governments," December 2007, available online at http://www.cbo.gov/ftpdocs/87xx/doc8711/12-6-Immigration.pdf (accessed November 4, 2010).

39. Katharine M. Donato, Charles M. Tolbert Jr., Alfred Nucci, and Yukio Kawano, "Recent Immigrant Settlement in the Nonmetropolitan United States: Evidence from Internal Census Data," *Rural Sociology* 72 (2007): 537–559; Helen B. Marrow, *New Destination Dreaming: Immigration, Race, and Legal Status in the Rural American South* (Stanford, Calif.: Stanford University Press, 2011).

40. For example, in 2005, the majority—59 of 99—of Iowa's counties were designated "medically underserved areas" due to the lack of medical providers, high poverty and the aging population: see Mark A. Grey, "State and Local Immigration Policy in Iowa," in *Immigration's New Frontiers: Experiences from the Emerging Gateway States,* ed. Greg Anrig Jr. and Tova Andrea Wang (New York: Century Foundation Press, 2006), 50.

41. Marc Cooper and Mark Grey, "The Heartland's Raw Deal," *Nation* 264 (1997): 11–17.

42. Jarnaal Abdul-Alim, "SAT Takers Grow More Diverse, Scores Stagnate," Diverse: Issues in Higher Education, September 14, 2010, available online at http://diverseeducation.com/article/14124 (accessed February 1, 2011).

43. J. Celeste Lay and Atiya Kai Stokes-Brown, "Put to the Test: Understanding Differences in Support for High-Stakes Testing," American Politics Research 37 (2009): 429–448.

44. Broadway and Stull, "Meat Processing and Garden City, KS."

45. Robert E. Park and Ernest W. Burgess, Introduction to the Science of Sociology (University of Chicago Press, 1969 [1921]), 360.

46. Katherine Fennelly, "Prejudice toward Immigrants in the Midwest," in New Faces in New Places: The Changing Geography of American Immigration, ed. Douglas Massey (New York: Russell Sage Foundation, 2008).

47. Thomas Tancredo, In Mortal Danger: The Battle for America's Border and Security. Nashville: Cumberland House, 2006), 203.

48. Robert A. Dahl, Who Governs? Democracy and Power in an American City (New Haven, Conn.: Yale University Press, 1961).

49. Larry Selinker, "Interlanguage," International Review of Applied Linguistics 10 (1972): 209–231.

50. Beverly Daniel Tatum, "Why Are All the Black Kids Sitting Together in the Cafeteria?": A Psychologist Explains the Development of Racial Identity (New York: Basic Books, 1997).

51. John Higham, Strangers in the Land: Patterns of American Nativism, 1860–1925 (New Brunswick, N.J.: Rutgers University Press, 2002); Peter Schrag, Not Fit for Our Society: Immigration and Nativism in America (Berkeley: University of California Press, 2010).

52. Richard Alba and Victor Nee, Remaking the American Mainstream: Assimilation and Contemporary Immigration (Cambridge, Mass.: Harvard University Press 2003).

53. Marrow, New Destination Dreaming, 14.

54. David Griffith, "New Midwesterners, New Southerners: Immigration Experiences in Four Rural American Settings," in New Faces in New Places: The Changing Geography of American Immigration, ed. Douglas Massey (New York: Russell Sage Foundation, 2008), 179–210; David Griffith, "Rural Industry and Mexican Immigration and Settlement in North Carolina," in New Destinations: Mexican Immigration in the United States, ed. Víctor Zúniga and Rubén Hernández-León (New York: Russell Sage Foundation, 2005), 50–75.

55. Personal interview with Dan Marburger, Perry, Iowa, May 24, 2010.

56. Tim Gallagher, "Storm Lake Choice Soars," Sioux City Journal, March 14, 2010.

57. Milton M. Gordon, Assimilation in American Life (New York: Oxford University Press, 1964); Ruby Jo Reeves Kennedy, "Single or Triple Melting Pot? Intermarriage Trends in New Haven, 1870–1950," American Journal of Sociology 58 (1952): 56–59; Lowry Nelson, "Intermarriage among Nationality Groups in a Rural Area of Minnesota," American Journal of Sociology 48 (1943) 585–592.

58. Tamara Henry, "Report: Greater Percentage of Americans Educated," USA Today, June 5, 2002.

59. Robert D. Putnam, "E Pluribus Unum: Diversity and Community in the Twenty-First Century, the 2006 Johan Skytte Prize Lecture," Scandinavian Political Studies 30 (2007): 163–164.

60. Interestingly, when I spoke to her in 2010, she had just received a violation due to the ordinance about mowing one's lawn. Her grass was more than six inches high, so she was fined. She described it as "puritanical" and "Eurocentric."

61. "Perry Buys Software to Translate Documents into Spanish," AP State and Local Wire, March 27, 2002.

CONCLUSION

Epigraph: Teresa Coenen, Principal, Storm Lake High School, 2010.

1. Nicholas A. Christakis and James H. Fowler, *Connected: The Surprising Power of Our Social Networks and How They Shape Our Lives* (New York: Little, Brown, 2009), 290.

2. Dennis Chong, *Rational Lives: Norms and Values in Politics and Society* (Chicago: University of Chicago Press, 1999).

3. Cynthia B. Struthers and Janet L. Bokemeier, "Myths and Realities of Raising Children and Creating Family Life in a Rural County," *Journal of Family Issues* 21 (2000): 17–46.

4. Robert Wuthnow, *Remaking the Heartland: Middle America since the 1950s* (Princeton, N.J.: Princeton University Press, 2011), 19.

5. Chong, *Rational Lives.*

6. "Immigrants in the Heartland," Targeted News Service, November 4, 2009.

7. William Claiborne, "Immigration Foes Find Platform in Iowa, National Groups Fight Governor on Recruiting Workers from Abroad," *Washington Post,* August 19, 2001, A3.

8. Mark A. Grey, "Immigrants, Migration, and Worker Turnover at the Hog Pride Pork Packing Plant," *Human Organization* 58 (1999): 25–26.

9. Tyson Foods, "Recognizing an Exceptional Workforce," 2010 Sustainability Report, available online at http://www.tysonfoods.com/Sustainability/2010/People/3_2/1.aspx (accessed June 13, 2011).

10. Helen B. Marrow, *New Destination Dreaming: Immigration, Race, and Legal Status in the Rural American South* (Stanford, Calif.: Stanford University Press, 2011), 237.

11. Jan Flora, Claudia Prado-Meza, Hannah Lewis, César P. Montalvo, and Frank Dunn, "The Impact of an Immigration and Customs Enforcement Raid on Marshalltown, Iowa," in *Latinos in the Midwest,* ed. Rubén O. Martinez (East Lansing: Michigan State University Press, 2011), 119–155.

12. My-Thuan Tran, "A Sharp Drop in Illegal Border Crossings Reported," *Los Angeles Times,* September 1, 2011, available online at http://articles.latimes.com/2010/sep/01/nation/la-na-immigration-20100902 (accessed January 17, 2012); Jordy Yager, "Obama's ICE Reports Record Number of Deportations of Illegal Immigrants," *The Hill,* October 18, 2011, available online at http://thehill.com/homenews/administration/188241-ice-announces-record-breaking-deportations (accessed January 17, 2012).

13. In considering their post–high school plans, rural young people decide where to live primarily on the basis of the local job opportunities and family ties. Very few students told us in the focus groups that they wanted to move far away. The majority of those intending to go to college planned to go Iowa State University, with a smaller group planning to go the University of Iowa, which was seen as "far away" for many youth in these central and western Iowa towns. Several young people said they wanted to stay in town but could not figure out how to do it and get a good job. See also Monica Kirkpatrick Johnson, Glen H. Elder Jr., and Michael Stern, "Attachments to Family and Community and the Young Adult Transition of Rural Youth," *Journal of Research on Adolescence* 15 (2005): 99–125.

14. Dale Maharidge and Michael Williamson, *Denison, Iowa: Searching for the Soul of America through the Secrets of a Midwest Town* (New York: Free Press, 2005), 88.

15. See also Nancy Brown Diggs, *Hidden in the Heartland: The New Wave of Immigrants and the Challenge to America* (East Lansing: Michigan State University Press, 2011).

16. Ken Belson and Jill P. Capuzzo, "Towns Rethink Laws against Illegal Immigrants," *New York Times,* September 26, 2007.

17. Dana Larsen, "Push On to Repeal 'English Only' but S[torm] L[ake] Officials See Little Impact," *Storm Lake Pilot Tribune,* January 29, 2008.

18. Janet M. Fitchen, *Endangered Spaces, Enduring Places: Change, Identity, and Survival in Rural America* (Boulder, Colo.: Westview Press, 1991).

19. Carolyn Dimitri, Anne Effland, and Neilson Conklin, *The 20th Century Transformation of U.S. Agriculture and Farm Policy,* Economic Information Bulletin no. 3, Economic Research Service, U.S. Department of Agriculture, Washington, D.C., June 2005.

20. Quoted in the "'Farm Town Futures': The New Homestead Act," *Nightly Business Report,* KQED World, episode no. 24048, May 27, 2004.

21. Chuch Hassebrook, "Speak Your Piece: Misguided Times," *Daily Yonder,* October 4, 2011, available online at http://www.dailyyonder.com/speak-your-piece-underinvesting -opportunity/2011/09/27/3538 (accessed October 21, 2011).

22. Richard E. Wood, *Survival of Rural America: Small Victories and Bitter Harvests* (Lawrence: University Press of Kansas, 2008), 139–147.

23. See Ron Nixon, "U.S. Spending Billions on Rural Jobs, but Impact Is Uncertain," *New York Times,* September 12, 2011, available at http://www.nytimes.com/2011/09/13/us/13rural.html?pagewanted=all (accessed January 19, 2012).

24. "Jobs and Economic Security for Rural America," report by the White House Rural Council, August 2011, available online at http://www.whitehouse.gov/sites/default/files/jobs_economic_security_rural_america.pdf (accessed September 18, 2011).

25. Lorri Glawe, "S[torm] L[ake] Charter School Success 'Beyond Wildest Imagination,'" *Storm Lake Pilot Tribune,* October 28, 2008.

Bibliography

Aboud, Frances E. *Children and Prejudice.* London: Blackwell, 1988.

Abramson, Paul R., and John H. Aldrich. "The Decline of Electoral Participation in America." *American Political Science Review* 76 (1982): 502–521.

Alba, Richard, and Victor Nee. *Remaking the American Mainstream: Assimilation and Contemporary Immigration.* Cambridge, Mass.: Harvard University Press, 2003.

Alesina, Alberto, Reza Baquir, and William Easterly. "Public Goods and Ethnic Divisions." *Quarterly Journal of Economics* 114 (1999): 243–285.

Alesina, Alberto, and Eliana La Ferrara. "Participation in Heterogeneous Communities." *Quarterly Journal of Economics* 115 (2000): 847–904.

———. "Who Trusts Others?" *Journal of Public Economics* 85 (2002): 207–234.

Allport, Gordon W. *The Nature of Prejudice.* Reading, Mass.: Addison-Wesley, 1954.

Almond, Gabriel, and Sidney Verba. *The Civic Culture.* Princeton, N.J.: Princeton University Press, 1963.

Alwin, Duane F., and Jon A. Krosnick. "Aging, Cohorts, and the Stability of Sociopolitical Orientations over the Life Span." *American Journal of Sociology* 97 (1991): 169–196.

Amato, Joseph. *To Call It Home: The New Immigrants of Southwestern Minnesota.* Marshall, Minn.: Crossings Press, 1996.

Andersen, Kristi. "In Whose Interest? Political Parties, Context and Incorporation of Immigrants." In *New Race Politics in America: Understanding Minority and Immigrant Politics,* ed. Jane Junn and Kerry L. Haynie, 17–38. New York: Cambridge University Press, 2008.

Anderson, Christopher J., and Aida Paskeviciute. "How Ethnic and Linguistic Heterogeneity Influence the Prospects for Civil Society: A Comparative Study of Citizenship Behavior." *Journal of Politics* 68 (2006): 783–802.

Arvizu, John R., and F. Chris Garcia. "Latino Voting Participation: Explaining and Differentiating Latino Voting Turnout." *Hispanic Journal of Behavioral Sciences* 18 (1996): 104–123.

Astin, Alexander W., Linda J. Sax, and Juan Avalos. "Long-Term Effects of Volunteerism during the Undergraduate Years." *Review of Higher Education* 22 (1999): 187–202.

Austin, Erica, and C. Leigh Nelson. "Influences of Ethnicity, Family Communication and Media on Adolescents' Socialization to U.S. Politics." *Journal of Broadcasting and Electronic Media* 37 (1993): 419–435.

Ayers, John W., C. Richard Hofstetter, Keith Schnakenberg, and Bohdan Kolody. "Is Immigration a Racial Issue? Anglo Attitudes on Immigration Policies in a Border County." *Social Science Quarterly* 90 (2009): 593–610.

Bailey, Benjamin. "Dominican-American Ethnic/Racial Identities and United States Social Categories." *International Migration Review* 35 (2001): 677–708.

Balch, George I. "Multiple Indicators in Survey Research: The Concept of 'Sense of Political Efficacy.'" *Political Methodology* 1 (1974): 1–43.

Bandura, Albert. "Perceived Self-Efficacy in Cognitive Development and Functioning." *Educational Psychologist* 28 (1993): 117–148.

———. *Self-Efficacy: The Exercise of Control.* New York: W. H. Freeman, 1997.

Barber, Benjamin. *Strong Democracy: Participatory Politics for a New Age.* Berkeley: University of California Press, 1984.

Bean, Frank D., B. Lindsay Lowell, and Lowell J. Taylor. "Undocumented Mexican Immigrants and the Earnings of Other Workers in the United States." *Demography* 25 (1988): 35–52.

Beane, James, Joan Turner, David Jones, and Richard Lipka. "Long-Term Effects of Community Service Programs." *Curriculum Inquiry* 11 (1981): 143–155.

Beck, Paul Allen, Russell J. Dalton, Steven Greene, and Robert Huckfeldt. "The Social Calculus of Voting: Interpersonal, Media and Organizational Influences on Presidential Choices." *American Political Science Review* 96 (2002): 57–74.

Beck, Paul Allen, and M. Kent Jennings. "Family Traditions, Political Periods, and the Development of Partisan Orientations." *Journal of Politics* 53 (1991): 742–763.

———. "Pathways to Participation." *American Political Science Review* 76 (1982): 94–108.

Beck, Roy. *The Case against Immigration.* New York: W. W. Norton, 1996.

Benjamin-Alvarado, Jonathan, Louis DeSipio, and Celeste Montoya. "Latino Mobilization in New Immigrant Destinations: The Anti-H.R. 4437 Protest in Nebraska's Cities." *Urban Affairs Review* 44 (2009): 718–735.

Bennett, Stephen E. "Why Young Americans Hate Politics, and What We Should Do about It." *PS: Political Science and Politics* 30 (1997): 47–53.

Benson, Janet. "Undocumented Immigrants and the Meatpacking Industry in the Midwest." In *Illegal Immigration in America: A Reference Handbook,* ed. David W. Haines and Karen E. Rosenblum, 172–193. Westport, Conn.: Greenwood Press, 1999.

Berelson, Bernard R., Paul F. Lazarsfeld, and William N. McPhee. *Voting: A Study of Opinion Formation in a Presidential Campaign.* Chicago: University of Chicago Press, 1954.

Berg, Justin Allen. "Core Networks and Whites' Attitudes toward Immigrants and Immigration Policy." *Public Opinion Quarterly* 73 (2009): 7–31.

Berkman, Lisa F. "The Role of Social Relations in Health Promotion." *Psychosomatic Medicine* 57 (1995): 245–254.

Beugelsdijk, Sjoerd. "A Note on the Theory and Measurement of Trust in Explaining Differences in Economic Growth." *Cambridge Journal of Economics* 30 (2006): 371–387.

Biographical History of Shelby and Audubon Counties, Iowa. Chicago: W. S. Dunbar, 1889.

Black, Jerome H. "The Practice of Politics in Two Settings: Political Transferability among Recent Immigrants to Canada." *Canadian Journal of Political Science* 20 (1987): 731–754.

Blalock, Hubert. *Toward a Theory of Minority Group Relations.* New York: John Wiley and Sons, 1967.

Bloom, Stephen G. *Postville: A Clash of Cultures in Heartland America.* Orlando, Fla.: Harcourt, 2000.

Blumer, Herbert. *Symbolic Interactionism: Perspective and Method.* Englewood Cliffs, N.J.: Prentice Hall, 1969.

Bobo, Lawrence. "Keeping the Linchpin in Place: Testing the Multiple Sources of Opposition to Residential Integration." *Revue Internationale de Psychologie Sociale* 2 (1989): 307–325.

Bobo, Lawrence, and Ryan A. Smith. "Antipoverty Policy, Affirmative Action, and Racial Attitudes." In *Confronting Poverty: Prescriptions for Change,* ed. Sheldon H. Danziger, Gary D. Sandefur, and Daniel H. Weinberg, 365–395. Cambridge, Mass.: Harvard University Press, 1994.

Bobo, Lawrence, and Camille L. Zubrinsky. "Attitudes on Racial Integration: Perceived Status Differences, Mere In-Group Preferences, or Racial Prejudice?" *Social Forces* 74 (1996): 883–909.

Books, John W., and Charles L. Prysby. *Political Behavior and the Local Context.* New York: Praeger, 1991.

Borjas, George J. "Do Blacks Gain or Lose from Immigration? In *Help or Hindrance? The Economic Implications of Immigration for African Americans,* ed. Daniel S. Hamermesh and Frank D. Bean, 51–74. New York: Russell Sage, 1998.

———. "The Economics of Immigration." *Journal of Economic Literature* 32 (1994): 1667–1717.

Borjas, George J., and Stephen J. Trejo. "Immigrant Participation in the Welfare System." *Industrial & Labor Relations Review* 44 (1991): 195–211.

Bourdieu, Pierre. "Cultural and Social Reproduction." In *Power and Ideology in Education,* ed. Jerome Karabel and A. H. Halsey, 487–511. New York: Oxford University Press, 1977.

———. "The Forms of Capital." In *Handbook of Theory and Research for the Sociology of Education,* ed. J. G. Richardson, 241–258. Westport, Conn.: Greenwood Press, 1985.

Bowler, Shaun, Francisco Pedraza, and Gary Segura. "The Efficacy and Trust of Juan Q. Public: How the Immigration Marches Reflect Surprising Support for American Institutions of Governance." Paper presented at the Western Political Science Conference, Las Vegas, March 8–11,, 2007.

Bradley, Martin B., Norman M. Green Jr., Dale E. Jones, Mac Lynn, and Lou McNeil. *Churches and Church Membership in the United States, 1990.* Atlanta: Glenmary Research Center, 1992.

Branton, Regina P., and Bradford S. Jones. "Re-examining Racial Attitudes: The Conditional Relationship between Diversity and Socioeconomic Environment." *American Journal of Political Science* 49 (2005): 359–372.

Brehm, John, and Wendy Rahn. "Individual-Level Evidence for the Causes and Consequences of Social Capital." *American Journal of Political Science* 41 (1997): 999–1023.

Broadway, Michael J. "Beef Stew: Cattle, Immigrants, and Established Residents in a Kansas Beefpacking Town." In *Newcomers in the Workplace: Immigrants and the Restructuring of the U.S. Economy,* ed. Louise Lamphere, Alex Stepick and Guillermo Grenier, 25–43. Philadelphia: Temple University Press, 1994.

Broadway, Michael J., and Donald D. Stull. "Meat Processing and Garden City, KS: Boom and Bust." *Journal of Rural Studies* 22 (2006): 55–66.

Broadway, Michael J., and Terry Ward. "Recent Changes in the Structure and Location of the U.S. Meatpacking Industry." *Geography* 76 (1990): 76–79.

Bronfenbrenner, Urie. *The Ecology of Human Development: Experiments by Nature and Design.* Cambridge, Mass.: Harvard University Press, 1979.

Bronfenbrenner, Urie, with P. A. Morris. "The Ecology of Developmental Processes." In *Handbook of Child Psychology: Volume 1: Theoretical Models of Human Development,* ed. William Damon and Richard M. Lerner, 993–1028. New York: John Wiley, 1998.

Brown, Rupert, and Miles Hewstone. "An Integrative Theory of Intergroup Contact." In *Advances in Experimental Social Psychology,* vol. 37, ed. Mark P. Zanna, 255–343. San Diego, Calif.: Academic Press, 2005.

Bryan, Frank M. *Politics in the Rural States: People, Parties, and Processes.* Boulder, Colo.: Westview Press, 1981.

Burbank, Matthew J. "The Psychological Basis of Contextual Effects." *Political Geography* 14 (1995): 621–635.

Burns, Nancy, Kay Lehman Schlozman, and Sidney Verba. *The Private Roots of Public Action: Gender, Equality and Political Participation.* Cambridge, Mass.: Harvard University Press, 2001.

Burns, Peter, and James G. Gimpel. "Economic Insecurity, Prejudicial Stereotypes, and Public Opinion on Immigration Policy." *Political Science Quarterly* 115 (2000): 201–225.

Burt, Ronald S. "The Contingent Value of Social Capital." *Administrative Science Quarterly* 42 (1997): 339–365.

———. "Social Contagion and Innovation: Cohesion versus Structural Equivalence." *American Journal of Sociology* 92 (1987): 1287–1335.

Bynner, John, and Sheena Ashford. "Politics and Participation: Some Antecedents of Young People's Attitudes to the Political System and Political Activity." *European Journal of Social Psychology* 24 (1994): 223–236.

Cain, Bruce, and Roderick Kiewiet. "California's Coming Minority Majority." *Public Opinion* 9 (1986): 50–52.

Campbell, Angus, Philip E. Converse, Warren E. Miller, and Donald E. Stokes. *The American Voter.* New York: John Wiley, 1960.

Campbell, Angus, Gerald Gurin, and Warren E. Miller. *The Voter Decides.* Evanston, Ill.: Row, Peterson, 1954.

Campbell, Bruce A. "A Theoretical Approach to Peer Influence in Adolescent Socialization." *American Journal of Political Science* 24 (1980): 324–344.

Campbell, David E. *Why We Vote: How Schools and Communities Shape Our Civic Life.* Princeton, N.J.: Princeton University Press, 2006.

Cantú, Lionel. "The Peripheralization of Rural America: A Case Study of Latino Migrants in America's Heartland." *Sociological Perspectives* 38 (1995): 399–414.

Card, David. "The Impact of the Mariel Boatlift on the Miami Labor Market." *Industrial and Labor Relations Review* 43 (1990): 245–257.

Carr, Patrick J., and Maria J. Kefalas. *Hollowing Out the Middle: The Rural Brain Drain and What It Means for America.* Boston: Beacon Press, 2009.

Carsey, Thomas. "The Contextual Effects of Race on White Voter Behavior: The 1989 New York City Mayoral Election." *Journal of Politics* 57 (1995): 221–228.

Castles, Stephen, and Mark J. Miller. *The Age of Migration.* Basingstoke: Palgrave Macmillan, 2003.

Chakraborti, Neil, and Jon Garland, eds. *Rural Racism.* Portland, Ore.: Willan Publishing, 2004.

Chapa, Jorge, Rogelio Saenz, Refugio I. Rochin, and Eileen Diaz McConnell. "Latinos and the Changing Demographic Fabric of the Rural Midwest." In *Apple Pie and Enchiladas: Latino Newcomers to the Midwest,* ed. Ann V. Millard and Jorge Chapa, 47–73. Austin: University of Texas Press, 2001.

Charles, Camille Z. "Neighborhood Racial-Composition Preferences: Evidence from a Multiethnic Metropolis." *Social Problems* 47 (2000): 379–407.

Chong, Dennis. *Rational Lives: Norms and Values in Politics and Society.* Chicago: University of Chicago Press, 1999.

———."Tolerance and Social Adjustment to New Norms and Practices." *Political Behavior* 16 (1994): 21–53.

Christakis, Nicholas A., and James H. Fowler. *Connected: The Surprising Power of Our Social Networks and How They Shape Our Lives.* New York: Little, Brown, 2009.

Cicourel, Aaron V., and John I. Kitsuse. "The School as a Mechanism of Social Differentiation." In *Power and Ideology in Education,* ed. Jerome Karabel and A. H. Halsey, 282–292. New York: Oxford University Press, 1977.

Cigler, Allan, and Mark R. Joslyn. "The Extensiveness of Group Membership and Social Capital: The Impact on Political Tolerance Attitudes." *Political Research Quarterly* 55 (2002): 7–25.

Citrin, Jack, Donald P. Green, Christopher Muste, and Cara Wong. "Public Opinion toward Immigration Reform: The Role of Economic Motivations." *Journal of Politics* 59 (1997): 858–881.

Claibourn, Michele P., and Paul S. Martin. "Trusting and Joining? An Empirical Test of the Reciprocal Nature of Social Capital." *Political Behavior* 22 (2000): 267–291.

Coffé, Hilde, and Benny Geys. "Community Heterogeneity: A Burden for the Creation of Social Capital?" *Social Science Quarterly* 87 (2006): 1053–1072.

Cohen, Jeffrey E., Patrick R. Cotter, and Philip B. Coulter. "The Changing Structure of Southern Political Participation: Matthews and Prothro 20 Years Later." *Social Science Quarterly* 64 (1983): 536–549.

Coladarci, Theodore, and Casey D. Cobb. "Extracurricular Participation, School Size, and Achievement and Self-Esteem among High School Students: A National Look." *Journal of Research in Rural Education* 12 (1996): 92–103.

Coleman, James. "Social Capital and the Creation of Human Capital." *American Journal of Sociology* 94 (1988): S95–S121.

Conover, Pamela J., and Donald Searing. "A Political Socialization Perspective." In *Rediscovering the Democratic Purposes of Education,* ed. Lorraine M. McDonnell, P. Michael Timpane, and Roger Benjamin, 91–126. Lawrence: University Press of Kansas, 2000.

Conover, Pamela J., Donald D. Searing, and Ivor M. Crewe. "The Deliberative Potential of Political Discussion." *British Journal of Political Science* 32 (2002): 21–62.

Converse, Philip E. "Attitudes and Nonattitudes: Continuation of a Dialogue." In *The Quantitative Analysis of Social Problems,* ed. Edward R. Tufte, 168–189. Reading, Mass.: Addison-Wesley, 1970.

Converse, Philip E., and Gregory B. Markus. "Plus ça change . . . The New CPS Election Study Panel." *American Political Science Review* 73 (1979): 32–49.

Conzen, Kathleen N., David A. Gerber, Ewa Morawska, George E. Pozzetta, and Rudolph J. Vecoli. "The Invention of Ethnicity: A Perspective from the USA." *Journal of American Ethnic History* 12 (1992): 4–51.

Cook, Stuart W. "Experimenting on Social Issues: The Case of School Desegregation." *American Psychologist* 40 (1985): 452–460.

Cooley, Charles H. *Human Nature and the Social Order.* New York: Scribner's, 1902.

Corzine, Jay, James Creech, and Lin Corzine. "Black Concentration and Lynchings in the South: Testing Blalock's Power-Threat Hypothesis." *Social Forces* 61 (1983): 774–795.

Costa, Dora L., and Matthew E. Kahn. "Civic Engagement and Community Heterogeneity: An Economist's Perspective." *Perspectives on Politics* 1 (2003): 103–111.

Craig, Stephen C., Richard G. Niemi, and Glenn E. Silver. "Political Efficacy and Trust: A Report on the NES Pilot Study Items." *Political Behavior* 12 (1990): 289–313.

Crispell, Diane. "Which Good Old Days?" *American Demographics* 18 (1996): 35.

Cromartie, John B., and Linda L. Swanson. "Census Tracts More Precisely Define Rural Populations and Areas." *Rural Development Perspectives* 11 (2001): 31–39.

Dahl, Robert A. "The City in the Future of Democracy." *American Political Science Review* 61 (1967): 953–970.

———. *Who Governs? Democracy and Power in an American City*. New Haven, Conn.: Yale University Press, 1961.

Dalla, Rochelle L., Amy Ellis, and Sheran C. Cramer. "Immigration and Rural America: Latinos' Perceptions of Work and Residence in Three Meatpacking Communities." *Community, Work, and Family* 8 (2005): 163–185.

Dalton, Russell J. "Reassessing Parental Socialization: Indicator Unreliability versus Generational Transfer." *American Political Science Review* 74 (1980): 421–431.

Damico, Alfonso J., Sandra Bowman Damico, and M. Margaret Conway. "The Democratic Education of Women: High School and Beyond." *Women and Politics* 19 (1998): 1–30.

Danbom, David B. *Born in the Country: A History of Rural America*. Baltimore: Johns Hopkins University Press, 1995.

de la Garza, Rodolfo. "Attitudes toward Immigration Policy." *Migration World Magazine* 21 (1993): 13–17.

de la Garza, Rodolfo, and Fujia Lu. "Explorations into Latino Voluntarism." In *Nuevos Senderos: Reflections on Hispanics and Philanthropy*, ed. Diana Comoamor, William A. Diaz, and Henry A. J. Ramos, 55–78. Houston: Arte Publico Press, 1999.

de la Garza, Rodolfo, Jerry L. Polinard, Robert D. Wrinkle, and Tomás Longoria. "Understanding Intra-Ethnic Attitude Variations: Mexican Origin Population Views of Immigration." *Social Science Quarterly* 72 (1991): 379–387.

Delhey, Jan, and Kenneth Newton. "Predicting Cross-national Levels of Social Trust: Global Pattern or Nordic Exceptionalism?" *European Sociological Review* 21 (2005): 311–327.

Delli Carpini, Michael X., and Scott Keeter. *What Americans Know about Politics and Why It Matters*. New Haven, Conn.: Yale University Press, 1997.

Denton, Nancy A., and Douglas S. Massey. "Residential Segregation of Blacks, Hispanics, and Asians by Socioeconomic Status and Generation." *Social Science Quarterly* 69 (1988): 797–817.

DeSipio, Louis. "Building America, One Person at a Time: Naturalization and Political Behavior of the Naturalized in Contemporary U.S. Politics." In *E Pluribus Unum? Immigrant, Civic Life, and Political Incorporation*, ed. John Mollenkopf and Gary Gerstle, 67–106. New York: Russell Sage, 2001.

DeSipio, Louis, Rodolfo O. de la Garza, and Mark Setzler. "Awash in the Mainstream: Latinos and the 1996 Elections." In *Awash in the Mainstream: Latinos and the 1996 Elections*, ed. Rodolfo de la Garza and Louis DeSipio, 3–46. Boulder, Colo.: Westview Press, 1999.

Devine, Patricia G., Margo J. Monteith, Julia R. Zuwerink, and Andrew J. Elliot. "Prejudice with and without Compunction." *Journal of Personality and Social Psychology* 60 (1991): 817–830.

Diamond, Jared, and James A. Robinson. *Natural Experiments of History*. Boston: Harvard University Press, 2010.

Diggs, Nancy Brown. *Hidden in the Heartland: The New Wave of Immigrants and the Challenge to America*. East Lansing: Michigan State University Press, 2011.

Dimitri, Carolyn, Anne Effland, and Neilson Conklin. *The 20th Century Transformation of U.S. Agriculture and Farm Policy*. Economic Information Bulletin no. 3, Economic Research Service, U.S. Department of Agriculture, Washington, D.C., June 2005.

Dixon, Jeffrey C. "The Ties That Bind and Those That Don't: Toward Reconciling Group Threat and Contact Theories of Prejudice." *Social Forces* 84 (2006): 2179–2204.

Dixon, Jeffrey C., and Michael S. Rosenbaum. "Nice to Know You? Testing Contact, Cultural, and Group Threat Theories of Anti-Black and Anti-Hispanic Stereotypes." *Social Science Quarterly* 85 (2004): 257–280.

Dixon, John. "Contact and Boundaries: 'Locating' the Social Psychology of Intergroup Relations." *Theory and Psychology* 11 (2001): 587–608.

Dixson, Adrienne D., and Celia K. Rousseau. "And We Are Still Not Saved: Critical Race Theory in Education Ten Years Later." In *Critical Race Theory in Education: All God's Children Got a Song,* ed. Adrienne D. Dixson and Celia K. Rousseau, 1–54. New York: Routledge, 2006.

Donato, Katharine M., Charles M. Tolbert Jr., Alfred Nucci, and Yukio Kawano. "Recent Immigrant Settlement in the Nonmetropolitan United States: Evidence from Internal Census Data." *Rural Sociology* 72 (2007): 537–559.

Dovidio, John F., Samuel L. Gaertner, and Ana Validzic. "Intergroup Bias: Status, Differentiation, and a Common In-Group Identity." *Journal of Personality and Social Psychology* 75 (1998): 109–120.

Dovidio, John F., Agata Gluszek, Melissa-Sue John, Ruth Ditlmann, and Paul Lagunes. "Understanding Bias toward Latinos: Discrimination, Dimensions of Differences, and Experience of Exclusion." *Journal of Social Issues* 66 (2010): 59–78.

Duncan, Cynthia M. *Worlds Apart: Why Poverty Persists in Rural America.* New Haven, Conn.: Yale University Press, 1999.

Dunning, Thad. "Improving Causal Inference: Strengths and Limitations of Natural Experiments." *Political Research Quarterly* 61 (2008): 282–293.

Durand, Jorge, Douglas S. Massey, and Chiara Capoferro. "The New Geography of Mexican Immigration." In *New Destinations: Mexican Immigration in the United States,* ed. Víctor Zúniga and Rubén Hernández-León, 1–20. New York: Russell Sage Foundation, 2005.

Easton, David, and Jack Dennis. "The Child's Acquisition of Regime Norms: Political Efficacy." *American Political Science Review* 61 (1967): 26–38.

Eccles, Jacquelynne S., and Bonnie Barber. "Student Council, Volunteering, Basketball, or Marching Band: What Kind of Extracurricular Involvement Matters?" *Journal of Adolescent Research* 14 (1999): 10–34.

Eliasoph, Nina. *Avoiding Politics: How Americans Produce Apathy in Everyday Life.* New York: Cambridge University Press, 1998.

Elder, Glen H., Jr. "Achievement Orientations and Career Patterns of Rural Youth." *Sociology of Education* 37 (1963): 30–58.

Elder, Glen H., Jr., and Rand D. Conger. *Children of the Land: Adversity and Success in Rural America.* Chicago: University of Chicago Press, 2000.

Ellison, Christopher, and Daniel A. Powers. "The Contact Hypothesis and Racial Attitudes among Black Americans." *Social Science Quarterly* 75 (1994): 385–399.

Emerson, Michael O., Karen J. Chai, and George Yancey. "Does Race Matter in Residential Segregation? Exploring the Preferences of White Americans." *American Sociological Review* 66 (2001): 922–935.

Erikson, Erik H. *Childhood and Society,* 2d ed. New York: W. W. Norton, 1963.

Erwin, Deborah O. "An Ethnographic Description of Latino Immigration in Rural Arkansas: Intergroup Relations and Utilization of Healthcare Services." *Southern Rural Sociology* 19 (2003): 46–72.

Espenshade, Thomas J., and Charles A. Calhoun. "An Analysis of Public Opinion toward Undocumented Immigration." *Population Research and Policy Review* 12 (1993): 189–224.

Falcon, Angelo. "Black and Latino Politics in New York City: Race and Ethnicity in a Changing Urban Context." *New Community* 14 (1988): 370–384.

Farley, Reynolds. "Residential Segregation in Urbanized Areas of the United States in 1970: An Analysis of Social Class and Racial Differences." *Demography* 14 (1977): 497–518.

Farley, Reynolds, Charlotte Steeh, Tara Jackson, Maria Krysan, and Keith Reeves. "Continued Racial Residential Segregation in Detroit: 'Chocolate City, Vanilla Suburbs' Revisited." *Journal of Housing Research* 4 (1993): 1–38.

Feagin, Joe R. *Racist America: Roots, Current Realities, and Future Reparations.* New York: Routledge, 2000.

Feldman, Lauren, and Vincent Price. "Confusion or Enlightenment? How Exposure to Disagreement Moderates the Effects of Political Discussion and Media Use on Candidate Knowledge." *Communication Research* 35 (2008): 61–87.

Fendrich, James Max, and Kenneth L. Lovoy. "Back to the Future: Adult Political Behavior of Former Student Activists." *American Sociological Review* 53 (1988): 780–784.

Fennelly, Katherine. "Prejudice toward Immigrants in the Midwest." In *New Faces in New Places: The Changing Geography of American Immigration,* ed. Douglas Massey, 151–178. New York: Russell Sage Foundation, 2008.

Fennelly, Katherine, and Christopher Federico. "Rural Residence as a Determinant of Attitudes toward U.S. Immigration Policy." *International Migration* 46 (2008): 151–190.

Fennelly, Katherine, and Helga Leitner. "How the Food Processing Industry Is Diversifying Rural Minnesota." Working paper no. 59, Julian Samora Research Institute, Michigan State University, East Lansing, 2002.

Festinger, Leon. *A Theory of Cognitive Dissonance.* Evanston, Ill.: Row, Peterson, 1957.

Fieldhouse, Edward, and David Cutts. "Does Diversity Damage Social Capital? A Comparative Study of Neighbourhood Diversity and Social Capital in the U.S. and Britain." *Canadian Journal of Political Science* 43 (2010): 289–318.

Fink, Deborah. *Cutting into the Meatpacking Line: Workers and Change in the Rural Midwest.* Chapel Hill: University of North Carolina Press, 1998.

Finifter, Ada W. "The Friendship Group as a Protective Environment for Social Deviants." *American Political Science Review* 68 (1974): 607–625.

Fitchen, Janet M. *Endangered Spaces, Enduring Places: Change, Identity, and Survival in Rural America.* Boulder, Colo.: Westview Press, 1991.

Flanagan, Constance, and Lonnie Sherrod. "Youth Political Development: An Introduction." *Journal of Social Issues* 54 (1998): 447–456.

Flora, Jan, Claudia Prado-Meza, Hannah Lewis, César P. Montalvo, and Frank Dunn. "The Impact of an Immigration and Customs Enforcement Raid on Marshalltown, Iowa." In *Latinos in the Midwest,* ed. Rubén O. Martinez, 119–155. East Lansing: Michigan State University Press, 2011.

Fossett, Mark A., and K. Jill Kiecolt. "The Relative Size of Minority Populations and White Racial Attitudes." *Social Science Quarterly* 70 (1989): 820–835.

Francia, Peter L., and Jody Baumgartner. "Victim or Victor of the 'Culture War'? How Cultural Issues Affect Support for George W. Bush in Rural America." *American Review of Politics* 26 (2005–2006): 349–367.

Frank, Thomas. *What's the Matter with Kansas? How Conservatives Won the Heart of America.* New York: Henry Holt, 2004.

Freudenberg, William. "The Density of Acquaintanceship: An Overlooked Variable in Community Research?" *American Journal of Sociology* 92 (1986): 27–63.

Frey, William H., and Kao-Lee Liaw. "Internal Migration of Foreign-Born Latinos and Asians: Are They Assimilating Geographically?" In *Geographic Perspectives on U.S.*

Migration: The Role of Population Movements in the Economic and Demographic Restructuring of Society, ed. Kavita Pandit and Suzanne Davies Winters, 212–230. Lanham, Md.: Rowman and Littlefield, 1999.

Friedberger, Mark. *Shake-Out: Iowa Farm Families in the 1980's.* Lexington: University of Kentucky Press, 1989.

Galston, William. "Political Knowledge, Political Engagement, and Civic Education." *Annual Review of Political Science* 4 (2001): 217–234.

Garcia, Carlos. "The Role of Quality of Life in the Rural Resettlement of Mexican Immigrants." *Hispanic Journal of Behavioral Science* 31 (2009): 446–467.

Garcia, F. Chris. "Hispanic Political Participation and Demographic Correlates." In *Pursuing Power: Latinos and the Political System,* 2d ed., ed. F. Chris Garcia, 187–199. South Bend, Ind.: University of Notre Dame Press, 1997.

Garcia Coll, Cynthia T., and Heidie A. Vazquez Garcia. "Developmental Processes and Their Influence on Interethnic and Interracial Relations." In *Toward a Common Destiny: Improving Race and Ethnic Relations in America,* ed. Willis D. Hawley and Anthony W. Jackson, 103–130. San Francisco: Jossey-Bass, 1995.

Garramone, Gina M., and Charles K. Atkin. "Mass Communication and Political Socialization: Specifying the Effects." *Public Opinion Quarterly* 50 (1986): 76–86.

Gastil, John. "Adult Civic Education through the National Issues Forums: Developing Democratic Habits and Dispositions through Public Deliberation." *Adult Education Quarterly* 54 (2004): 308–328.

Gastil, John, and James P. Dillard. "The Aims, Methods, and Effects of Deliberative Civic Education through the National Issues Forums." *Communication Education* 48 (1999): 179–192.

Gay, Claudine. "Seeing Difference: The Effect of Economic Disparity on Black Attitudes toward Latinos." *American Journal of Political Science* 50 (2006): 982–997.

George, Rosalyn. "Urban Girls' 'Race' Friendship and School Choice: Changing Schools, Changing Friendships." *Race, Ethnicity, and Education* 10 (2007): 115–129.

Gilens, Martin. "Racial Attitudes and Opposition to Welfare." *Journal of Politics* 57 (1995): 994–1014.

———. *Why Americans Hate Welfare: Race, Media, and the Politics of Antipoverty Policy.* Chicago: University of Chicago Press, 2000.

Gilens, Martin, Paul M. Sniderman, and James H. Kuklinski. "Affirmative Action and the Politics of Realignment." *British Journal of Political Science* 28 (1998): 159–183.

Giles, Michael, and Kaenan Hertz. "Racial Threat and Partisan Identification." *American Political Science Review* 88 (1994): 317–326.

Gimpel, James G., Joshua J. Dyck, and Daron R. Shaw. "Registrants, Voters and Turnout Variability across Neighborhoods." *Political Behavior* 26 (2004): 343–375.

Gimpel, James G., and Kimberly A. Karnes. "The Rural Side of the Urban–Rural Gap." *PS: Political Science and Politics* 39 (2006): 467–472.

Gimpel, James G., and J. Celeste Lay. "Political Socialization and Reactions to Immigration-related Diversity in Rural America." *Rural Sociology* 73 (2008): 180–204.

Gimpel, James G., J. Celeste Lay, and Jason Schuknecht. *Cultivating Democracy: Civic Environments and Political Socialization in America.* Washington, D.C.: Brookings Institution Press, 2003.

Glaeser, Edward L., David Laibson, Jose A. Scheinkman, and Christine L. Soutter. "Measuring Trust." *Quarterly Journal of Economics* 115 (2000): 811–846.

Glanville, Jennifer L. "Political Socialization or Selection? Adolescents' Extracurricular Participation and Political Activity in Early Adulthood." *Social Science Quarterly* 80 (1999): 279–290.

Glynn, Carroll J., Andrew F. Hayes, and James Shanahan. "Perceived Support for One's Opinions and Willingness to Speak Out: A Meta-analysis of Survey Studies on the Spiral of Silence." *Public Opinion Quarterly* 61 (1997): 452–461.

Goldthwait, Nathan E., ed. *History of Boone County, Iowa,* vols. 1–2. Chicago: Pioneer Publishing, 1914.

Goodhart, David. "Too Diverse?" *Prospect* 95 (2004): 30–37. Available online at http://www.cceia.org/media/goodhart.pdf.

Gordon, Milton M. *Assimilation in American Life.* New York: Oxford University Press, 1964.

Granovetter, Mark. "The Strength of Weak Ties." *American Journal of Sociology* 78 (1973): 1360–1380.

Greeley, Andrew. "Coleman Revisited: Religious Structures as a Source of Social Capital." *American Behavioral Scientist* 40 (1997): 587–594.

Green, Donald P., Dara Strolovich, and Janelle Wong. "Defended Neighborhoods, Integration, and Racially Motivated Crime." *American Journal of Sociology* 104 (1998): 372–403.

Green, Melanie C., Penny S. Visser, and Philip E. Tetlock. "Coping with Accountability Cross-Pressures: Low-Effort Evasive Tactics and High-Effort Quests for Complex Compromises." *Personality and Social Psychology Bulletin* 26 (2000): 1380–1391.

Greenberg, Edward S., Leon Grunberg, and Kelley Daniel. "Industrial Work and Political Participation: Beyond 'Simple Spillover.'" *Political Research Quarterly* 49 (1996): 305–330.

Grey, Mark A. "Immigrants, Migration, and Worker Turnover at the Hog Pride Pork Packing Plant." *Human Organization* 58 (1999): 16–27.

———. "Meatpacking and the Migration of Refugee and Immigrant Labor in Storm Lake, Iowa." *Changing Face* 2, no. 3 (1996), available online at http://migration.ucdavis.edu/cf/comments.php?id=154_0_2_0.

———. "Pork, Poultry and Newcomers in Storm Lake, Iowa." In *Any Way You Cut It: Meat Processing and Small-Town America,* ed. Donald D. Stull, Michael J. Broadway, and David Griffith, 109–127. Lawrence: University of Kansas Press, 1995.

———. "State and Local Immigration Policy in Iowa." In *Immigration's New Frontiers: Experiences from the Emerging Gateway States,* ed. Greg Anrig Jr. and Tova Andrea Wang, 33–66. New York: Century Foundation Press, 2006.

Grey, Mark A., Michele Devlin, and Aaron Goldsmith. *Postville, U.S.A.: Surviving Diversity in Small-Town America.* Boston: GemmaMedia, 2009.

Grey, Mark A., and Anne C. Woodrick. "'Latinos Have Revitalized Our Community': Mexican Migration and Anglo Responses in Marshalltown, Iowa." In *New Destinations: Mexican Immigration in the United States,* ed. Víctor Zúniga and Rubén Hernández-León, 133–154. New York: Russell Sage Foundation, 2005.

Griffith, David. "New Midwesterners, New Southerners: Immigration Experiences in Four Rural American Settings." In *New Faces in New Places: The Changing Geography of American Immigration,* ed. Douglas Massey, 179–210. New York: Russell Sage Foundation, 2008.

———. "Rural Industry and Mexican Immigration and Settlement in North Carolina." In *New Destinations: Mexican Immigration in the United States,* ed. Víctor Zúniga and Rubén Hernández-León, 50–75. New York: Russell Sage Foundation, 2005.

———. "Social and Cultural Bases for Undocumented Immigration into the U.S. Poultry Industry." In *Illegal Immigration in America: A Reference Handbook,* ed. David W. Haines and Karen E. Rosenblum, 157–171. Westport, Conn.: Greenwood Press, 1999.

Ha, Shang E. "The Consequences of Multiracial Contexts on Public Attitudes toward Immigration." *Political Research Quarterly* 63 (2010): 29–42.

Hanks, Michael, and Bruce K. Eckland. "Adult Voluntary Associations and Adolescent Socialization." *Sociological Quarterly* 19 (1978): 481–490.

Hardin, Russell. *Trust.* Cambridge: Polity, 2006.

Haubert, Jeannie, and Elizabeth Fussell. "Explaining Pro-Immigrant Sentiment in the U.S.: Social Class, Cosmopolitanism, and Perceptions of Immigrants." *International Migration Review* 40 (2006): 489–507.

Henry, P. J., and David O. Sears. "The Crystallization of Contemporary Racial Prejudice across the Lifespan." *Political Psychology* 30 (2009): 569–590.

———. "The Symbolic Racism 2000 Scale." *Political Psychology* 23 (2002): 253–283.

Hero, Rodney. *Social Capital and Racial Diversity: Equality and Community in America.* Cambridge: Cambridge University Press, 2007.

———. "Social Capital and Racial Inequality in America." *Perspectives on Politics* 1 (2003): 113–122.

Hero, Rodney, F. Chris Garcia, John Garcia, and Harry Pachon. "Latino Participation, Partisanship and Office Holding." *PS: Political Science and Politics* 33 (2000): 529–534.

Herreros, Francisco. *The Problems of Forming Social Capital: Why Trust?* New York: Palgrave, 2004.

Hess, Robert D., and Judith V. Torney. *The Development of Political Attitudes in Children.* Chicago: Aldine, 1967.

Higham, John. *Strangers in the Land: Patterns of American Nativism, 1860–1925.* New Brunswick, N.J.: Rutgers University Press, 2002.

Hill, Kim Quaile, and Jan E. Leighley. "Racial Diversity, Voter Turnout and Mobilizing Institutions in the United States." *American Political Quarterly* 27 (1999): 275–295.

Hood, M. V., III, and Irwin L. Morris. "Amigo o Enemigo? Context, Attitudes, and Anglo Public Opinion toward Immigration." *Social Science Quarterly* 78 (1997): 309–323.

Hood, M. V., III, Irwin L. Morris, and Kurt A. Shirkey. "'Quedate o Vente!' Uncovering the Determinants of Hispanic Public Opinion toward Immigration." *Political Research Quarterly* 50 (1997) 627–647.

Hopkins, Daniel J. "The Diversity Discount: When Increasing Ethnic and Racial Diversity Prevents Tax Increases." *Journal of Politics* 71 (2009): 160–177.

———. "Politicized Places: Explaining Where and When Immigrants Provoke Local Opposition." *American Political Science Review* 104 (2010): 40–60.

Hoskin, Marilyn, and William Mishler. "Public Opinion toward New Migrants: A Comparative Analysis." *International Migration* 21 (1983): 440–462.

Hossler, Donald, John Braxton, and G. Coopersmith. "Understanding Student College Choice." In *Higher Education: Handbook of Theory and Research,* vol. 5, ed. John C. Smart, 231–288. New York: Agathon, 1985.

Hossler, Donald, and Karen S. Gallagher. "Studying Student College Choice." *College and University* 62 (1987): 207–221.

House, James S., Karl R. Landis, and Debra Umberson. "Social Relationships and Health." *Science* 241 (1988): 540–545.

Hritzuk, Natacha, and David Park. "The Question of Latino Participation: From an SES to a Social Structural Explanation." *Social Science Quarterly* 81 (2000): 151–166.

Huckfeldt, Robert. "Political Loyalties and Social Class Ties." *American Journal of Political Science* 28 (1984): 399–417.

———. "The Social Communication of Political Expertise." *American Journal of Political Science* 28 (2001): 425–479.

———. "Social Contexts, Social Networks, and Urban Neighborhoods: Environmental Constraints on Friendship Choice." *American Journal of Sociology* 89 (1983): 651–669.

Huckfeldt, Robert, Paul Allen Beck, Russell J. Dalton, and Jeffrey Levine. "Political Environments, Cohesive Social Groups, and the Communication of Public Opinion." *American Journal of Political Science* 39 (1995): 1025–1054.

Huckfeldt, Robert, Paul E. Johnson, and John Sprague. "Individuals, Dyads and Networks: Autoregressive Patterns of Political Influence." In *The Social Logic of Politics: Personal Networks as Contexts for Political Behavior*, ed. Alan Zuckerman, 21–48. Philadelphia: Temple University Press, 2005.

Huckfeldt, Robert, and John Sprague. *Citizens, Politics, and Social Communication.* Cambridge: Cambridge University Press, 1995.

Huddle, Donald. *The Net National Cost of Immigration in 1993.* Washington, D.C.: Carrying Capacity Network, 1994.

Hughes, Diane, James Rodriguez, Emilie P. Smith, Deborah J. Johnson, Howard C. Stevenson, and Paul Spicer. "Parents' Ethnic-Racial Socialization Practices: A Review of Research and Directions for Future Study." *Developmental Psychology* 42 (2006): 747–770.

Huntington, Samuel P. *Who Are We? The Challenges to America's National Identity.* New York: Simon and Schuster, 2004.

Hurh, Won Moo, and Kwang Chung Kim. "The 'Success' Image of Asian Americans: Its Validity, and Its Practical and Theoretical Implications." *Ethnic and Racial Studies* 12 (1989): 514–561.

Irwin, Michael, Charles M. Tolbert, and Thomas A. Lyson. "There's No Place Like Home: Nonmigration and Civic Engagement." *Environment and Planning* 31 (1999): 2223–2238.

Iyengar, Shanto. "Subjective Political Efficacy as a Measure of Diffuse Support." *Public Opinion Quarterly* 44 (1980): 249–256.

Jackman, Mary R., and M. Crane. "'Some of My Best Friends are Black . . .' Interracial Friendship and Whites' Racial Attitudes." *Public Opinion Quarterly* 50 (1986): 459–486.

Jackson, Robert A. "Latino Political Connectedness and Electoral Participation." *Journal of Political Marketing,* 8 (2009): 233–262.

Jennings, M. Kent. "Generation Units and the Student Protest Movement in the United States: An Intra- and Intergenerational Analysis." *Political Psychology* 23 (2002): 303–324.

———. "Political Knowledge over Time and across Generations." *Public Opinion Quarterly* 60 (1996): 228–252.

Jennings, M. Kent, and Gregory B. Marcus. "Partisan Orientations over the Long Haul: Results from the Three-Wave Political Socialization Panel Study." *American Political Science Review* 78 (1984): 1000–1018.

Jennings, M. Kent, and Richard G. Niemi. "Continuity and Change in Political Orientations: A Longitudinal Study of Two Generations." *American Political Science Review* 69 (1975): 1316–1335.

———. *Generations and Politics.* Princeton, N.J.: Princeton University Press, 1981.

———. *The Political Character of Adolescence: The Influence of Families and Schools.* Princeton, N.J.: Princeton University Press, 1974.

———. "The Transmission of Political Values from Parent to Child." *American Political Science Review* 62 (1968): 169–184.

Jennings, M. Kent, Jan W. van Deth, Samuel Barnes, Dieter Fuchs, Felix Heunks, Ronald Inglehart, Max Kaase, Hans-Dieter Klingemann, and Jacques Thomassen. *Continuities in Political Action: A Longitudinal Study of Political Orientations in Three Western Democracies.* New York: de Gruyter, 1989.

Johnson-Webb, Karen D. "Employer Recruitment and Hispanic Labor Migration: North Carolina Urban Areas at the End of the Millennium." *Professional Geographer* 54 (2002): 406–421.

Johnson, Monica Kirkpatrick, Glen H. Elder Jr., and Michael Stern. "Attachments to Family and Community and the Young Adult Transition of Rural Youth." *Journal of Research on Adolescence* 15 (2005): 99–125.

Jones-Correa, Michael. *Between Two Nations: The Political Predicament of Latinos in New York City.* Ithaca, N.Y.: Cornell University Press, 1998.

Kahne, Joseph, and Joel Westheimer. "The Limits of Political Efficacy: Educating Citizens for a Democratic Society." *PS: Political Science and Politics* 39 (2006): 289–296.

Kandel, William, and John Cromartie. *New Patterns of Hispanic Settlement in Rural America.* Rural Development Research Report, no. 99. Economic Research Service, U.S. Department of Agriculture, Washington, D.C., 2004.

Kasinitz, Philip, Mary Waters, John Mollenkopf, and Jennifer Holdaway. *Inheriting the City: The Children of Immigrants Come of Age.* New York: Russell Sage Foundation, 2009.

Katz, Phyllis A. "Development of Children's Racial Awareness and Intergroup Attitudes." *Current Topics in Early Childhood Education* 4 (1982): 17–54.

Kaufmann, Karen M. "Cracks in the Rainbow: Group Commonality as a Basis for Latino and African-American Coalitions." *Political Research Quarterly* 56 (2003): 199–210.

———. "Divided We Stand: Mass Attitudes and the Prospects for Black/Latino Urban Political Coalitions." In *Black and Latino/a Politics: Issues in Political Development in the United States,* ed. William E. Nelson Jr. and Jessica Lavareiga Monforti, 158–168. Miami: Barnhardt and Ashe, 2006.

———. "Immigration and the Future of Black Power in U.S. Cities." *Du Bois Review* 4 (2007): 79–96.

———. *The Urban Voter: Group Conflict and Mayoral Voting Behavior in American Cities.* Ann Arbor: University of Michigan Press, 2004.

Kaufmann, Karen M., and Antonio Rodriguez. "The Future of Latino Involvement in U.S. Politics: Why Immigrant Destinations Matter." Unpublished ms.

Kelley, Jonathan, and Ian McAllister. "Social Context and Electoral Behavior in Britain." *American Journal of Political Science* 29 (1985): 564–586.

Kellstedt, Lyman. "Ethnicity and Political Behavior: Inter-group and Inter-generational Differences." *Ethnicity* 1 (1974): 393–415.

Kennedy, Ruby Jo Reeves. "Single or Triple Melting Pot? Intermarriage Trends in New Haven, 1870–1950." *American Journal of Sociology* 58 (1952): 56–59.

Kenny, Chris B. "Political Participation and Effects from the Social Environment." *American Journal of Political Science* 36 (1992): 259–267.

Kerwin, James F. *My Hometown, Carroll, Iowa.* Glidden, Iowa: Ferguson, 1992.

Kesler, Christel, and Irene Bloemraad. "Does Immigration Erode Social Capital? The Conditional Effects of Immigration-Generated Diversity on Trust, Membership, and Participation across 19 Countries, 1981–2000." *Canadian Journal of Political Science* 43 (2010): 319–347.

Key, V. O. *Southern Politics in State and Nation.* New York: Alfred A. Knopf, 1949.

Kinder, Donald R., and Cindy D. Kam. *Us versus Them: Ethnocentric Foundations of American Opinion.* Chicago: University of Chicago Press, 2009.

Kinder, Donald R., and Lynn M. Sanders, *Divided by Color: Racial Politics and Democratic Ideals.* Chicago: University of Chicago Press, 1996.

Kinder, Donald R., and David O. Sears. "Prejudice and Politics: Symbolic Racism versus Racial Threats to the Good Life." *Journal of Personality and Social Psychology* 40 (1981): 414–431.

King, Gary. "Why Context Should Not Count." *Political Geography* 15 (1996): 159–164.

Kinzler, Katherine D., Kristin Shutts, Jasmine DeJesus, and Elizabeth S. Spelke. "Accent Trumps Race in Guiding Children's Social Preferences." *Social Cognition* 27 (2009): 623–634.

Klapper, Joseph T. *The Effects of Mass Communication.* New York: Free Press, 1960.

Knack, Stephen. "Social Capital and the Quality of Government: Evidence from the United States." *American Journal of Political Science* 46 (2002): 772–785.

Knack, Stephen, and Philip Keefer. "Does Social Capital Have an Economic Payoff? A Cross-country Investigation." *Quarterly Journal of Economics* 112 (1997): 251–288.

Knight, Jack, and James Johnson. "Aggregation and Deliberation: On the Possibility of Democratic Legitimacy." *Political Theory* 22 (1994): 277–296.

Korean American Coalition. "Population Change by Race and Ethnicity, 1990–2000: USA, California, Southern California, LA County, Orange County, Koreatown," July 2, 2003. Available at http://www.calstatela.edu/centers/ckaks/census/7203_tables.pdf (accessed August 15, 2011).

Krissman, Fred. "Immigrant Labor Recruitment: U.S. Agribusiness and Undocumented Migration from Mexico." In *Immigration Research for a New Century,* ed. Nancy Foner, Ruben G. Rumbaut, and Steven J. Gold, 277–321. New York: Russell Sage Foundation, 2000.

Lamare, James W. "The Political Integration of Mexican-American Children: A Generational Analysis." *International Migration Review* 16 (1982): 169–188.

Lamphere, Louise, Alex Stepick, and Guillermo Grenier, eds., *Newcomers in the Workplace: Immigrants and the Restructuring of the U.S. Economy.* Philadelphia: Temple University Press, 1994.

Langton, Kenneth P., and M. Kent Jennings. "Political Socialization and the High School Civics Curriculum in the United States." *American Political Science Review* 62 (1968): 852–867.

Lasley, Paul, F. Larry Leistritz, Linda M. Lobao, and Katherine Meyer. *Beyond the Amber Waves of Grain: An Examination of Social and Economic Restructuring in the Heartland.* Boulder, Colo.: Westview Press, 1995.

Lay, J. Celeste, and Atiya Kai Stokes-Brown. "Put to the Test: Understanding Differences in Support for High-Stakes Testing." *American Politics Research* 37 (2009): 429–448.

Lazarsfeld, Paul F., Bernard Berelson, and Hazel Gaudet. *The People's Choice: How the Voter Makes Up His Mind in a Presidential Campaign* (1944). New York: Columbia University Press, 1968.

Leach, Mark A., and Frank D. Bean. "The Structure and Dynamics of Mexican Migration to New Destinations in the United States." In *New Faces in New Places: The Changing Geography of American Immigration,* ed. Douglas Massey, 51–74. New York: Russell Sage Foundation, 2008.

Lee, Everett S. "A Theory of Migration." *Demography* 3 (1966): 47–57.

Lee, Yueh-Ting, and Victor Ottati. "Attitudes toward U.S. Immigration Policy: The Roles of In-Group–Out-Group Bias, Economic Concern and Obedience to Law." *Journal of Social Psychology* 142 (2002): 617–634.

Leighley, Jan. *Strength in Numbers? The Political Mobilization of Racial and Ethnic Minorities.* Princeton, N.J.: Princeton University Press, 2001.

Leitner, Helga. "The Political Economy of International Labor Migration." In *Companion Guide to Economic Geography,* ed. Eric Sheppard and Trevor J. Barnes, 450–567. Oxford: Blackwell, 2000.

Lewis, Amanda E. "There Is No 'Race' in the Schoolyard: Color-Blind Ideology in an (Almost) All-White School." *American Educational Research Journal* 38 (2001): 781–811.

Lewis-Beck, Michael, and Peverill Squire. "Iowa: The Most Representative State?" *PS: Political Science and Politics* 42 (2009): 39–44.

Lin, Nan. "Social Networks and Status Attainment." *Annual Review of Sociology* 25 (1999): 467–487.

Lindemann, Stephanie. "Koreans, Chinese, or Indians? Attitudes and Ideologies about Non-native English Speakers in the United States." *Journal of Sociolinguistics* 7 (2003): 348–364.

———. "Who Speaks 'Broken English'? U.S. Undergraduates' Perceptions of Non-native English." *International Journal of Applied Linguistics* 15 (2005): 187–212.

Lippi-Green, Rosina. *English with Accents: Language, Ideology, and Discrimination in the United States.* New York: Routledge, 1997.

Loewen, James W. *Sundown Towns: A Hidden Dimension of American Racism.* New York: New Press, 2005.

Longworth, Richard C. *Caught in the Middle: America's Heartland in the Age of Globalism.* New York: Bloomsbury, 2008.

Lopez, Mark Hugo, and Karlo Barrios Marcelo. "The Civic Engagement of Immigrant Youth: New Evidence from the 2006 Civic and Political Health of the Nation Survey." *Applied Developmental Science* 12 (2008): 66–73.

Lutkus, Anthony D., and Andrew R. Weiss. *The Nation's Report Card: Civics 2006* U.S. Department of Education, National Center for Education Statistics, NCES 2007-476. Washington, D.C.: U.S. Government Printing Office, 2007.

Luttmer, Erzo F. P. "Group Loyalty and the Taste for Redistribution." *Journal of Political Economy* 109 (2001): 500–528.

Maharidge, Dale, and Michael Williamson. *Denison, Iowa: Searching for the Soul of America through the Secrets of a Midwest Town.* New York: Free Press, 2005.

Mahoney, Joseph L., and Robert B. Cairns. "Do Extracurricular Activities Protect against Early School Leaving?" *Developmental Psychology* 33 (1997): 241–253.

Majka, Theo J., and Linda C. Majka. "Institutional Obstacles to Incorporation: Latino Immigrant Experiences in a Midsized Rust-Belt City." In *Latinos in the Midwest,* ed. Rubén O. Martinez, 87–118. East Lansing: Michigan State University Press, 2011.

Marrow, Helen B. "New Destinations and Immigrant Incorporation." *Perspectives on Politics* 3 (2005): 781–799.

———. *New Destination Dreaming: Immigration, Race, and Legal Status in the Rural American South.* Stanford, Calif.: Stanford University Press, 2011.

Marschall, Melissa J., and Dietlind Stolle. "Race and the City: Neighborhood Context and the Development of Generalized Trust." *Political Behavior* 26 (2004): 125–153.

Marsh, Herbert W. "Extracurricular Activities: Beneficial Extension of the Traditional Curriculum or Subversion of Academic Goals?" *Journal of Educational Psychology* 84 (1992): 553–562.

Marwell, Gerald, Michael T. Aiken, and N. J. Demerath III. "The Persistence of Political Attitudes among 1960s Civil Rights Activists." *Public Opinion Quarterly* 51 (1987): 359–375.

Massey, Douglas S. "Why Does Immigration Occur? A Theoretical Synthesis." In *Handbook of International Migration,* ed. Charles Hirschman, Philip Kasinitz, and Joshua DeWind, 34–52. New York: Russell Sage Foundation, 1999.

Massey, Douglas S., Rafael Alarcon, Jorge Durand, and Humberto Gonzalez. *Return to Aztlan: The Social Process of International Migration from Western Mexico.* Berkeley: University of California Press, 1987.

Massey, Douglas S., and Chiara Capoferro. "The Geographic Diversification of American Immigration." In *New Faces in New Places: The Changing Geography of American Immigration,* ed. Douglas Massey, 25–50. New York: Russell Sage Foundation, 2008.

Massey, Douglas S., and Nancy A. Denton. *American Apartheid: Segregation and the Making of the Underclass.* Cambridge, Mass.: Harvard University Press, 1993.

Massey, Douglas S., Jorge Durand, and Nolan J. Malone. *Beyond Smoke and Mirrors: Mexican Immigration in an Age of Economic Integration.* New York: Russell Sage Foundation, 2002.

Massey, Douglas S., Luin Goldring, and Jorge Durand. "Continuities in Transnational Migration: An Analysis of Nineteen Mexican Communities." *American Journal of Sociology* 99 (1994): 1492–1533.

Matthews, Donald R., and James W. Prothro. *Negroes and the New Southern Politics.* New York: Harcourt Brace, 1966.

Matthews, Hugh, Mark Taylor, Kenneth Sherwood, Faith Tucker, and Melanie Lamb. "Growing Up in the Countryside: Children and the Rural Idyll." *Journal of Rural Studies* 16 (2000): 141–153.

McClain, Paula D., Niambi M. Carter, Victoria M. DeFrancesco Soto, Monique L. Lyle, Jeffrey D. Grynaviski, Shayla C. Nunnally, Thomas J. Scotto, J. Alan Kendrick, Gerald F. Lackey, and Kendra Davenport Cotton. "Racial Distancing in a Southern City: Latino Immigrants' View of Black Americans." *Journal of Politics* 68 (2006): 571–584.

McClurg, Scott D. "The Electoral Relevance of Political Talk: Examining Disagreement and Expertise Effects in Social Networks on Political Participation." *American Journal of Political Science* 50 (2006): 737–754.

———. "Political Disagreement in Context: The Conditional Effect of Neighborhood Context, Disagreement, and Political Talk on Electoral Participation." *Political Behavior* 28 (2006): 349–366.

———. "Social Networks and Political Participation: The Role of Social Interaction in Explaining Political Participation." *Political Research Quarterly* 56 (2003): 448–464.

McConnell, Eileen Diaz, and Faranak Miraftab. "Sundown Town 'Little Mexico': Old-Timers and Newcomers in an American Small Town." *Rural Sociology* 75 (2009): 605–629.

McDevitt, Michael. "The Partisan Child: Developmental Provocation as a Model of Political Socialization." *International Journal of Public Opinion Research* 18 (2006): 67–70.

McGrath, Daniel J., Raymond R. Swisher, Glen H. Elder Jr., and Rand D. Conger. "Breaking New Ground: Diverse Routes to College in Rural America." *Rural Sociology* 66 (2001): 244–267.

McGuire, William J. "Personality and Attitude Change: An Information Processing Theory." In *Psychological Foundations of Attitudes,* ed. Anthony C. Greenwald, Timothy C. Brock, and Thomas M. Ostrom, 171–196. San Diego, Calif.: Academic Press, 1968.

McKee, Seth C. "Rural Voters in Presidential Elections, 1992–2004." *The Forum* 5 (2007): art. 2.

McNeal, Ralph B. "Extracurricular Activities and High School Dropouts." *Sociology of Education* 68 (1995): 62–81.

McPhee, William N. *Formal Theories of Mass Behavior.* New York: Macmillan, 1963.

Meer, Bernard, and Edward Freedman. "The Impact of Negro Neighborhoods on White Home Owners." *Social Forces* 45 (1966): 11–19.

Meirick, Patrick C., and Daniel B. Wackman. "Kids Voting and Political Knowledge: Narrowing Gaps, Informing Voters." *Social Science Quarterly* 85 (2004): 1161–1177.

Michelson, Melissa R. "Getting Out the Latino Vote: How Door-to-Door Canvassing Influences Voter Turnout in Rural Central California." *Political Behavior* 25 (2003): 247–263.

——. "Political Efficacy and Electoral Participation of Chicago Latinos." *Social Science Quarterly* 81 (2000): 136–150.

Milbrath, Lester W., and M. Lal Goel. *Political Participation: How and Why Do People Get Involved in Politics?* 2d ed. Chicago: Rand McNally, 1977.

Millard, Ann V., and Jorge Chapa. "*Aqui* in the Midwest." In *Apple Pie and Enchiladas: Latino Newcomers to the Midwest,* ed. Ann V. Millard and Jorge Chapa, 1–21. Austin: University of Texas Press, 2001.

Millard, Ann V., Jorge Chapa, and Eileen Diaz McConnell. "'Not Racist Like Our Parents': Anti-Latino Prejudice and Institutional Discrimination." In *Apple Pie and Enchiladas: Latino Newcomers to the Midwest,* ed. Ann V. Millard and Jorge Chapa, 102–124. Austin: University of Texas Press, 2001.

——. "Ten Myths about Latinos." In *Apple Pie and Enchiladas: Latino Newcomers to the Midwest,* ed. Ann V. Millard and Jorge Chapa, 22–25. Austin: University of Texas Press, 2001.

Miller, David L., ed. *The Individual and the Social Self: Unpublished Essays by G. H. Mead.* Chicago: University of Chicago Press, 1982.

Miller, Lawrence W., Jerry L. Polinard, and Robert D. Wrinkle. "Attitudes toward Undocumented Workers: The Mexican American Perspective." *Social Science Quarterly* 65 (1984): 482–492.

Miller, Norman, and Hugh J. Harrington. "Social Categorization and Intergroup Acceptance: Principles for the Design and Development of Cooperative Learning Teams." In *Interaction in Cooperative Groups,* ed. Rachel Hertz-Lazarowitz and Norman Miller, 203–227. New York: Cambridge University Press, 1992.

Moreno, Dario. "Cuban-American Political Empowerment." In *Pursuing Power: Latinos and the Political System,* ed. F. Chris Garcia, 208–226. Notre Dame, Ind.: University of Notre Dame Press, 1997.

Morrell, Michael E. "Deliberation, Democratic Decision-making, and Internal Political Efficacy." *Political Behavior* 27 (2005): 49–69.

Morris, Charles W., ed. *Mind, Self, and Society.* Chicago: University of Chicago Press, 1934.

Mueller, John. *Quiet Cataclysm: Reflections on the Recent Transformation of World Politics.* New York: HarperCollins, 1995.

Mutz, Diana C. "Cross-Cutting Social Networks: Testing Democratic Theory in Practice." *American Political Science Review* 96 (2002): 111–126.

——. *Hearing the Other Side: Deliberative versus Participatory Democracy.* Cambridge: Cambridge University Press, 2006.

——. *Impersonal Influence: How Perceptions of Mass Collectives Affect Political Attitudes.* New York: Cambridge University Press, 1998.

Mutz, Diana C., and Jeffrey Mondak. "Dimensions of Sociotropic Behavior: Group-Based Judgments of Fairness and Well-Being." *American Journal of Political Science* 41 (1997): 284–308.

Myrdal, Gunnar. *An American Dilemma: The Negro Problem and Modern Democracy.* New York: Harper and Brothers, 1944.

Nannestad, Peter. "What Have We Learned about Generalized Trust, If Anything?" *Annual Review of Political Science* 11 (2008): 413–435.

Ndura, Elavie, Michael Robinson, and George Ochs. "Minority Students in High School Advanced Placement Courses: Opportunity and Equity Denied." *American Secondary Education* 32 (2003): 21–38.

Nelson, Dale C. "Ethnicity and Socioeconomic Status as Sources of Participation: The Case for Ethnic Political Culture." *American Political Science Review* 73 (1979): 1024–1038.

Nelson, Lisa, and Nancy Hiemstra. "Latino Immigrants and the Renegotiation of Place and Belonging in Small Town America." *Social and Cultural Geography* 9 (2008): 319–342.

Nelson, Lowry. "Intermarriage among Nationality Groups in a Rural Area of Minnesota." *American Journal of Sociology* 48 (1943) 585–592.

Nesdale, Drew. "Developmental Changes in Children's Ethnic Preferences and Social Cognition." *Journal of Applied Developmental Psychology* 20 (1999): 501–519.

———. "Social Identity Processes and Children's Ethnic Prejudice." In *The Development of the Social Self,* ed. Mark Bennett and Fabio Sani, 219–246. East Sussex: Psychology Press, 2004.

Nevins, Joseph. *Operation Gatekeeper: The Rise of the "Illegal Alien" and the Making of the U.S.–Mexico Boundary.* New York: Routledge, 2003.

Nie, Norman, Jane Junn, and Kathleen Stehlik-Barry. *Education and Democratic Citizenship in America.* Chicago: University of Chicago Press, 1996.

Niemi, Richard G., and M. Kent Jennings. "Issues and Inheritance in the Formation of Party Identification." *American Journal of Political Science* 35 (1991): 970–988.

Niemi, Richard G., and Jane Junn. *Civic Education: What Makes Students Learn.* New Haven, Conn.: Yale University Press, 1998.

Nisbet, Matthew C., and Dietram A. Scheufele. "Political Talk as a Catalyst for Online Citizenship." *Journalism and Mass Communication Quarterly* 81 (2004): 877–896.

Noelle-Neumann, Elizabeth. "The Spiral of Silence: A Theory of Public Opinion." *Journal of Communication* 24 (1974): 43–51.

———. *The Spiral of Silence: Public Opinion—Our Social Skin,* 2d ed. Chicago: University of Chicago Press, 1993.

Oliver, J. Eric. *Democracy in Suburbia.* Princeton, N.J.: Princeton University Press, 2001.

———. *The Paradoxes of Integration: Race, Neighborhood, and Civic Life in Multiethnic America.* Chicago: University of Chicago Press, 2010.

Oliver, J. Eric, and Tali Mendelberg. "Reconsidering the Environmental Determinants of White Racial Attitudes." *American Journal of Political Science* 44 (2000): 574–589.

Oliver, J. Eric, and Janelle Wong. "Intergroup Prejudice in Multiethnic Settings." *American Journal of Political Science* 47 (2003): 567–582.

Olsen, Marvin E. "Social and Political Participation of Blacks." *American Sociological Review* 35 (1970): 682–687.

Olzak, Susan. *The Dynamics of Ethnic Competition and Conflict.* Stanford, Calif.: Stanford University Press, 1992.

Orrenius, Pia M. "The Effect of U.S. Border Enforcement on the Crossing Behavior of Mexican Migrants." In *Crossing the Border: Research from the Mexican Migration Project,* ed. Jorge Durand and Douglas S. Massey, 281–290. New York: Russell Sage Foundation, 2005.

Osajima, Keith. "Asian Americans as the Model Minority: An Analysis of the Popular Press Image in the 1960s and 1980s." In *Reflections on Shattered Windows,* ed. Gary Y. Okihiro, John M. Liu, Arthur A. Hansen, and Shirley Hune, 165–174. Pullman: Washington State University Press, 1988.

Pacheco, Julianna Sandell. "Political Socialization in Context: The Effect of Political Competition on Youth Voter Turnout." *Political Behavior* 30 (2008): 415–436.

Park, Robert E., and Ernest W. Burgess. *Introduction to the Science of Sociology* (1921). University of Chicago Press, 1969.

Parrado, Emilio A., and William A. Kandel. "Hispanic Population Growth and Rural Income Inequality." *Social Forces* 88 (2010): 1421–1450.

Pasek, John, Lauren Feldman, Daniel Romer, and Kathleen Hall Jamieson. "Schools as Incubators of Democratic Participation: Building Long-term Political Efficacy with Civic Education." *Applied Developmental Science,* 12 (2008): 26–37.

Passel, Jeffery S., and Rebecca L. Clark. "How Much Do Immigrants Really Cost? A Reappraisal of Huddle's 'The Costs of Immigrants.'" Urban Institute, Washington, D.C., 1994.

Pastor, Manuel, Jr., and Enrico Marcelli. "Somewhere over the Rainbow? African Americans, Unauthorized Mexican Immigration and Coalition Building." *Review of Black Political Economy* 31 (2003): 125–155.

Pateman, Carole. *Participation and Democratic Theory.* New York: Cambridge University Press, 1970.

Patterson, Marjorie. *A Town Called Perry: Midwest Life in Small-town Iowa.* Perry, Iowa: Fullhart-Carnegie Museum Trust, 1997.

Pettigrew, Thomas F. "Intergroup Contact Theory." *Annual Review of Psychology* 49 (1998): 65–85.

Pettigrew, Thomas F., and Linda R. Tropp. "A Meta-Analytic Test of Intergroup Contact Theory." *Journal of Personality and Social Psychology* 90 (2006): 751–783.

Pinkelton, Bruce E., and Erica Austin. "Individual Motivations, Perceived Media Importance, and Political Disaffection." *Political Communication* 18 (2001): 321–334.

———. "Media Perceptions and Public Affairs Apathy in the Politically Inexperienced." *Mass Communication and Society* 7 (2004): 319–337.

Plutzer, Eric. "Becoming a Habitual Voter: Inertia, Resources and Growth in Young Adulthood." *American Political Science Review* 96 (2002): 41–56.

Popkin, Samuel L., and Michael Dimock. "Knowledge, Trust and International Reasoning." In *Elements of Reason: Cognition, Choice and the Bounds of Rationality,* ed. Arthur Lupia, Michael McCubbins, and Samuel L. Popkin, 214–238. New York: Cambridge University Press, 2000.

Portes, Alejandro, and Robert L. Bach. *Latin Journey: Cuban and Mexican Immigrants in the United States.* Berkeley: University of California Press, 1985.

Portes, Alejandro, and Rubén G. Rumbaut. *Immigrant America: A Portrait.* Berkeley: University of California Press, 1996.

———. *Immigrant America: A Portrait,* 3d ed. Berkeley: University of California Press, 2006.

———. *Legacies: The Story of the Immigrant Second Generation.* Berkeley: University of California Press, 2001.

Poterba, James M. "Demographic Structure and the Political Economy of Public Education." *Journal of Policy Analysis and Management* 16 (1997): 48–66.

Pulera, Dominic. *Visible Differences: Why Race Will Matter to Americans in the 21st Century.* New York: Continuum International, 2002.

Putnam, Robert D. *Bowling Alone: The Collapse and Revival of American Community.* New York: Simon and Schuster, 2000.

———. "*E Pluribus Unum*: Diversity and Community in the Twenty-First Century, the 2006 Johan Skytte Prize Lecture." *Scandinavian Political Studies* 30 (2007): 137–174.

———. *Making Democracy Work: Civic Traditions in Modern Italy.* Princeton, N.J.: Princeton University Press, 1993.

Ramakrishnan, S. Karthick, and Mark Baldassare. *The Ties That Bind: Changing Demographics and Civic Engagement in California.* San Francisco: Public Policy Institute of California, 2004.

Ramirez-Barranti, Chrystal C. "The Grandparent/Grandchild Relationship: Family Resource in an Era of Voluntary Bonds." *Family Relations* 34 (1985): 343–352.

Ramsey, Patricia G. "Young Children's Thinking about Ethnic Differences." In *Children's Ethnic Socialization,* ed. Jean S. Phinney and Mary Jane Rotheram, 56–72. Newbury Park, Calif.: Sage, 1987.

Rapoport, Ronald B. "Partisanship Change in a Candidate-Centered Era." *Journal of Politics* 59 (1997): 185–199.

Rice, Tom W., and Jan L. Feldman. "Civic Culture and Democracy from Europe to America." *Journal of Politics* 59 (1997): 1143–1172.

Rice, Tom W., and Brent Steele. "White Ethnic Diversity and Community Attachment in Small Iowa Towns." *Social Science Quarterly* 82 (2001): 397–407.

Rosenberg, Morris. "Some Determinants of Political Apathy." *Public Opinion Quarterly* 18 (1954–1955): 349–366.

Rosenfeld, Michael, and Marta Tienda. "Mexican Immigration, Occupational Niches and Labor Market Competition: Evidence from Los Angeles, Chicago and Atlanta, 1970–1990." In *Immigration and Opportunity: Race, Ethnicity, and Employment in the United States,* ed. Frank D. Bean and Stephanie Bell-Rose, 64–105. New York: Russell Sage Foundation, 1999.

Rosenstone, Steven J., and John Mark Hansen. *Mobilization, Participation, and Democracy in America.* New York: Macmillan, 1993.

Saenz, Rogelio. "The Changing Demography of Latinos in the Midwest." In *Latinos in the Midwest,* ed. Rubén O. Martinez, 33–55. East Lansing: Michigan State University Press, 2011.

Salamon, Sonya. "Culture." In *Encyclopedia of Rural America: The Land and People,* ed. Gary A. Goreham. Santa Barbara, Calif.: ABC-Clio, 1997.

Sampson, Robert J. "Crime and Public Safety: Insights from Community-Level Perspectives on Social Capital." In *Social Capital and Poor Communities,* ed. Susan Saegert, J. Phillip Thompson, and Mark R. Warren, 89–114. New York: Russell Sage Foundation, 2001.

———. "Disparity and Diversity in the Contemporary City: Social (Dis)Order Revisited." *British Journal of Sociology* 60 (2009): 1–31.

Sampson, Robert J., and Stephen W. Raudenbush. "Seeing Disorder: Neighborhood Stigma and the Social Construction of Broken Windows." *Social Psychology Quarterly* 67 (2004): 319–342.

Sampson, Robert J., Steven W. Raudenbush, and Felton Earls. "Neighbourhoods and Violent Crime: A Multilevel Study of Collective Efficacy." *Science* 277 (1997): 918–924.

Sanchez-Jankowski, Martin. "Minority Youth and Civic Engagement: The Impact of Group Relations." *Applied Developmental Science* 6 (2002): 237–245.

Schofield, Janet Ward. "The Impact of Positively Structured Contact on Intergroup Behavior: Does It Last under Adverse Conditions?" *Social Psychology Quarterly* 42 (1979): 280–284.

Schrag, Peter. *Not Fit for Our Society: Immigration and Nativism in America.* Berkeley: University of California Press, 2010.

Sears, David O. "The Persistence of Early Political Predispositions: The Role of Attitude Object and Life Stage." In *Review of Personality and Social Psychology,* vol. 4, ed. Ladd Wheeler and Philip Shaver, 79–116. Beverly Hills, Calif.: Sage, 1983.

Sears, David O., Jack Citrin, Sharmaine V. Cheleden, and Colette van Laar. "Cultural Diversity and Multicultural Politics: Is Ethnic Balkanization Psychologically Inevitable?" In *Cultural Divides: Understanding and Overcoming Group Conflict,* ed. Deborah A. Prentice and Dale T. Miller, 35–132. New York: Russell Sage Foundation, 1999.

Sears, David O., and P. J. Henry. "The Origins of Symbolic Racism." *Journal of Personality and Social Psychology* 85 (2003): 259–275.

Sears, David O., and Victoria Savalei. "The Political Color Line in America: Many 'Peoples of Color' or Black Exceptionalism?" *Political Psychology* 27 (2006): 895–924.

Sears, David O., and Nicholas A. Valentino. "Politics Matters: Political Events as Catalysts for Preadult Socialization." *American Political Science Review* 91 (1997): 45–65.

Sears, David O., Colette van Laar, M. Carrillo, and R. Kosterman. "Is It Really Racism? The Origins of White Americans' Opposition to Race-Targeted Policies." *Public Opinion Quarterly* 61 (1997): 16–53.

Seeman, Teresa E. "Social Ties and Health: The Benefits of Social Integration." *Annals of Epidemiology* 6 (1996): 442–451.

Segovia, Francine, and Renatta Defever. "The Polls-Trends: American Public Opinion on Immigrants and Immigration Policy." *Public Opinion Quarterly* 74 (2010): 374–394.

Selinker, Larry. "Interlanguage." *International Review of Applied Linguistics* 10 (1972): 209–231.

Sewell, William H., and Robert M. Hauser. *Education, Occupation, and Earnings: Achievement in the Early Career.* New York: Academic Press, 1975.

Shaw, Daron, Rodolfo O. de la Garza, and Jongho Lee. "Examining Latino Turnout in 1996: A Three-State, Validated Survey Approach." *American Journal of Political Science* 44 (2000): 338–346.

Sherif, Muzafer, O. J. Harvey, B. J. White, W. R. Hood, and Carolyn W. Sherif. *Intergroup Conflict and Cooperation: The Robber's Cave Experiment.* Norman: University of Oklahoma Book Exchange, 1961.

Sigelman, Lee, and Susan Welch. "The Contact Hypothesis Revisited: Black-White Interaction and Positive Racial Attitudes." *Social Forces* 71 (1993): 781–795.

Simmel, Georg. *The Metropolis and Mental Life.* In *Simmel: On Individuality and Social Forms,* ed. Donald Levine, 324–339. Chicago: University of Chicago Press, 1971.

Simon, Rita J. "Immigration and American Attitudes." *Public Opinion* 10 (1987): 47–50.

Slavin, Robert E. "Cooperative Learning and Intergroup Relations." In *Handbook of Research on Multicultural Education,* ed. James A. Banks and Cherry A. McGee Banks, 628–634. New York: Simon and Schuster-Macmillan, 1996.

———. "Enhancing Intergroup Relations in Schools: Cooperative Learning and Other Strategies." In *Toward a Common Destiny: Improving Race and Ethnic Relations in America,* ed. Willis D. Hawley and Anthony W. Jackson, 291–314. San Francisco: Jossey-Bass, 1995.

Smith, Robert C., and Richard Seltzer. *Contemporary Controversies and the American Racial Divide.* Lanham, Md.: Rowman and Littlefield, 2000.

Solis, Dianne. "Farmers Branch Files Federal Appeal on Immigration Ordinance," *Dallas Morning News,* January 6, 2011.

St. John, Craig, and Nancy A. Bates. "Racial Composition and Neighborhood Evaluation." *Social Science Research* 1 (1990): 47–61.

Stein, Robert M., Stephanie Shirley Post, and Allison Rinden. "Reconciling Context and Contact Effects on Racial Attitudes." *Political Research Quarterly* 53 (2000): 285–303.

Stepick, Alex. *Pride against Prejudice: Haitians in the United States.* Boston: Allyn and Bacon, 1998.

Stepick, Alex, and Carol Dutton Stepick. "Becoming American, Constructing Ethnicity: Immigrant Youth and Civic Engagement." *Applied Developmental Science* 6 (2002): 246–257.

Stepick, Alex, Carol Dutton Stepick, Emmanuel Eugene, Deborah Teed, and Yves Labissiere. "Shifting Identities and Inter-generational Conflict: Growing Up Haitian in Miami." In *Ethnicities: Children of Immigrants in America,* ed. Ruben Rumbaut and Alejandro Portes, 229–266. Berkeley: University of California Press, 2001.

Stokes, Atiya Kai. "Latino Group Consciousness and Political Participation." *American Politics Research* 31 (2003): 361–378.

Stoll, Michael A., Edwin Melendez, and Abel Valenzuela. "Spatial Job Search and Job Competition among Immigrant and Native Groups in Los Angeles." *Regional Studies* 35 (2002): 97–112.

Struthers, Cynthia B., and Janet L. Bokemeier. "Myths and Realities of Raising Children and Creating Family Life in a Rural County." *Journal of Family Issues* 21 (2000): 17–46.

Sue, Stanley, and Harry H. L. Kitano. "Stereotypes as a Measure of Success." *Journal of Social Issues* 29 (1973): 83–98.

Suro, Roberto, and Audrey Singer. "Latino Growth in Metropolitan America: Changing Patterns, New Locations." Center on Urban and Metropolitan Policy of the Brookings Institution and Pew Hispanic Center, Washington, D.C., 2002.

Taeubur, Karl E. "The Effect of Income Redistribution on Racial Residential Segregation." *Urban Affairs Quarterly* 4 (1965): 5–14.

Tancredo, Thomas. *In Mortal Danger: The Battle for America's Border and Security*. Nashville: Cumberland House, 2006.

Tatum, Beverly Daniel. *"Why Are All the Black Kids Sitting Together in the Cafeteria?" A Psychologist Explains the Development of Racial Identity*. New York: Basic Books, 1997.

Tauxe, Caroline. "Heartland Community: Economic Restructuring and the Management of Small Town Identity in the Central U.S." *Identities* 5 (1998): 335–377.

Taylor, Marylee C. "How White Attitudes Vary with the Racial Composition of Local Populations: Numbers Count." *American Sociological Review* 63 (1998): 512–535.

Tedin, Ken L. "Assessing Peer and Parent Influence on Adolescent Political Attitudes." *American Journal of Political Science* 24 (1980): 136–153.

Tolbert, Charles M., Michael D. Irwin, Thomas A. Lyson, and Alfred R. Nucci. "Civic Community in Small-Town America: How Civic Welfare Is Influenced by Local Capitalism and Civic Engagement." *Rural Sociology* 67 (2002): 90–113.

Torney-Purta, Judith. "The School's Role in Developing Civic Engagement: A Study of Adolescents in Twenty-Eight Countries." *Applied Developmental Science* 6 (2002): 203–212.

Torney-Purta, Judith, Carolyn H. Barber, and Britt Wilkenfeld. "Latino Adolescents' Civic Development in the United States: Research Results from the IEA Civic Education Study." *Journal of Youth and Adolescence* 36 (2007): 111–125.

Torney-Purta, Judith, Rainer Lehmann, Hans Oswald, and Wolfram Schulz. *Citizenship and Education in Twenty-Eight Countries: Civic Knowledge and Engagement at Age Fourteen*. Amsterdam: International Association for the Evaluation of Educational Achievement, 2001.

Trainor, Jennifer S. *Rethinking Racism: Emotion, Persuasion and Literacy Education in an All-White High School*. Carbondale: Southern Illinois University Press, 2008.

Uhlaner, Carole J., Bruce E. Cain, and D. Roderick Kiewiet. "Political Participation of Ethnic Minorities in the 1980s." *Political Behavior* 11 (1989): 195–231.

Uslaner, Eric M. "The Foundations of Trust: Macro and Micro." *Cambridge Journal of Economics* 32 (2008): 289–294.

———. *The Moral Foundations of Trust*. Cambridge: Cambridge University Press, 2002.

Uslaner, Eric M., and Mitchell Brown. "Inequality, Trust, and Civic Engagement." *American Politics Research* 31 (2003): 1–28.

Vaca, Nicolas Corona. *The Presumed Alliance: The Unspoken Conflict between Latinos and Blacks and What It Means for America*. New York: Rayo, 2004.

Valentino, Nicholas A., Krysha Gregorowicz, and Eric W. Groenendyk. "Efficacy, Emotions, and the Habit of Participation." *Political Behavior* 31 (2009): 307–330.

Valentino, Nicholas A., and David O. Sears. "Event-Driven Political Socialization and the Preadult Socialization of Partisanship." *Political Behavior* 20 (1998): 127–154.

Van Ausdale, Debra, and Joe R. Feagin. *The First R: How Children Learn Race and Racism.* Lanham, Md.: Rowman and Littlefield, 2001.

van Deth, Jan W. "Politicization and Political Interest." In *Eurobarometer: The Dynamics of European Public Opinion,* ed. Karlheinz Reif and Ronald Inglehart, 201–213. New York: St. Martin's Press, 1991.

Vargas, Zaragosa. *Proletarians of the North: A History of Mexican Industrial Workers in Detroit and the Midwest, 1917–1933.* Berkeley: University of California Press, 1993.

Vega, Arturo, Rubén O. Martinez, and Tia Stevens. "*Cosas Políticas*: Politics, Attitudes and Perceptions by Region," in *Latinos in the Midwest,* ed. Rubén O. Martinez, 57–86. East Lansing: Michigan State University Press, 2011.

Verba, Sidney, and Norman H. Nie. *Participation in America: Political Democracy and Social Equality.* New York: Harper and Row, 1972.

Verba, Sidney, Kay Schlozman, and Henry Brady. *Voice and Equality: Civic Voluntarism in American Politics.* Cambridge, Mass.: Harvard University Press, 1995.

Voss, D. Stephen. "Beyond Racial Threat: Failure of an Old Hypothesis in the New South." *Journal of Politics* 58 (1996): 1156–1170.

——. "Huddled Masses or Immigrant Menace? The Black Belt Hypothesis Did Not Emigrate." *American Review of Politics* 22 (2001): 217–232.

Waldinger, Roger, ed. *Strangers at the Gates: New Immigrants in Urban America.* Berkeley: University of California Press, 2001.

Walsh, Katherine Cramer. *Talking about Politics: Informal Groups and Social Identity in American Life.* Chicago: University of Chicago Press, 2004.

Warren, Wilson J. *Tied to the Great Packing Machine: The Midwest and Meatpacking.* Iowa City: University of Iowa Press, 2007.

Welch, Susan, Lee Sigelman, Timothy Bledsoe, and Michael Combs. *Race and Place: Race Relations in an American City.* Cambridge: Cambridge University Press, 2001.

White, Stephen, Neil Nevitte, Andre Blais, Elisabeth Gidengil, and Patrick Fournier. "The Political Resocialization of Immigrants: Resistance of Lifelong Learning." *Political Research Quarterly* 61 (2008): 268–281.

Whiteley, Paul F. "Economic Growth and Social Capital." *Political Studies* 48 (2000): 443–466.

Wilcox, Jerry, and W. Clark Roof. "Percent Black and Black–White Status Inequality: Southern versus Non-Southern Patterns." *Social Science Quarterly* 59 (1978): 421–434.

Wilner, Daniel M., Rosabelle Price Walkley, and Stuart W. Cook. *Human Relations in Interracial Housing: A Study of the Contact Hypothesis.* Minneapolis: University of Minnesota Press, 1976.

Wolfinger, Raymond E., and Steven J. Rosenstone. *Who Votes?* New Haven, Conn.: Yale University Press, 1980.

Wong, Janelle S. *Democracy's Promise: Immigrants and American Civic Institutions.* Ann Arbor: University of Michigan Press, 2006.

——. "The Effects of Age and Political Exposure on the Development of Party Identification among Asian American and Latino Immigrants in the United States." *Political Behavior* 22 (2000): 341–371.

Wong, Janelle S., and Vivian Tseng. "Political Socialisation in Immigrant Families: Challenging Top-Down Parental Socialisation Models." *Journal of Ethnic and Migration Studies* 34 (2008): 151–168.

Wong, Paul, Chienping Faith Lai, Richard Nagasawa, and Tieming Lin. "Asian Americans as a Model Minority: Self-Perceptions and Perceptions by Other Racial Groups." *Sociological Perspectives* 41 (1998): 95–118.

Wood, Richard E. *Survival of Rural America: Small Victories and Bitter Harvests*. Lawrence: University Press of Kansas, 2008.

Works, Ernest. "The Prejudice-Interaction Hypothesis from the Point of View of the Negro Minority Group." *American Journal of Sociology* 67 (1961): 47–52.

Wrinkle, Robert D., Joseph Stewart Jr., Kenneth J. Meier, and John R. Arvizu. "Ethnicity and Nonelectoral Participation." *Hispanic Journal of Behavioral Sciences* 18 (1996): 142–151.

Wuthnow, Robert. *Remaking the Heartland: Middle America since the 1950s*. Princeton, NJ: Princeton University Press, 2011.

Youniss, James, Jeffrey A. McLellan, and Miranda Yates. "What We Know about Engendering a Civic Identity." *American Behavioralist Scientist* 40 (1997): 620–631.

Zak, Paul J., and Stephen Knack. "Trust and Growth." *Economics Journal* 111 (2001): 295–321.

Zaller, John. *The Nature and Origins of Mass Opinion*. New York: Cambridge University Press, 1992.

Zarate, Michael A., and Moira P. Shaw. "The Role of Cultural Inertia in Reactions to Immigration on the U.S./Mexico Border." *Journal of Social Issues* 66 (2010): 45–57.

Zhou, Min. "Ethnicity as Social Capital: Community-based Institutions and Embedded Networks of Social Relations." In *Ethnicity, Social Mobility and Public Policy: Comparing the U.S.A. and U.K.,* ed. Glenn C. Loury, Tariq Modood, and Steven Teles, 131–159. New York: Cambridge University Press, 2005.

Zubrinsky, Camille L., and Lawrence Bobo. "Prismatic Metropolis: Race and Residential Segregation in the City of the Angels." *Social Science Research* 25 (1996): 335–374.

Zuckerman, Alan S., ed. *The Social Logic of Politics: Personal Networks as Contexts for Political Behavior*. Philadelphia: Temple University Press, 2005.

Zuckerman, Alan S., Laurence Kotler-Berkowitz, and Lucas A. Swaine. "Anchoring Political Preferences: The Importance of Social and Political Contexts and Networks in Britain." *European Journal of Political Research* 33 (1998): 285–322.

Zukin, Cliff, Scott Keeter, Molly Andolina, Krista Jenkins, and Michael X. Delli Carpini. *A New Engagement? Political Participation, Civic Life, and the Changing American Citizen*. New York: Oxford University Press, 2006.

Index

Page numbers followed by the letter f *or* t *refer to figures or tables, respectively.*

J. Celeste Lay is an Assistant Professor of Political Science at Tulane University.